D0199695

MADUMO

ADAM ASHFORTH

MADUMO

A MAN BEWITCHED

THE UNIVERSITY OF CHICAGO PRESS

CHICAGO AND LONDON

The University of Chicago Press, Chicago 60637
The University of Chicago Press, Ltd., London

Paperback edition 2005
Printed in the United States of America

18 17 16 15 14 8 9

ISBN-13: 978-0-226-02972-6
ISBN-10: 0-226-02972-7

Library of Congress Cataloging-in-Publication Data

Ashforth, Adam.
Madumo, a man bewitched / Adam Ashforth.
p. cm.

1. Witchcraft—South Africa—Soweto—Case studies. 2. Madumo. 3. Soweto (South Africa)—Religious life and customs. 4. Soweto (South Africa)—Social life and customs—20th century. I. Title.

BF1584.S6 Z7 2000
299′.64—dc21
[B]

99-057325

♾ The paper used in this publication meets the minimum requirements of the American National Standard for Information Sciences—Permanence of Paper for Printed Library Materials, ANSI Z39.48-1992.

CONTENTS

A NOTE TO THE READER

In this book I tell a story, arising from a decade-long friendship, about a young man named Madumo struggling to free himself from the curse of witchcraft in Soweto, South Africa, at the close of the twentieth century. It is based upon our shared experiences and taped conversations; interviews and discussions with others; journals and letters (both Madumo's and mine); together with my own observations, recollections, and speculations leavened with a good measure of gossip deriving from times in Soweto since 1990—not to mention books I have read and things I've forgotten. These materials have here been edited and translated, shaped and reshaped, in an effort to present an accessible narrative for an English-speaking reader.

Although the book had its origins in Madumo's own desire to make a "case study" of his plight, the result is nothing of the sort. Indeed, Madumo was rather surprised when he saw what I'd made of his story, for he said he was expecting more of a "documentary," something more "academic." I was pleased, however, that he adjudged my tale a "true story" despite the bits of "fabrication" (his term) supplied here and there to "appetize the reader." I present this book, then, not as a scientific treatise nor as a transcript from a court of law, but rather as a story, particular and personal, drawn from life. Of course, names, dates, and telltale details of scene and action have been changed in an effort to protect the privacy of the people concerned. It is a true story, nonetheless, and I have made my best efforts to make it seem so. I hope that none of these alterations will seem like errors or injustice to my friends.

1

WHERE'S MADUMO?

No one answered when I tapped at the back door of Madumo's home on Mphahlele Street a few days after my return to Soweto, so I pushed the buckling red door in a screeching grind of metal over concrete and entered calling, "Hallo?" From behind the bedroom door to the left of the kitchen Madumo's sister, Ouma, peered out, her head wrapped in a faded blue towel. She greeted me and gestured towards the sitting room before returning to her bath.

I perched myself on the edge of the large overstuffed cranberry-colored velvet sofa, still sheathed in its clear plastic cover, and waited. The old four-room "matchbox" house, an icon of oppression in apartheid-era Soweto, had been recently extended by pushing out the front wall and installing floor-to-ceiling windows in place of the old metal-framed glass panels. In each of the two windows, large framed photographs of the Bishops Lekganyane, the founder of the Zion Christian Church and his son and successor, faced out to the front yard, greeting anyone who ventured past the heavy steel gate with a sign of the power and piety protecting the house. A new display cabinet, pale pink and glossy, was stocked to overflowing with bottles of generic spirits and ersatz liqueurs rarely tasted in these beer-drinking parts. A family of china cats were nestled amongst the liquor. On the kitchen table, splaying perilously on the yellow plastic surface, a dozen or so bottles of Carling Black Label beer were racked in a rickety wooden wine stand. Why so much liquor in a house of Zionists, I wondered as I sank back into the crackling plastic, since Zionists are pledged to abstain?

When I last visited this house, two years ago, the place was submerged in a sea of hand-crocheted lace doilies. Hundreds of them in all sizes and patterns covered every available surface. In the corner, freshly laundered doilies had been stacked in a neatly tapering tower nearly two feet high. The mother of this house was a great one for doilies. I used to feel self-conscious about walking over them in my heavy boots until Madumo told me not to worry: "There's nowhere to walk without walking on them," he said, "so walk." In the kitchen doilies covered the coal stove, the electric hotplate, the table, and every inch of cutting space: "You can't fry an egg without folding fifty doilies first," Madumo used to complain. His mother had been crocheting them for years. She was not a well woman—"sugar diabetes, plus high blood, and nerves"—or so I was told at the time. Piling up her doilies day by day, she awaited her husband's return. The father of her family never did return, though the pile of doilies grew and grew.

"Where's Madumo?" I asked when his sister finally emerged from her room carrying a blue plastic basin full of sudsy water to the drain outside.

"He's no more staying here," Ouma replied, glancing down across the delicate balance of her basin to where I floated on the sofa. Her manner was arch and offhand, habitually disdainful in the manner of a woman who knows she's considered proud but is confirmed in her belief, as she takes an afternoon bath, that she has much to feel proud about.

"I heard you chased him away," I said.

"No, we didn't chase him. He just left after our mother passed away. He was doing funny things. *Too* much . . ."

I followed her out to the tap in the backyard, where she proceeded to tell me a convoluted tale of Madumo's misdeeds. I couldn't follow all the details. She spoke as if recalling a malicious private pleasure. It seemed my friend had borrowed money from a relative to buy counterfeit banknotes and then failed to repay the debt. "Six thousand rands," she said. "Imagine!" When I asked her to explain she merely snorted: "You must ask him yourself when you see him."

"Where's he staying?" I asked. The tap gushed as she wiped the basin with her washcloth.

"Who knows?" she replied, shaking the basin free of water in an arc of rapid-fire drops to the hard red clay, as if to indicate that the interview was over. "He's no more coming this side."

"Well, if you see him, tell him I'm looking for him."

"Okay," she replied, though I could see she wasn't hoping to see him soon.

I could easily have found Madumo myself. Mpho, our mutual friend, had told me where his room was—somewhere on the first street this side of Vusi's shebeen in Mapetla East. He'd also told me he wouldn't help me find our old friend. "The man has changed," Mpho had said when I asked after an absent Madumo upon my arrival. "He's no more like he used to be." Friends were crowding that day into the house in Lekoka Street where I always stayed, to welcome me back to Soweto. Neighbors stopped in to enjoy the beer; the kitchen was bustling with women; the street and the yard were an uproar of children . . . but there was no sign of Madumo. "Where's Madumo?" I had asked, only to receive a collective shrug. Mpho tried to tell me not to expect him. I pressed for reasons. "He's changed," he said again, outlining the details of a long, complicated squabble that sounded to me like something I should rise above, "and I very much doubt that he's been going to school. No, my man, I very much doubt it. I heard he's selling drugs and fakes." Mpho would say no more.

I knew the street where Madumo was said to be staying, and

it would not have been difficult to walk over and ask around until I found his room. No doubt I would have met people along the way surprised to find a lone white man on foot asking after a local guy in "Deep" Soweto. But although I'd been away I was still well known in Mapetla, so before long someone would have been sure to recognize me and help me locate my friend. At least it wouldn't have been too difficult in the daylight hours; I wouldn't risk being out on those streets alone after dark. Yes, I could have found Madumo easily enough. But I couldn't be bothered. For like everyone else I encountered as I asked after Madumo, I was angry with him too. I resented the fact that he hadn't come to greet me on my arrival, especially as I'd sent him the money for his school fees some months before and never received any thanks in reply. Still, I wanted to see him again—if only to hear his story and vent my spleen.

We have long been like brothers, Madumo and me. In the face of danger and death, which is never far away for young men in Soweto, there is no question that we stand together. But like many brothers, our connection is rarely untroubled. When I am away from Soweto, Madumo seems always to be with me. Fond, loving memories I carry—to be sure—but memories of Madumo are often a troubling presence in my life, like a broken bone of years ago or an old scar that can be worn as a trophy until the weather changes and an unsettled night brings on the ache anew. Whenever word of Madumo reaches me in New York, and it inevitably arrives secondhand as he doesn't have a phone and rarely writes unless desperate for money, it always carries news of catastrophe: he's been stabbed and robbed, or beaten, or chased away from home. I have worried about him for years, of course. But thoughts of Madumo regularly rouse something else in me, something far less satisfying than plain, unvarnished feelings of friendship and concern. I wouldn't say my feelings at such times are guilt, exactly, although I sometimes still feel guilty wondering if I couldn't do more for him. Nor could I call it exasperation, though such a feeling is a frequent presence when Madumo himself is around. It's rather that I find myself keeping these other feelings at bay by exploiting a certain distance or detachment in myself, a certain reserve. And for that, after all we've been through together, I can't help but feel guilty. It's not a simple story to tell.

I first met Madumo on June 16, 1990, the anniversary of the famous 1976 Soweto Revolt. Madumo, along with Mpho, was a former schoolmate of a friend of mine in the United States named Marks, whom I had met when he was a student in northern Minnesota—a solitary black South African in a land of snow and Scandinavians—and I was a visiting Australian teaching at the local university. When Marks heard I would be traveling to South Africa on a research trip to study the transition to democracy, he deputed his friends at home to show me Soweto and asked his mother to arrange a place for me to stay. She contacted the Mfetes, who were happy to host a visitor from overseas at their house in Lekoka Street, to show him life under apartheid, although they were unsure of the reception a white man would receive in the black township. They prepared for the worst. I was only intending to stay overnight before returning to the university in the white suburbs to continue with my research, but I hadn't reckoned on the warmth of the welcome I would find, nor the power of this place to pull me ever more firmly into its orbit. Soweto opened for me as a world quite different from anything I had ever read about in books, yet it seemed strangely familiar as well. It took many years for me to learn how to live there, and though I now know how to do that well enough, Soweto always finds ways to confound me.

Madumo was twenty-five when we first met; Mpho, twenty-one; I, thirty-one. Where Mpho offers a clear, open face to the world and a trusting look that inspires trust in return, Madumo's brow seems perpetually furrowed or teetering on the edge of a frown, as if grappling with a problem he can't yet identify, something that might be deep inside him or way off in the distance. His is a restless intelligence, and he has a philosopher's cast of mind: blessed with the ability to doubt and cursed with the capacity to question. Strangers routinely misread his contemplation or his mischievous provocative questions for hostility and respond in kind. He is often mistaken for a thug, though he doesn't sport the scars of a seasoned criminal. Like most young men in Soweto, he has tried his hand at crime, but found he lacks the taste for cruelty requisite for success. In fact he is the gentlest of souls. Madumo always seems to inspire distrust. Once, at the airport, when I left him to mind my cases for a moment, a kindly lady intervened and warned me not to trust him. She was white, as it happened, but she could just as easily have been a Sowetan. Madumo often seems to have that effect on people. Mostly it amuses him. At times, however, perplexed and depressed, he wonders why he is so marked. Mpho never has such troubles. He is always well-liked.

The day I arrived in Soweto was the first anniversary of the '76 Revolt to be celebrated in what used to be called the "new" South Africa, the first to be addressed by leaders of the newly legalized African National Congress, who were fresh from exile and prison. Mpho met me in Johannesburg, and we traveled by minibus taxi back to the township, to the rally at Jabulani Amphitheater. From every corner of Soweto the comrades came bedecked in the green, gold, and black colors of the liberation movements, marching through the dusty streets to Jabulani with their banners and flags, "toyi-toyi"-ing in their martial high-stepping dance and singing their slogans of struggle. "*Siyaya ePitoli,*" they sang. We are going to Pretoria! "*Shaya 'maBulu,*" they chanted. Hit the Boers! Kill the Boers! Kill the farmers! Everyone was a Comrade, and we saluted each other with clenched fists—"Com!" From the streets of Soweto it seemed as if the Young Lions had roared and the regime of the Boers was at bay. Freedom seemed close at hand.

Jabulani Amphitheater was crammed to overflowing that day with legions of exuberant youths. Revered elders of the ANC and assorted emissaries from around the world addressed the crowd and the cameras, celebrating the Youth of Soweto and their Struggle while imploring them to be disciplined and patient with the "talks about talks." When the bands began to play at the end of the day, the dignitaries and journalists departed, leaving fifty thousand Sowetans singing the songs of freedom as if with one voice. As darkness settled onto the coal-fire orange of a Soweto winter's sunset, I joined the serpentine threads of young Sowetans weaving through the pathways in the long dry grass. My new friends, along with a detachment of their comrades, escorted me to Mapetla and into another world. I could never have dreamt, as we went out on the town in Soweto that night, that in the years to come this place would seem like home and the people I was with would become like family. Nor could I have foretold that in becoming part of their world mine would be changed forever.

To say I was a center of attention in those days when I first encountered Soweto would be an understatement, and to claim it didn't turn my head would be a lie. Here I was in a place that was at the center of one of the great moments in twentieth-century world history—the last chapter in the history of white domination in Africa, a final closing of the book on five hundred years of European colonialism—and I was being welcomed as a white man into a place made for Blacks under the auspices of white racism. Until recently it had been illegal for a white person to stay overnight in a black township. Even to visit during the day required a permit. The only white faces usually encountered in Soweto, apart from one or two in clerical garb, belonged to policemen or government officials and were hated. Yet all I had to do was be there as a friend—and the fact that I *was* there was taken by most to mean that I must be a friend—in order to be celebrated as a symbol of the new South Africa. I was feted as a sign that black and white could in fact live together, an implicit rebuke to the segregationists who had ruled this place for so long. Of course I felt like a fraud.

In all that clamor over the novelty of a white man living in Soweto, it took time to discover who my true friends were. It took time to learn how to live in a place where the risk of violent death is so great and the chances of securing justice through recourse to public authorities are so slim; where the struggle for the basic necessities of life is so hard. It took time, too, to learn that the essence of friendship in such a place is premised not just upon emotional or intellectual affinity but upon the unquestioned willingness to face death for one another and to share willingly whatever bounty good fortune might dispense. Over time Madumo and I, along with Mpho and Thabo, the eldest son of the family with whom I stayed, became like brothers. We faced the risk of death together and survived. We helped each other in whatever ways we could without question. And when we quarreled, we reconciled and made peace because we were brothers.

In the years following 1990, as South Africa stumbled towards democracy, Soweto like other places was torn apart by war between ANC supporters and members of the Zulu-nationalist Inkatha Freedom Party. Residents suffered mysterious terrorist attacks on their homes and in trains. Beloved leaders were killed. It seemed as if secret forces within the government were mounting a concerted conspiracy to thwart the political birthright of the people. With freedom at last so close to hand, the pace of constitutional negotiations seemed glacial. When the ANC took its place in the limelight, first as a partner in negotiations in 1990 and finally, after 1994, as the government, the sense of a historic moment having arrived was palpable. But the flurry of hopeful expectations in Soweto gradually dissipated into an abiding sense of disappointment as the leaders reaped the reward of the struggle while times got tougher for those who had risked their lives and sacrificed their schooling for freedom.

With the ending of apartheid, profound transformations in everyday life in Soweto began. The greater opportunities afforded to Africans in government and business exacerbated rapidly growing inequalities within black populations, which in previous generations had been compelled to live in conditions of relative socio-economic parity. At the same time, the community solidarity fashioned through political opposition to an oppressive regime fragmented into a frenzy of individualistic consumerism. Opportunities greatly expanded for the new black elite and the swelling middle classes, accelerating a trend that had been underway for more than a decade, but the benefits expected from democracy failed to materialize for the majority of the population. Jobs were few; wages were low. The value of the rand fell, resulting in a steep rise in the price of the imported consumer goods that are so essential to marking status. The young men who had been feted as the Young Lions of the Struggle were now left to loiter on street corners. They soon found other avenues for expressing themselves and securing the means of status; crime and violence remained rampant.

Despite the dawning of democracy, then, people were still suffering. Yet the task of interpreting the meaning of misfortune was becoming more complex. Hithertofore, the misfortunes of individuals and families in a place like Soweto could be reckoned not only by reference to particular causes but also to a general name hanging over the suffering of all black people—Apartheid. Now, with apartheid gone, the sorrows of an unfair fate could only be measured, case by case, against the conspicuous "progress" and good fortune of particular relatives, colleagues, and neighbors, not to mention the ubiquitous images in the media of black people who had made it, and advertisements tailored to their desires. Such post-apartheid developments fed undercurrents of jealousy and envy—a dangerous development in a place such as Soweto, where physical and spiritual security is so precarious. There, jealousy is widely considered to be the primary motivation not only of physical violence, but also of witchcraft, and witchcraft, loosely understood as the capacity to cause harm or accumulate wealth by illegitimate occult means, permeates every aspect of everyday life.

Through good fortune with research grants and leave from my teaching job, I was able to stay in Soweto for most of the time until the first democratic elections of 1994. After that I had to return to work in New York and have only been able to return to Soweto for three months each northern summer. As the years passed, the bonds of fraternity that once bound us so close—Mpho, Madumo, Thabo, and me—became fractured and strained.

Such was the situation, then, when I returned to Soweto and failed to find Madumo. A week passed after my visit to Madumo's home, then another, with no sign of my erstwhile friend. I was still nursing my resentment at his neglect when Thabo "organized" a car, a Mazda of the variety known in these parts as *iDombolo*—the dumpling—after its resemblance to a local dish, a football-sized dough ball steamed in a plastic bag in a pot on the stove top. Thabo and I bought the car from a couple of young Indian guys in a town to the west of Soweto. They told us it was their father's, but the documents referred to a man with a Tswana name living in a hospital in North-West Province. It didn't cost us much and was guaranteed by virtue of its age not to attract hijackers. Plus, as a car favored by maGents, the typical Soweto guys (at least, those who can't afford BMWs), it would signify a degree of belonging that my white skin would normally belie. The Indians must have had good contacts in the traffic department because all the papers were in order.

We were mobile and it was Saturday night.

"Should we check Madumo?" Thabo asked as we drove through Mapetla.

"Why not?" replied Mpho.

Though angry with Madumo, Mpho was nostalgic for the nights when we four roamed together through Soweto, drinking and dancing and playing cat-and-mouse with the police. It wouldn't be the same going out on a Saturday night without Madumo, aka Madube, aka Madume, aka Mad-Dumo, or just the plain old Madman. We call him the Madman because his eccentricities and enthusiasms many times had brought us close to disaster. Most people don't appreciate Madumo's irreverence and taste for irony—like the time when he decided to reinterpret the New Testament in a loud voice in a crowded shebeen in this deeply religious place to prove that Jesus was a criminal who was justly punished for, amongst other lesser crimes, counterfeiting wine out of water.

We pulled into Rakuba Street. Dusk had not long settled over the rows of matchbox houses, and mothers were still at their gates calling children from their dusty play. Music was blaring from the stereo of a car parked near another under which a mechanic was working while his friends loitered nearby, drinking beer. Madumo was strolling down the street towards us, his shoulders hunched against the winter chill as it cut through his tattered blue Giants shirt. Thabo drove at him as if to run him down. The car skidded to a halt in a cloud of dust.

Madumo stopped, peered into the car, opened the door, and climbed in. "Howzit gents?" he said. That was all: "Howzit gents?"

"So-Where-To?" asked Thabo.

"Soweto!" echoed Mpho, clapping his hands onto the back of Thabo's seat, and for another Saturday night it was almost like the old days.

But it wasn't the old days. Soweto had changed; we had changed. The old townships of Apartheid were no longer blazing with protest and promise. We were no longer youths without cares. My friends were all fathers now. Thabo had a permanent job and was facing the prospect of a wedding. Mpho had almost completed his law degree and was about to start work. I was a junior professor facing down the tenure clock in New York. And Madumo had been accused of using witchcraft to murder his mother.

"I've been having troubles," said Madumo when we finally found a space to sit in a corner of Philly's crowded shebeen. "Troubles I tell you, too many troubles. *Too* many . . ."

Before he could begin to tell of these troubles, Thabo plonked six large bottles of Castle lager on the table and Madumo's words drowned in the Saturday night noise. He promised to come to my place on Monday and tell me his story.

2

MADUMO'S CURSE

On Monday afternoon Madumo came with his story. We sat alone in the backyard of the Mfetes' house, the house that I long ago came to think of as home in Soweto.

"I've been having troubles," he said. "Ever since my mother passed away, nothing but troubles. *Too* many troubles . . ." He picked at a thread fraying from the hem of his shorts. We sat in silence. Neither of us was in the mood for idle chatter, and yet neither of us could find a way to begin the conversation we both approached with a sense of foreboding.

Though the sun was bright, the air carried a wintery chill. An acrid stench wafted over the wall from a neighbor's yard, where women were burning the hair off sheeps' feet prior to boiling them to sell as a sticky-meat delicacy. Madumo was perched on the polish-blackened concrete washtub, leaning back against the outhouse wall. I sat on the table that Hendry, the father of the house, had salvaged from the wreckage of Seanna Marena High School back in '93, when the school was being torn apart by vandals. To the metal frame of a classroom desk, Hendry had fixed boards from a packing case and sanded them smooth before painting the whole an alarming vermillion red. He must have bought the red paint cheap because everything else in the yard that might have needed a coat of paint, from the big metal storage box to the toilet door, was painted in the same dramatic color. The yard was surrounded by tall grey cinder-block walls. Years ago, when I first came to this house, everything was open to the neighbors' gaze, and the neighbors were expected to intervene if ever they should see something amiss. The old man next door used to sit under his tree all afternoon, watching all, while his granddaughter swept and polished. Now the old man is long dead, and high walls topped with razor wire cut us off from the neighbors and the street. These barriers, which in the old days would have been considered an insult to the neighborhood and an invitation to criminals to do their deeds free from scrutiny, now signify status and assist with privacy and security.

I could see that my friend had changed. On Saturday night, though animated and amusing as of old, there had been a dispiriting gravity about him that I'd never seen before, a somberness that reasserted itself whenever the mask of conviviality slipped—as if the weight of his calamity was too much to bear. In the past, even when troubles were upon him, he would always find a way to make light of them and make us laugh. And he'd always had some perverse little mantra garnered from the accidental fruits of everyday chatter that he would interject into conversations whenever the earnest seemed too self-important. "Government is a crook" was one of his favorites. He had plucked it from the conversation of our friend Mr. Dladla one night when we were drinking in Dladla's shebeen with a visitor from America. Mr. Dladla had been stumbling in his limited English for an explanation of the plight of black people under apartheid when he landed upon the felicitous phrase: Government is a crook. Madumo seized upon the phrase and repeated it endlessly, twisting it into absurdity whenever the level of political bombast became intolerable, as it often did in those days—only he would use it to suggest that no matter what might happen after Mandela became president, Government would always be a crook. Another favorite phrase he pilfered from a radio call-in show during the tumultuous aftermath of Chris Hani's assassination in 1993, when the country came close to exploding in rage over the killing of a beloved leader by a white assassin. A white woman had phoned in to a program hosted by a right-wing fanatic—choice listening for Madumo—to opine that Hani's death confirmed that black people lived like cockroaches, so they should die like cockroaches. Madumo loved that phrase, only he transposed it into the rustic Zulu pronunciation of our friend Mr. Dladla: "like koka-loaches" Whenever he felt in need of a laugh he would expostulate, usually to some utterly perplexed interlocutor: "You live like a kokaloach, you must die like a kokaloach!" It was enough for Madumo that he enjoyed his own sardonic joke. Now Mr. Dladla was dead, murdered by thugs near Merafe Hostel, and Madumo's imitations could only remind us how much we missed him.

Although we came to know each other at first through the accident of his having been Marks's schoolmate, it was Madumo's taste for irony, not to say cynicism, that attracted me to him and brought us closer over the years. In 1994, inspired by Mandela's call for the youth to return to school, Madumo conceived a desire to try the matriculation examination one more time so that he could go to university, get a degree, and build himself a better life, consonant with the promise of the new South Africa. He asked me for support. I happily paid for his classes at Damelin College, a private correspondence school for adults. At first his mother was hostile to his plans, but he persisted and she relented. After the matriculation, Madumo enrolled in a bachelor of commerce course by correspondence with the University of South Africa. I continued to finance him. I had been reluctant to do so at first, as the course he had chosen was expensive and I had other commitments at the time. But he persuaded me of his determination, so I found the money. When last I had seen him, he'd been a student full of eager promise. But the Madumo sitting opposite me in MaMfete's yard this crisp June day was a shadow of the man I once knew. He looked painfully thin, sallow and unkempt. Defeated.

I tried to muster the remnants of my resentment: "So what's this I hear about you selling drugs and fakes?" I asked.

"It's true," he replied without hesitation. "I was doing that business, but no more."

"Why?"

Madumo began to tell his story. I sunned myself on the table and listened. Sometimes I would ask a question, though mostly I remained quiet. He talked for hours. He told me how his mother died after a long and debilitating illness; how his younger brother, a member of the Zion Christian Church, had been told by a prophet at church that their mother's death had been caused by witchcraft directed against her by someone inside the family. The prophet had described the death as an "inside job." Madumo was fingered as the culprit. Madumo and this brother had long been on bad terms. He told me how he had been accused of bewitching his mother and was chased away from his home. He spoke of the hardships he'd endured, of the friends he'd made when down and out, of his career in crime.

"Everything went wrong when my mother died," he said, recapitulating his tale while easing himself from his perch on the washtub to stretch a cramped leg. "I've had no peace since then. None at all. To speak truly, I consider myself cursed. There's nothing I can do."

"So what happened to your studies?" I asked.

"I dropped out," he replied. "When they chased me from home, I had nowhere to stay. Nowhere to study my books."

"And the money I sent for fees?"

"No. I've still got it. It's in the bank—fixed-term deposit. I can't touch it."

I didn't doubt he was telling the truth. It was exactly the sort of thing Madumo would do: lock his money away for the long term to get a better rate of interest while cadging pennies day to day to survive.

"Why didn't you let me know about all this?" I asked. "Why didn't you write?"

"I wrote you a letter," he said, "explaining everything. But I never sent it."

"Why?" When I'm away from Soweto my correspondence with Madumo is desultory, but I usually hear from him in times of trouble.

"I don't know." He turned to run the tap, drinking from a hand cupped under the stream. "I wanted to write you the whole story, but I never finished it. I started it after you sent me that article you wrote, the one about witchcraft. I wanted to write it all down, my whole story, so you could use it as a case study in your classes in New York." He glanced at his feet and bent over to retie a shoelace. "I've still got it," he said.

He was referring to my paper about witchcraft and power in Soweto, which I'd sent to him and to Mpho and some other friends, asking for their comments. In it I argue that the political and intellectual imperatives of the struggle against apartheid, coupled with a habitual white derogation of African culture as backward, created a situation in which the fact that most black people in South Africa live in a world where "witchcraft" is an everyday reality has become an enormous public secret. Over years of living in Soweto, I had slowly come to appreciate that most people here understand the powers spoken of as "witchcraft" as palpable realities that are utterly commonplace and yet shrouded in the utmost secrecy, and that every aspect of social life, including politics, is permeated by these powers. Premature death, such as that which struck Madumo's mother in her early fifties, is generally considered a plain sign that witchcraft is at work. It seemed to me that these matters could not be treated as simply manifestations of ignorance and superstition, as the modernist "enlightened" disposition would have it. (Although, in a place where education—in the indigenous knowledge and traditions of Africa as well as those of the West—is generally inferior, ignorance and superstition should not be underestimated.) In addition to chronic poverty and violence, the context of everyday life in Soweto is marked by more or less acute forms of spiritual insecurity, of which "witchcraft" is a part. And this insecurity cannot be divorced from the religious, cultural, and political history of the place and its people. Mpho had responded to my paper with a long commentary endorsing my basic argument while contesting a number of propositions (particularly my tendency to conflate the powers of witches with the morally opposed forces of healers and ancestors, folding them all into a single category of "invisible forces"). He had provided many concrete examples to illustrate his case. Madumo had written nothing. I was beginning to understand why.

"Why don't you finish that letter," I said when the clanking of the gate being unlatched signaled the end of our privacy. "Write it all down and maybe I *will* make a case study."

"I will," he said.

A few days later he came with his letter:

It all started after we buried my late mother, only a few days after. We buried her on the 29th of August. At the beginning of September the show started.

I was told by my brother that I am not gonna be spoiled like before. My younger sister too was in support of my brother. There were two aunties staying with us. They were the ones who were pulling strings. Adam, it sometimes happens in black families that when the mother passes away, or the father, a lot of drama will go on. Useless accusations, lies, and jealousy in all sorts of forms.

These two aunties were not aware that I have been trying to pick myself up through thick and thin. Firstly they began with their "University-thing" comments: "Why do you go to school? Who gives you money for schooling? How do you know that white man? Boys of your age are having kids, wives, cars, and houses, and they are earning a living. Why do you have to strain yourself with these studies whilst here in Soweto people are having money without schooling? And you are too old to be punishing yourself with those books. At the end of the day you will just be talking your high-flowing English in local shebeens and working odd jobs like being sent to buy beer cases from a liquor store. Or else, you'll be a hobo."

That was what my aunties and my brother and sister were saying. I took it lightly at first, but eventually it exploded and turned into a serious challenge. I could not study during the night. They would complain about the lights, asking, Who is going to pay the electricity bill if you are busy wasting electricity? Then I was told to look for a job or else nobody will be buying and cooking for me. I was given food only once a day. That soft porridge, that was all. I was restricted in my use of toiletries, of television, and the phone. What I was supposed to do was to wake up—as early as 5:30 am—wash myself, and go. No sitting in the sitting room. Coming back, I must not waste more than thirty minutes in the house. Just put my books in the house and go. Sunset, straight to the bedroom and sleep.

But that was not the worst. The other thing they were saying was that I had killed my mother. They said my father was collaborating with our elder brother and I was one of the conspirators; that I had made an inside job. They said my father gave our elder brother a herb that he then gave to me because I am very close with my mother. So they said I was the one who knew where to pour the herb in her food where it will be effective to kill her. To kill our mother. My younger brother is a staunch member of the Zion Christian Church. A prophet at church told him that.

So, Adam, they said that I am a murderer. That I used witchcraft to kill my mother. This is what I was told three days after the funeral. I was told point-blank that they were not gonna let me stay in the house. . . .

Madumo's letter, after chronicling his life on the streets, ended on an upbeat note, of sorts: *I know that one day I will make it in life even if I regard myself as cursed.*

Madumo had been exceedingly fond of his mother. Although she had initially greeted his efforts to return to school with the same contempt as the rest of his family, she slowly came to respect his determination and supported him against the resentment of his siblings. Robbed of the right to mourn her death, Madumo was driven to the brink of madness. He tried to kill himself. He took himself down to the bridge at Merafe Station to jump in front of a train. But his nerve failed him, so he rode the trains aimlessly into the city and drifted into the underworld of Johannesburg. He had no doubt that someone had bewitched his mother. Only Madumo knew that he was not the culprit. But if not him, then who?

After reading Madumo's letter I went to visit him in his room in Rakuba Street, behind MaDudu's shebeen. The matchbox shebeen had a typical two-room-and-garage addition built in the yard behind it in the manner that became popular in the 1980s, when Sowetan householders discovered they could earn significant income from subtenants while boycotting their own rent payments to the "puppets of apartheid" in the Soweto City Council as part of the Struggle. I knocked at the kitchen door to greet the people in the main house. Although it was barely noon, a gathering of stalwarts, evidently regulars, was hunched over beers in the front room. An old man named Boy recognized me from years past and greeted me with the usual pleasantries. I declined his offer of beer by saying "I'm coming," the Sowetan manner of departing while avoiding farewells. I tapped on the door of the outside room I'd been told was Madumo's and heard a voice say, "Come in."

Madumo's room, the middle of three, was about ten feet square. A double bed took up most of the floor space. At the foot of the bed, a wooden cabinet was stacked with books, papers, and groceries. I could see the well-thumbed copy of the *Columbia History of the World* that I had given him for Christmas in '92 sitting on a pile of commerce texts and assorted books I'd left behind with him in years past. He has an autodidact's thirst for knowledge, and so, as books are expensive and hard to find here,

I try to keep him supplied. In the corner by the window a couple of large garbage bags kept his clothes free of dust. Indifferent now towards politics, Madumo is passionate about clothes. He knows the work of all the great couturiers, which he studies in his collection of jealously guarded secondhand fashion magazines. He loves nothing better than to debate the relative merits of Giorgio Armani and Gianni Versace or, better still, the Italians in general versus the French. Under his bed, stuffed with newspaper and awaiting a special day, he keeps his pair of special shoes, black Church's brogues—his most valuable possession. Ten years ago, when he bought them, they were worth the equivalent of two months' wages for an average Sowetan worker (which Madumo was not). He bought them with his winnings from the dice game at the corner by Mr. Matodzhi's shop, from a guy who'd pilfered them from a shoe shop in town. A pair of orange curtains sagged on a string across the windows. An old and battered two-ring hotplate sat glowing red on top of two concrete blocks. Madumo was in bed, wrapped in blankets.

"Hey, this room is fucken cold," he said after we had greeted each other. "No ceiling." He gestured towards the exposed underside of the tin roof, where a single electric bulb hung precariously from fraying wires. "And I haven't even opened the windows today."

I warmed my hands over the rings of the stove. A small aluminum pot, pushed aside, was encrusted still with the previous night's rice.

"Who pays the electricity?" I asked.

"Included in the rent."

"Lucky for you," I said. He agreed, adding that his landlady was always complaining about his use of electricity. We chatted idly for a while about women and the weather. The talk ebbed. A baby cried in the house next door.

"Listen," I said. "I read your letter. . . ." He nodded as I spoke. I couldn't think what next to say.

"No," he said, interrupting my fumbling for words with the

customary negative affirmation of these parts, "you
case study."

"What do you mean?"

"You know, a case study. An example of witchc
your classes in New York."

"Not likely," I laughed. "They've got me teaching American government now." He seemed disappointed. "But more to the point," I said, "what are *you* going to do?"

He sank back into his blankets.

"There's nothing I can do," he said.

"What do you mean?" He didn't answer. "*Hmmm?*" I demanded.

"It's like I said in the letter," he replied, his voice barely a whisper. "My life has been cursed."

"What do you mean 'cursed'?" I spat, losing patience. "What kind of bullshit is that? You've had bad luck? Everyone has bad luck sometimes."

"You don't understand," he said, slumping back again. I immediately regretted my outburst; he looked so thoroughly defeated.

"So tell me," I said, feeling the weight of his gloom settle upon me. "What *do* you mean by 'cursed'?"

"It's difficult," he replied, raising himself upon an elbow. "It's difficult to explain. . . . It's more than bad luck. You see, for me, I'm relating this thing to the people that are called ancestors. I'm asking why can't they take me out of this trouble? Why can't they protect me?" He found a cigarette loose on top of the cabinet, the last of three he'd bought on his way home the night before, struck a match, and drew deeply on his smoke. He exhaled a long slow sigh of smoke. "Because I'm in a fucked-up situation. Down and out. Down and out." He drew again on his cigarette. "Have you ever known me like this before? No. I'm telling you, something is seriously wrong. *Seriously* wrong. And I've tried so hard. But look what happened. Look at me! I'm an outcast. Even my family have turned their backs on me. Even my friends. Why?"

He inhaled again. "There must be a reason. There must. So that is why I'm questioning about these ancestors." He paused and looked up from where he had been studying a scorch mark in the blanket. I met his eyes but had nothing to say. "You know yourself, Adam, I never used to be thinking too much about these things of witchcraft and ancestors, even if my mother *was* spiritually inclined. But now, I have to face it. Something is wrong. Seriously wrong. I can't deny it."

"So you blame your ancestors?"

"It's not blame, exactly," he explained. "It's like they are forgetting me. Forgetting me because they think I've forgotten them." I must have looked skeptical. "According to our tradition, you know, we must visit our ancestors' graves, at least sometimes, and make a feast. Otherwise, it's like they despair and lose their powers to protect us, their descendants. They forget you. It's like we say, when someone is run over by a car, say, we say their ancestors have forgotten them. They didn't make you aware that the car was coming."

"So they're punishing you?"

"No. It's just that they won't protect me. You know, my mother used to be always telling me to go to the graves. Both my brothers went. Things came good for them. Especially the firstborn: good job, wife, children . . . house in the suburbs. But I didn't listen. I didn't have time for those people, the ancestors. Besides, we were too short of transport at home. No money. And those graves are in the rural areas, the real *bunduland*."

The ancestors of his parents lie in graves about a day's journey from Soweto, each family in opposite directions: father's to the west, mother's to the east.

"We were really short of transport," he said, "and my father wasn't prepared to take us there."

"Why?" I asked.

"I don't know," he replied. When he spoke of his father, a bitter sadness descended upon Madumo. "Maybe he was scared that if we went there, we would come up, succeed in life, like.

Become a challenge to him. Actually, when I say I'm cursed it's my father that has created this whole situation."

"Why don't you go to the graves now, then?" I suggested.

"That's my plan, of course," he replied. "The problem is, it's expensive. You have to make a feast to communicate with your ancestors." He stubbed his cigarette on a cracked saucer perched on the blanket over his knees, tipping it over in the process. "Shit!" he muttered as the butts and ashes cascaded over the bed. He busied himself with clearing them up.

In this part of the world a person can't just walk into a graveyard and start talking to the ancestors. These things must be properly arranged through the living elders of the family. A feast must be made. A beast must be slaughtered—a sheep, or a goat, if there's no money for a cow—and sorghum beer must be brewed. All who arrive at the house on that day must be fed. And throngs will arrive. Such feasts cost money; Madumo has no money. The relatives on his father's side, who should preside over such feasting, are poor too, so no aid could be expected from them. Some of the ancestors know my friend personally; others, like the great-grandfather after whom he was named—who appeared to Madumo's mother in a dream while she was pregnant, announcing the name for her child—died before he was born.

"Surely the ancestors understand that you're short of money?" I said. "Wouldn't they appreciate it anyway if you just made some sort of effort, say by going to their graves even if you can't make a feast?" It seemed to me that these ancestors were somewhat lacking in the way of charity and compassion for my sad friend, their descendant. "Besides, didn't you tell me once that you had an ancestor who was an Irishman? He's not going to mind what you do, surely."

Madumo grunted, almost laughed: "Yeah, on my mother's side we are Coloureds. Partially. That's why she was having her own way of doing things, which people this side, in Soweto, didn't understand. But those other ancestors, they'll still want their feast." He picked at a few last specks of ash clinging to the blanket. "I supposed I *could* make some kind of an alternative reservation," he mused. "Maybe I could slaughter a chicken, make some home-brew beer . . . communicate that way. But it won't work. The seniors of the family will tell me that I'm still owing. They'll say there are too many ancestors for just one chicken. Besides, my grandfather was having many cattle. So they'll say I should buy two cows and a goat, that I must come back and make the whole thing straight."

"So tell me, Madumo," I said, "if you believe so much in these ancestors, why didn't you make an effort to connect up with them before? Why did you wait?"

"Ah," sighed Madumo, "that's the problem. You know, the problem with this ancestorship business is that we Africans, myself included, when life picks up and things are going smooth for us, we normally forget about ancestors. Because we are trying to follow Western culture. We think we have done those things—got a job, maybe, or a degree—on our own. But when the job is finished, we'll go back and say, 'Oh, my ancestors, my ancestors! Why have you forgotten me?' I mean, I should have made this feast long ago."

"And you know how to do it?" I asked. "You know the proper procedures for communicating with the ancestors?"

Madumo paused. "I don't," he replied. "In a true sense, I don't know these things. Not at all. You know, Adam, our tradition is really dead. To tell you the honest truth, it's dead. Dead. Because with this thing of feasts for our ancestors, we are talking about tradition. And tradition, really, we don't know it. Say if I take ten elders and tell them that I've made a feast, and I've given people a chicken, two out of ten will support me. The other eight will say I've done a wrong thing. So what am I supposed to do? All I know is that I am supposed to do *something*."

In Madumo's reading of the predicament, there was no way around the expense of a feast. And it would be worse, he reasoned, to make a small feast with the promise of a better one to follow than to offer nothing at all. For a small feast would merely awaken the ancestors without satisfying them, risking their wrath as well as their neglect. They might then become so inclined as to lead him into some kind of danger, such as allowing him be stabbed by thugs in the street, in order to make him realize that they are still waiting for their feast. When they are simply neglected, as Madumo had neglected them, communication breaks down, and the ancestors are unable to provide the protection that is their duty towards their descendants. But, he felt certain, they wouldn't go out of their way to make things worse.

"So what do the ancestors need from you that you should spend all your money making them a feast?" I asked.

"Our presence and acknowledgment," he replied, "that's all."

"Sounds like plenty," I said, "if you have to come with cows."

As we talked it became clear to me that if Madumo was cursed as he believed, his only chance of rectifying the situation would be if I provided the money to make a feast. But I was by no means certain that I wanted to bankroll such an undertaking. For one thing, my friend was not exaggerating when he lamented the costs. For another, I had had enough experience in Soweto over the years to know that these feasts do not always produce the desired results. Misfortune has a habit of persisting in the face of feasts. If you make a feast for the ancestors and then discover later that the real problem is witchcraft, you might please the ancestors, but you are throwing your money away. Serious problems of witchcraft require specialist treatment by healers who are expert in divining the cause of affliction and repelling witchcraft. And when it comes to specialists in the relief of misfortune, there are legions of them in Soweto—almost as many as the misfortunes they confront in this place of poverty and suffering. They will all happily proffer their remedies and take your money.

"How do you know this is the cause of your problems, Madumo?" I asked. "How do you really know it's this 'ancestorship' that has caused the curse? I mean, I could take you right now to a priest I know who will tell you that this talk of ancestors is nonsense. He'll tell you that all you need to do is to pray to Jesus and the Holy Spirit, repent your sins, and have faith. Then all will be well. And it won't cost you anything." I had in mind an Anglican priest from nearby Senaoane, a young African man who understands well the spiritual complexity of this place but who has no truck with ancestors or the rituals for their appeasement. This priest recognizes the power of evil in the world and the reality of witchcraft, certainly, but confirms prayer, based upon faith in Jesus as Savior and Protector, as the most effective means of combating it.

"Ah, really," sighed Madumo, "I won't tolerate that priest. Because I've studied this Bible. And I know how this Bible came to our place here in Africa with this whole Christianity setup." He paused for a moment, considering the matter. "The way I was brought up was in the sense of ancestorship, even if I've neglected them since. Unless somebody from the family, unless a very close somebody from the family who knows our surname, who knows our beliefs, can tell me that I should pray, I'll just ignore him. I won't believe a priest."

"So how do you know it's the ancestors that are causing your problems?" I asked, returning to my theme. "You hear so many different things about these African ancestors: someone says they do this, others say they don't do that. . . ."

"No, this thing of ancestorship is what we are having at our home. That is our belief. But *hhayi!* You're right. It's hard to know what to believe. Like, some people strongly believe that if you get money, you must go straight to the grave to thank the ancestors. Others say, if you do that, they'll think you are satisfied with that little bit of money and you won't get any more. Even me, most of the time I don't want to think about this ancestorship." He fell silent, slowly rubbing a speck of cigarette ash into his blanket. "It's difficult."

I gazed at my morbid friend languishing in his bed as he pondered the dilemmas of an unfair fate, our silence punctuated by the shouts of children playing in a neighboring yard, and I wondered again whether I shouldn't offer to help. Somehow or other he had to get back to his studies. His schooling had been derailed by the death of his mother and would clearly go nowhere until this matter of the life cursed by neglected ancestors was resolved. I wondered if I should say something about wanting to help. Madumo interrupted my reverie.

"All I know," he said quietly, "is that I am in an urban area, and my ancestors are in the rural areas. Communication has broken down. If I can get some money, I *will* go to their graves."

Suddenly the atmosphere of the room seemed unbearably squalid.

"Fine," I said. "Go to their graves. But for fuck's sake get out of that bed first. Come on. Let's get out of here and get something to eat."

Madumo sprang out of his bed and dressed quickly. I resolved not to mention the possibility of helping him until I'd discussed his situation with MaMfete, the woman I call Mother in Soweto.

3

IN THE CITY

Madumo had not been easily dislodged from the family home. When accused of killing his mother he vehemently denied using witchcraft, demanding proof, which none could produce—not brothers, nor sister, nor aunts. Inside the house the atmosphere grew ever more poisonous. Yet Madumo hung on, for he had nowhere else to stay, and besides, as he insisted in the face of his brother's rage, this was his home and he had a right to stay under the family's roof. In the interests of peace, though, he kept out of everyone's way, leaving the house early in the morning and returning quietly at night, tapping on his sister's window and waiting quietly for her to open the kitchen door. For two months he carried on thus, spending his days in libraries or at the University of South Africa campus in Pretoria—two hours north of Soweto—preparing for his exams.

Two days before the exams, his brother broke the stalemate in the house. Madumo returned from a day of study to find his blankets burnt and his clothes, books, and belongings dumped in a heap in the yard behind the house. The door was locked. He tapped on his sister's window. No answer. He sank to his arse on the cold concrete stoep, leant against the door, and wept like a baby. No one answered his cries. He rapped on the door again, hard, and then harder. No one answered. He staggered to his feet and kicked the resonant metal door with enough force to buckle it in at the bottom and leave him hopping and cursing with bruised toes. Vagrant wisps of acrid smoke from the pile of blankets still smoldering in the corner of the yard burnt into his eyes, blinding him with anger and anguish.

He had no option but to go, but he had nowhere to go to. He wandered down to the station determined to throw himself from the bridge and into the path of an onrushing train. A train pulled out of the station as he climbed the stairs of the overpass. He waited for another. It was getting late, and cold. At that hour on a Saturday night in Soweto, trains are few. The station was deserted. In the distance he could see Merafe Hostel. He closed his eyes and revisited the days when Zulu *impis,* phalanxes of armed warriors, would surge through the hostel gates and massacre commuters on their way to work. He closed his eyes and willed such an attack, an attack that would leave him a hero: dead and mourned by strangers heaping his grave with pity and ire. None came. The Zulus were sleeping and the hostel had been quiet for years.

The next train to arrive found him huddling on the platform with the wind whipping thin trousers around his sockless ankles. He climbed into the warmth and rode to Naledi, the next station and the end of the line. At Naledi another train waited across the platform. He boarded the train and fell asleep. Thereupon he dreamt a marvelous dream in which his mother came to him and smiled. When he awoke the train was in motion and the last traces of his dream were scattering across a sleeping Soweto. In the harsh flourescent glare of the overhead light, Madumo realized that he was the only passenger and was on his way into the city with neither a ticket nor a penny in his pocket.

Disembarking before dawn at Park Station in downtown Johannesburg, he wandered the deserted streets aimlessly, kicking scraps of garbage north towards Hillbrow. On Pretoria Street he came upon two men by a fire, eating bananas. He greeted them in Zulu, formally, as a young man should, and they replied with the formality of those unaccustomed to the language. The taller man gestured for Madumo to join them at the fire. As the flames devoured the cardboard that he was stripping from a fruit box, his shadow danced ever larger on the wall behind. Madumo noticed a deep scar running the length of the man's cheek to the crimson white of a bulbous eye. The other man, small and very dark, said nothing beyond the greeting and retreated into his oversized greatcoat and onto an upturned tin to sleep.

The fire-tender was talkative and glad to have company. He pointed to a pile of bananas, rotten bananas discarded the night before from a street vendor's stall, and told the newcomer to eat. The bottles at his feet were empty. "Finished!" he said, catching the drift of Madumo's gaze. They were watchmen, he explained, gesturing towards the boarded-up building behind him with an elbow interrupted from the tearing of the box. Madumo ate hungrily and felt a faint stirring of relief. While the small man slept, the fire-tender introduced himself as Ben. Pointing to his companion, he muttered, "Ike." Both seemed to be in their middle forties and were dressed in the manner of men whom life was not treating kindly.

"Where do you stay?" Madumo asked after offering his own name.

"Here," replied Ben. "And you?"

Madumo explained that he lived in Mapetla, Soweto, though it crossed his mind to say "here," too. He warmed his hands over the flames, feeling himself drawn into the graceful dance of the fire as it swept up the side of the drum with each feed of cardboard to lick at the edges of the fading night. He tried in vain to remember his dream, to grasp his mother's message. All that remained was the image of her face, fading now with the dawn's slow entry upon the tawdry Hillbrow streetscape. He lost track of Ben's talk, pondering instead his own life and sorrows.

Madumo felt he'd had more than his share of misfortune. As

a boy, he'd been regarded as one of the brightest students at school. But he came of age in interesting times, the mid-eighties, when South Africa and Soweto were all a tumult of uproar and protest in the struggle against apartheid. Madumo's school, Morris Isaacson, was famous as the headquarters of the '76 Revolt. Though too young for the glory of '76, Madumo was an activist in his day. Every youth was a combatant in those times, a comrade. Madumo was known as Comrade COSAS, after his role in the swiftly banned Congress of South African Students. "Liberation before Education" was their slogan. He was arrested a couple of times during the States of Emergency, but never tortured, nor imprisoned, nor forced into exile. Education denied was his contribution to the price of freedom. In 1985, when his turn to attack the dreaded Matric arrived, the exams were canceled because of the political turmoil. He sat for them the following year, but failed. Narrowly. He tried the next year but again, no luck. For the next five years he loitered around Mapetla, unable to find work or build a future in the dying days of apartheid. In 1991 he scored a job selling tickets at a cinema in Shareworld, a theme park designed to bring all races and cultures together. But business was poor and Shareworld went bankrupt. Madumo never saw a pay packet again.

Madumo's father drove trucks, long-distance semi-trailers, up and down the country. He earned good money. His firstborn became a teacher, later moving into banking. He even encouraged his daughter to attend college after she passed her Matric. Madumo, after despairing of passing his, traveled the country with his father, hoping to be taught how to drive. But the trucking company bosses banned the carrying of passengers before Madumo got his chance behind the wheel. In '92, his father disappeared. Two years later Madumo heard he was in the western Transvaal, in a rural place, with a new wife and family. Madumo, along with his younger brother and sister—then all in their twenties—remained with their mother. They were dependent upon the charity of the firstborn son, their older brother, who was working but was married to a woman who resented her relatives.

Their mother fell ill and was confined to the house. Madumo was pressured to find work, but there was no work to be found—especially not for a young man of Soweto with neither qualifications nor experience. Then his mother died and he was blamed. He found himself on the street. He found himself cursed.

"You don't look the type," said Ben, interrupting himself from a soliloquy that was drifting into a long, detailed, and unrequited argument about auto electronics. He eyed Madumo's windbreaker. "Ski Jackson Hole," it said.

Madumo didn't know quite what type the older man was referring to, but explained that he was a student from Soweto whose mother had died recently, leaving him at the mercy of hateful relatives who had chased him away from his home. Ben nodded in sympathy.

"It's part of life," Madumo concluded.

"There's nothing we can do," said Ben.

Madumo agreed. He said nothing about the witchcraft.

"Life is too tough," said Ben. He gave Madumo his story: Before these hard times arrived, seven years ago, he'd crossed the border, eluding the lions of the Kruger Park, to come to Joburg from Maputo. He worked as an auto electrician, for a Boer, until the workshop was liquidated in the downturn of '92. When he lost his job and fell into difficulties, he couldn't pay rent, so the landlord threw his things into the street. His girlfriend disappeared. "She was South African," said Ben. "Xhosa." He lingered on that word, that "tribal" designation, as if to affirm both his status and her fickleness in one breath. Madumo understood. Nodding towards his sleeping friend, Ben said, "From Zimbabwe. Used to be policeman . . ." Madumo nodded.

The fire had died and so had Ben's interest in feeding it. Silence descended.

"This place is no good," he said, slowly studying his new companion with a prolonged sidelong glance that made the scar on his cheek turn his smile to a fearsome grimace. "You can't be staying on these streets."

Madumo looked away.

"Come with us," Ben said, rousing his sleeping companion with a gentle nudge.

Madumo followed his new friends down Pretoria Street, wondering what was in store. He was too tired to distrust, too cold to care. Hillbrow was still sleeping. Street boys were resting in doorways under cardboard, waiting for the traffic to return and give them work guarding parking spots. Shops, boarded up against the life of the night, crouched beneath tattered buildings terraced with flapping laundry. Whites used to say Hillbrow went to the dogs when the Blacks were allowed in and the place turned "grey," long before the repeal of the Group Areas Act that was supposed to keep everyone in their places. Now the Blacks are ruling South Africa, and people are appalled by the influx of "Africans," black foreigners they disparage as *maKwerekwere.* As in the old days of apartheid "influx control," the police try to stem the tide of migration to the city, challenging people for papers and deporting foreigners by the thousands every month. Sometimes they have "crime sweeps" and round up the immigrants in droves. Other times local hawkers rampage through the city to clear the streets of foreign competition. Madumo studied the pavement and burped a fragrant banana as he followed a pair of *Kwerekwere* to their home.

Ben and Ike, watchmen, had commandeered a derelict Indian linen store some few months back and installed themselves as landlords. The three-story building was slated for demolition, but no one seemed in a hurry to build in Hillbrow these days and their occupancy had been, so far, undisturbed. As they climbed the stairs, a small girl in a tattered red T-shirt reaching to her knees descended from the darkness, gingerly taking one step at a time and steadying herself against the wall as the contents of a bright yellow bucket slopped before her. Neither water nor electricity were supplied by Ike and Ben. A baby cried in the farther reaches. The rent, Ben explained as they reached the top of the stairs, was twenty rands per person per week.

Looking about him in the dim morning light, Madumo could see that the place was home to some three dozen people. Bodies under blankets were everywhere.

"Be at home," said Ben.

Madumo said he had no money. Ike stared unblinking while Ben nodded amiably and listened to the younger man promising to pay at the end of the week. Ben said, "Okay." Ike said nothing. He handed Madumo a blanket and retreated to his own corner, behind a curtain. For the rest of that Sunday Madumo remained wrapped in his solitude as the life of the flat unfolded around him.

On Monday morning, hours before dawn, Madumo awoke from a fitful sleep. Though born a mere dozen miles from the city, he had never before slept beyond the bounds of Soweto. He washed himself with a basin of cold water and a rag borrowed from Ben, took some more bananas, and set out for the two-hour walk back down the road to Soweto to the National Sports and Recreation Centre, where his examinations were to be held. UNISA, the University of South Africa, draws students by correspondence from all around the country. Forty thousand of them, or more, each year. At exam time they congregate for assessment in any sort of space big enough for a multitude.

For the next three weeks Madumo struggled through seven papers until his exams were completed—accounting, business management, business economics. . . . By the time he was finished, he owed Ben eighty rands for rent. Ben had been supportive throughout, telling Madumo that he felt like an uncle to him and could see that he was trying to improve himself, so he wouldn't harass him for the rent. Just to be on the safe side, though, he held Madumo's ID and school books as surety against the debt.

After the exams Madumo wandered the streets in search of work. He ventured once back to Soweto, to his home. No one was there and the door was locked, but he was relieved to discover his precious books still secreted neatly in the corner of the big tin storage box in the backyard where he had left them. He returned to town. Christmas was approaching, and with it the annual market for New Year fireworks. One morning in the downtown regions of the city, where the streets are crowded with hawkers, he chanced upon a Chinese trader setting up a fireworks stall on the pavement outside a store and asked him for a job. Madumo told the trader that he was an immigrant from Zimbabwe, for Ben had advised that if he was known as a Sowetan he would never be trusted. The trader, whom Madumo only ever knew as the Chinaman, or *uChina*—for he never gave himself a name and was happy to call Madumo "Boy"—told him to come back early in the morning. Maybe there would be a job.

Next morning, early, Madumo was there, waiting for the trader to set up shop. He was given instructions to sell the fireworks and told he'd be paid on commission. Every morning the trader would arrive to find Madumo waiting. They would set up two long tables outside the store and display the stock in neat rows: "crickets" at one end, rockets at the other. Madumo amused himself arraying the brightly packaged explosives in combinations of color, reds against yellows over greens. After three days of diligent service, Madumo's boss trusted him well. Madumo seemed like a good Boy, grateful for the twenty rands he was given each day. He could be left alone in charge of the wares while the Chinaman attended to other stalls. By overcharging the customers in the boss's absence and pocketing the profit, Madumo quickly repaid his debt to Ben and retrieved his belongings. He even bought his landlord a half-jack of brandy as a gift of thanks. Life was smooth but going nowhere. He was obsessed with the task of not thinking about his mother.

Early one afternoon Ben strolled past Madumo's stall, idling the hours before sunset when he would become a watchman again. He arrived just as the sky was darkening in readiness for thunder. Friday afternoon crowds were hurrying through the city. Hawkers scurried to gather up their goods. The Chinaman had instructed Madumo that if the weather changed he should pack up the fireworks. Under pressure from the impending storm, Ben helped him stash the crackers in their plastic bags. When the tables were clear and the bags sealed, the two men looked up from their work and suddenly it seemed obvious that they should flee down Jeppe Street with the stock and the cash, so they did. A wave of thunder and water followed in their wake, sweeping them up in an exhilarating rush before dumping them sodden, panting, and shrieking with laughter in the shelter of a downtown verandah.

Assessing the weight of their catch, Ben said he knew an Indian who sold stuff to hawkers in the townships. The rain soon ceased and they found the Indian in his store on Diagonal Street. They demonstrated a couple of crackers in the crowded street and haggled for an eternity before the Indian consented to paying six hundred rands for the lot—a fraction of their value to the Chinaman. There was no question but that the proceeds would be divided equally, and there was no question that it was time to celebrate. Ben insisted they buy brandy, Mellow Wood brandy—a "straight" each. They returned to the flat in triumph.

Ben presided over the brandy. A steadily thickening knot of tenants stopped by for a nip, braving his shouts of "Buy your own fokken liquor!" Everyone was thirsty; no one was denied. When the bottles were empty, Ben sent a young boy out with cash for more. Madumo sat and pondered his future. A woman in the twilight beyond the circle of merriment shifted her weight to bring her grandchild from her back before despatching the drinkers a look of contempt. She glanced at Madumo, who by this time had been implicated in the heroic feats Ben was spreading before his tenants, boasting of their exploits. "And you?" she demanded, her voice, though stern, was quiet enough not to distract the others. "A kaffir is a kaffir," declaimed Madumo with a grin. In the sudden silence that greeted his statement, he felt the weight of the company's contempt slowly settle upon him, and it was good. Ben intervened over the murmuring to tell them the boy was alright. Madumo returned to contemplating his future.

With the three hundred from the fireworks, his fortune now totaled slightly more than seven hundred rands. It was a sizable sum for the residents of Ben and Ike's place, but not enough to go far. He was not optimistic about the exam results; even less so about finding the money for next year's fees. He figured that if he failed he could hardly ask for more help. He felt tired. For years he'd been studying on his own—first for the Matric at Damelin, then with UNISA while his mother sickened and died. The words of his aunt came to him again: "You're too old to be punishing yourself with those books." She was right; he'd had enough.

In the first moment of clarity that arrived with the third glass of brandy, Madumo made a decision. He had to get away from there, he reasoned. Since leaving Soweto he'd been living in a daze. All his energy had been devoted to not thinking about his mother and to containing his bitterness and desire for revenge against his younger brother. Even when writing his exams he had thought of little else. Yet in the surge of excitement he'd felt sprinting down Jeppe Street this afternoon with the Chinaman's fireworks, his anger and despair had become as droplets of spittle on a red-hot stove top. Now was the time to set things straight, he told himself. He tapped his empty glass against an empty hand and gazed down on the fresh bottle of Mellow Wood around which the drinkers circled. Somebody set down two bottles of beer to add to the festivity. Madumo felt gloom pressing in upon him again. He stared at his glass. One more and he would be drawn into whatever it was that his companions were debating as the brandy began to spike their talk with passion and fill their lungs with bellowing laughter. As if from a great distance he could hear Ben begin his favorite disquisition on the virtues of fuel injection. Revolving his glass slowly Madumo aligned both edges of the rim through a single squinting eye and found that he could achieve silence despite the hubbub all around. He would take advantage of the fireworks windfall, he told himself, and make amends with his family.

When the drinkers were deep into the Mellow Wood and bellowing at each other in an endless spiral of inanity—"No, my man! It's the BMW that's faster, I'm telling you. . . ."—Madumo set his glass down, retrieved his bag of books, slipped away from the flat without a word, and booked into a cheap hotel on Quartz Street, promising himself he would return on Christmas Day to celebrate again with his *Kwerekwere* friends. With seven hundred rands he could have bought ten days in the hotel, but he only needed two. He'd made a plan. As he finished a final, peaceful cigarette, he relaxed into the pillow and rehearsed his plan for the coming weekend. Tomorrow: buy the groceries—meat, rice, toiletries . . . some nice talcum powder for his sister. And a cake. A nice big cake. Then early in the morning on Sunday take the first taxi back to Soweto, before anyone can leave the house for church. Offer the hand of forgiveness, he told himself as he pictured his brother at the door: "We must forgive and forget." Forgive and forget. . . . He drifted into sleep while the well-drawn butt of his cigarette memorialized itself on the laminate of the bedside table.

But Madumo had forgotten that he was not the one to dispense forgiveness, for he was the one who had killed their mother—or so the brother insisted. Angry at being awoken by an insistent early morning knocking, he had dragged himself out of a warm bed to find Madumo at the door with his bags. Their sister had seemed at first less unforgiving—or perhaps more distracted by the offerings of peace. While the brothers ranted about who should repent, she carefully stowed the groceries before retreating to the bedroom. Madumo found himself defeated again. His cake sat sadly in its cellophane wrapper in the middle of the kitchen table, dwarfed by a rack of beer. Sitting in a chair by the door, like a stranger from the street, Madumo slowly gazed around the kitchen. The doilies were gone. Gone for good. His brother stood with folded arms in the doorway to the sitting room as if to guard the interior, his bland smooth face smug and self-righteous. Madumo could see he was not welcome; he would never be welcome. He resolved to go but his legs weren't with him. His brother stood there; hateful, silent and still. Madumo suppressed his welling tears and stared at his thin canvas shoes. Then stooping as if to clear a low-slung lintel, he pushed through the door and stumbled off the polished red concrete stoep. With tears flooding his face, he fled his childhood home once more and wandered aimlessly into Mapetla.

Months passed in a blur. Seldom sleeping in the same place twice and wearing out his welcome as he went, Madumo wandered through the underworlds of Soweto and Johannesburg. Through a friend named Lucky, who had a friend who knew a warder from Soweto, he began selling drugs to inmates in Johannesburg's Diepkloof Prison, the lockup nicknamed "Sun City" by the gallows humorists of Soweto after the famous resort in the former homeland of Bophutatswana. Business was good until one day a class of new recruits from the school for warders was sent to the prison to conduct strip searches of all the inmates. Madumo and Lucky's stock was confiscated. At least that was the warder's story. Another business venture involved selling counterfeit currency. Madumo knew some guys who acted as intermediaries for printers specializing in hundred-rand notes. Together with Lucky, who knew a Zimbabwean with real cash, they concocted a scheme to buy fakes for themselves and went into business. Before long they had a million rands in counterfeit banknotes, a "meter," to sell. Unfortunately, when Lucky tried to arrange a sale he was betrayed to the police, losing their real money as well as the fakes in the process. Luckily for Lucky, however, he was arrested while the counterfeits were in a rubbish bin some distance away and not actually on his person, so with the aid of a smart lawyer he was able to avoid conviction. The experience sobered Madumo's assessment of the risks of crime and further convinced him that he labored under a curse. He sold his last few thousand counterfeits (poor quality off-cuts from the main pile) to a friend who planned to pass them off on unsophisticated retailers in the rural areas and concentrated on finding himself a room of his own. After a long and dispiriting search he settled into the dreary room behind MaDudu's shebeen in Mapetla East, not far from his family home, and sank into hapless despondency, surviving on handouts and loans to pay off loans. I found him some six months later, his mind churning in a ceaseless lament for his mother and his own bitter fortune.

4

BREAKFAST STORIES

"I know you, Adam," said MaMfete, looking up from her breakfast, "you'll make up your own mind." Her voice trailed off into silence. She paused for a moment, fixing me with a gaze at once kindly and judicious. "Don't you think you've done enough already?"

I knew what she was thinking. I'd told her Madumo's story as we sat together at her kitchen table eating breakfast, told her I was thinking of ways to help him, and asked her advice about what I should do. But MaMfete had heard the rumors about Madumo selling drugs, and she has no tolerance for criminals of any kind. With the rumors confirmed, Madumo was now beyond the pale as far as she was concerned. I reserved judgement. My loyalty to Madumo was forged in the crucible of life on Soweto's streets and could not be dissolved merely by his misdemeanors of selling drugs and fakes. Back in '93, for instance, when thugs came with an AK-47 to "discipline" me (I'd chastised their friend for whipping a young neighbor of mine whom he called his girlfriend), Madumo, along with Mpho and Thabo, helped talk them out of it. There was no question then that we stood together. I would not find it easy to desert him now.

"I know what you're thinking," I said. From the livingroom I could hear the Sotho radio station, MaMfete's favorite, blaring out the sounds of an African gospel choir. "But he's no longer selling drugs."

"Oh," she said, looking unconvinced. She paused for a moment as she spooned the last of the oatmeal from her plate. Despite her disapproval she couldn't easily withhold her sympathy for my friend, especially because Madumo had loved his mother dearly. "There are too many pathetic stories here," she sighed, handing me her plate so I could stack it on mine. She smoothed the faded red tablecloth back into place and returned the vase of plastic flowers to the center of the table. Whenever I come to her with a story that has moved me, she'll remind me that there are many pathetic stories here, as if to say, "I've heard it all before," while at the same time lamenting afresh the suffering that is so much part of life here.

"Should I offer him the money for a feast then?" I asked again. "Maybe it would help if he could satisfy his ancestors. He's really in bad shape, you know. I've never seen him like this before. He used to say before that he was cursed, but it was like he was joking. Now it's different. He really believes it. He says his ancestors have forgotten him. He's a mess."

"It can be that he should do that feast," MaMfete replied. "But the problem is one: if he's not on good terms with his family, how is he going to make a feast? You can't do a feast on your own, you know."

"He wants to go to the rural areas, where his father's people come from," I explained. "Wouldn't that work?"

"Maybe." She didn't seem convinced and continued smoothing the tablecloth. "But that will be costly."

"Perhaps I should offer to take him to an *inyanga* or a prophet instead," I suggested.

"Sometimes that can help," she said. "But you know, Adam, some people here think when they see a white man they're looking at a money tree. They just want to shake him. So if the *inyanga* sees that Madumo has a white man backing him up, sponsoring him, he can try to make an overcharge."

"Madumo wouldn't allow that," I insisted, rising to clear the breakfast dishes. MaMfete smiled. I filled the kettle for tea.

Every morning—except on Saturdays, which are given over to funerals, and Sundays, which she saves for church—I prepare breakfast for MaMfete and we swap stories over tea at her kitchen table. Her kitchen at the rear of the house in Lekoka Street is both a sanctuary and a way station, a place where we linger over breakfast, where neighbors come to gossip, and where joys and calamities break first into the house. The walls are now painted a bold cherry red, with ceiling, floor, and cupboards in contrasting shades of white. The whole effect, punctuated by the red door handles on the cupboards, echoes the colors of MaMfete's uniform for the Methodist Ladies' Prayer Manyano, of which she has long been a staunch and devoted member. When the bright African sun filters through the red-and-white checkered curtains, the room feels warm, vibrant, and strong—a fitting domain for a woman such as MaMfete.

When I first began staying in Soweto in 1990 as the guest of MaMfete, who was accommodating me for her friend and coworker from the Carlton Hotel, the mother of my friend in New York, it seemed like a good joke to her—and she enjoys nothing better than a hearty laugh—to insist that the tall white man living in her house was her son. I didn't mind. I learnt to call her Mother in return. At first I was merely adopting, as instructed, the customary African requirement of according respect to one's elders. Everyone over a certain age is your mother or father here. After a short while in MaMfete's house in Lekoka Street, however, it really did seem as if I had been adopted into the family as a son and brother. We use this formidable and odd-sounding word "adoption" with a smile when we talk about our connection now because there were no formal procedures, nor paperwork, and nothing has ever been said or done to make our affinity seem like anything out of the ordinary nor to suggest that I might not be perfectly happy with the family I was born into at home somewhere else.

In families here it is not at all uncommon to find people unrelated by birth being assimilated into the roles, rights, and responsibilities of kinship. Indeed, MaMfete has another such "child," a woman named Naome, who enjoys referring to me as her twin brother, as we are the same age, if about as physically different as it is possible for two people to be. MaMfete's eldest daughter, Seipati, met Naome in a taxi one afternoon a dozen or so years ago. Naome was distraught because she had no place to stay and had to return to work knowing no one who could look after her newborn baby during the day. Seipati brought her home to her mother, and MaMfete opened her home to Naome and her two young children. They stayed for four or five years as part of the family before getting a place of their own. I arrived shortly after Naome left. We both remain part of the family.

"So what do you think Madumo means when he says his life is cursed?" I asked as I returned to the table with MaMfete's tea. "Do you think there really is something happening with his ancestors? Or could it be that he has been bewitched?"

"You don't believe in witches, do you?" she asked, chuckling.

"But seriously," I pressed. "I know Madumo believes in witchcraft."

"Well, Adam," she said, squeezing her spoon against the tea bag to extract the last drops of liquid, "I don't really know. It could be either way. Two/two chances." She set the tea bag on a saucer. After scooping sugar into her mug, she paused to think while her spoon circled in the tea, tinkling distractedly against the sides. "You know, in our culture, it's been like this for ages. There *is* witchcraft. And we should be very much aware of it as we go through life. So really," she said, rolling the "rrr" gently in the manner of a Sotho speaker, "it might be true that Madumo's mother was witched. And it might be true that Madumo has been bewitched in some way, too. You never know." She paused, ladling spoonfuls of steaming tea from the mug and watching the liquid fall back to its source.

Whenever something puzzles or excites me about life in Soweto, I crave the opportunity to sit with MaMfete in her kitchen after breakfast and talk it through. We've talked about witchcraft many times over the years, especially when I was new to Soweto and the topic seemed so exotic and weird. At times there has been an urgency to our talk. Years ago a mutual friend was dying and asked me to drive her on a wearying round of visits to healers, both witchdoctors and prophets of the indigenous African Christian churches founded upon spiritual healing. For weeks, I drove our friend to healers all over Soweto while suppressing my mounting disquiet at the parade of outlandish cures. I begged her to seek treatment at the hospital as well. "No one comes out of there alive," she would say in refusal, echoing a common sentiment. Sure enough, by the time she did get to the hospital it was too late. MaMfete encouraged me to assist in this quest for a spiritual cure and helped me to understand why it was necessary. She also encouraged me to keep trying to persuade our friend to visit medical doctors as well. Madumo's situation, however, seemed less straightforward. He might just be delinquent and depressed.

MaMfete looked up from her tea. Our eyes met. She sipped from her mug and placed it back on the table, stroking her chin in a pensive gesture that also served to mask the fact that she'd not yet installed her dentures. She frowned for a moment.

"As for me," she said quietly through her fingers, her voice soft and musical, "I'm not really deep into believing in witchcraft. But sometimes, you know, when I see things turning out in an awkward way, when nothing in life goes right, I find myself looking back and thinking that maybe it's something like witchcraft that's messing up life."

Again, she studied her tea. Again, she frowned. It seemed as if a fleeting cloud of memory was darkening her day. Then she smiled. I clasped my teacup in both hands, drawing comfort from its warmth. Although we'd often spoken about witchcraft, I realized I'd never heard MaMfete talk of being afflicted by occult forces herself. So I asked, "Have you ever been bewitched?"

"Me?" she replied, chuckling softly. "I don't think so!" She began preparing her morning "smoke" of snuff. Placing the round black Ntsu snuff box on the table, she scooped a small mound of the pungent ground tobacco onto the yellow plastic lid and sniffed with a capacious snort. Snuff is the sole legitimate vice for grandmothers here. When the grannies finish their boxes of Ntsu, young boys collect them to make wheels for the toy cars they fashion from pieces of wire. Dabbing a welling tear with a wad of tissue as the nicotine worked its magic, she continued:

"Have I ever been bewitched? No, I don't think so. Although there was a time while we were growing up when we once heard some funny noises at night—sounds of people singing in our yard—and the next morning we saw funny footprints and places where water had been thrown onto the yard, right around the yard. We were told that it was from people who were bewitching us. But apart from that, I don't think so." She was interrupted by the cries of her young grandson awaking from his morning sleep in the next room.

While MaMfete attended to the child, I remembered the time a pair of *inyangas* had come to the house to protect us from witchcraft. It was about five years back. They came from Alexandra, the black township in the middle of Johannesburg's expensive northern suburbs, arriving at our house one evening shortly after sundown with the husband of MaMfete's cousin. About two months earlier we had made the trip out to Alexandra ourselves to consult one of them for a cure for MaMfete's high blood pressure. She had spent the weekend with extremely high blood pressure and probably suffered a minor coronary attack. Although she is not a big fan of "traditional healing," MaMfete's regular doctor, Dr. Mohasoane, our local general practitioner, had failed to produce a cure, so she was prepared to try the *inyangas.* Her cousin in Alexandra spoke highly of this one, so we squeezed into taxis and made our way north. In Alexandra the *inyanga* threw his divining bones, identified the cause of her problem, and gave her a mixture of barks to boil up and drink. Her health, which a year earlier had become so poor as to force her to resign from her job in the Carlton Hotel's laundry, improved dramatically. (At the time I insisted that the improvement had nothing to do with witchdoctors but was the result of my preparing her healthy breakfasts of oats and fresh fruit. She smiled and told me she was happy to eat my "donkey food.")

After a while the Alexandra *inyanga*'s herbs became less effective, so a neighbor took MaMfete to consult MaBanana, a hugely popular herbalist in Soweto at the time. MaBanana was running an assembly-line operation, with scores of assistants brewing up hundreds of gallons of herbal mixtures each week and selling it in bulk at ten rands per gallon. Her house was besieged daily by hundreds of patients seeking cures. Everyone in Soweto had heard of MaBanana. MaBanana stuffed all the ten-rand notes in a plastic bag. Rumor has it that she went out of business after having been robbed too many times. MaBanana wasted little time on consultation or diagnosis, merely doling out bucketfuls of her mixtures: one for "high blood," another for "nerves," "running stomach," and so on. MaMfete had to wait for more than four hours before getting her *muthi.* It didn't do her much good. Eventually she returned to Dr. Mohasoane's pills, which at least kept the condition manageable, although the stresses of everyday life regularly undermined the pharmaceuticals.

When we were in Alexandra consulting the *inyanga* that time, he promised that as soon as he could he would come to our place for a house call. So although we were surprised to see them when they turned up that Thursday evening in December just as we were sitting down to dinner, they were not altogether unexpected. The *inyanga* from Alexandra whom MaMfete had consulted previously was a tall handsome man in his late thirties, dressed in a grey suit and looking every inch like an insurance broker. He was accompanied by an older man, who told me he had been in the healing business for forty-five years. We put rugs down on the lounge room floor so that we could sit without getting wet from the flood that had inundated the livingroom during the previous night's storm.

The *inyangas* prepared their "bones," an assortment of sheep and goat "knuckle bones" mixed with cowry shells, and asked Hendry, the father, and Thabo, the firstborn son, to throw them. In the fall of these bones, the *inyangas* promptly divined the presence of a *tokoloshe*—a short, hairy creature with enormous genitals and a voracious appetite for using them—at work about the house. The younger *inyanga* asked me if I had been hearing noises in the night. No, I replied. Hendry was less certain. A few weeks back he'd asked me if I'd heard anything on the roof during the night. I hadn't; not recently. When I first moved into the outside room, I had joked about a ghostly leopard running around on my roof, keeping me awake at night. The problem was solved by removing the loose sheets of corrugated tin stored on the roof, which had been rattling in the wind. I hadn't heard any sounds after that and arrogantly dismissed Hendry's worries about nocturnal visitations as a product of the sort of habitual drinking that has been known to make less hardened imbibers see pink elephants and spiders climbing their walls. Hendry was somewhat obsessed with the roof because for the past two months, since the summer rains began, he had been engaged in a prolonged and futile battle against the leaks that had left the ceiling and carpets sodden with rainwater and reeking with the pungent smell of the tar he'd been smearing as a sealant over the tin. So I wasn't convinced about the *tokoloshe.*

As the *inyangas* began to interpret the words of the ancestors written in the bones on our lounge room floor, discussing their layout and asking questions of the family, it became clear to them that someone had bewitched us and sent this *tokoloshe* to plague our lives. The fact that only Hendry, the father of the house, was aware of its presence (even though he'd often told me he didn't believe in such things) proved, apparently, that we were in mortal peril. As far as I was aware, no one in the house had any knowledge of such a creature on the premises, and most of us were skeptical about its existence, though we went along with the procedure nonetheless. The *inyangas* were not prepared to tell us who had bewitched us, saying they didn't want to cause trouble in the community. They did, however, warn Thabo to stop roaming around late at night and informed him that his ex-wife was planning to go to the police to enforce maintenance payments for their four-year-old son.

When the diagnosis was established, the *inyangas* prepared a mixture of herbs to protect us from the *tokoloshe.* They carried with them briefcases full of roots and powders. Within minutes the room was transformed into a veritable apothecary. Some of the powders were in canisters, others in plastic pill bottles; some in paper envelopes, others in animal-skin pouches. The *inyangas* seemed to know what they were doing and nobody asked questions. The older man told me again that he had been studying herbs since 1948, the year when the National Party was elected to office on its program of apartheid. In order to effect full protection, they told us, the house had to be shielded and the family "operated" on.

The younger *inyanga,* the one who looked like a broker, mixed about ten different herbs from his sachets and canisters into a basin filled with river sand that Thabo had pilfered for him from a building site down the road. He then took twenty bluestone pebbles, also procured from the same site, coated them with Stork table margarine, and powdered them with the herbs. For a while I thought we might be obliged to eat this stuff, so I was very relieved to discover it was just for sprinkling around the outside of the house, on the roof, and over the cars. Then came the "operation." Each member of the family in turn was cut with a razor blade on the chest, shoulders, elbows, wrists, ankles, knees, and feet; the mixture of herbs and margarine rubbed into the incisions. The whole procedure took a couple of hours, and the *inyangas* departed two hundred rands richer after doling out packets of herbs for this and that to each of the family. We got their services cheap. Usually they charge six to eight hundred rands. Once, they told me, they had been called to de-*tokoloshe* a white lady's house in the suburbs because none of her maids would stay there. The fee that time was fifteen hundred rands. Luckily we had money for them, as I had been to the bank the day before to get money for our monthly expedition to the supermarket at Highgate Mall, beyond the borders of Soweto. Their fees would have bought us groceries sufficient for almost a month. They said we must leave the sand in the yard for a week. To the best of my knowledge, no one was troubled by a *tokoloshe* after that.

"So tell me," I said to MaMfete when she returned with the child, "do you believe there really are bad things that people can do by means of witchcraft?" Throughout her life MaMfete has been a devout Methodist, yet she cherishes the culture of her ancestors. When the family endures times of trouble, separation, or death—or comes together in celebration of weddings and births—MaMfete presides over the rituals, communicating with the ancestors, and guides the family, myself included, in abiding by the rules and prohibitions appropriate to the occasion. She integrates these rituals and rules relating to ancestors into a religious faith that situates Jesus Christ and the Father at the center of all creation after the manner of the eighteenth-century English evangelist John Wesley, founder of the church to which she is devoted. Though the rituals and symbols of the Sunday service were imported from England, in the prayer *manyano* that occupies her prayerfulness for the rest of the week MaMfete gathers with other women from her church to pray and sing and preach the scriptures—often for healing ailments of body and spirit—in a way that seems to me distinctively African.

"There are," she replied. "There *are* things that are done by witchcraft." The child on her knee gurgled merrily, experimenting with his first forays into speech. MaMfete stroked his soft, tight curls. He dropped his bottle on the floor and reached for MaMfete's unfinished mug of tea, which was deftly pushed beyond his reach.

"Such as?" I asked.

"There are herbs, *muthis,* which can really harm other people's lives. Maybe they can put it into your food and poison you. They call it *isidliso.* And there *is* such a thing, because even doctors are finding this thing inside people. What do they call it in English? Black Poison. Well, actually they used to be calling it Kaffir Poison, but that's a racist remark, really. So they could put that in your food, these witches. Even at the hospital they are knowing this thing."

"So is it just a poison, like rat poison, or does it work spiritually, or by magic?" Over the years I've heard countless versions of these techniques of the witch's craft, but I've never found anyone who could tell me exactly how such powers are put to work.

"*Hawu,*" she replied, laughing. "Don't ask me, *I*'m not a witch. But I know they can do it. Or they could sprinkle those herbs on the ground so that when you are walking on your way you'll pass over them, and they will just do something bad to you. Or while it's quiet at night and you are sleeping, witches can do their magic around your home. The next morning, when you wake up, you'll go outside and then you'll step over those herbs and then find yourself in a difficult situation." The child on her lap, who had been blinking at me quietly down the length of an upturned bottle, lowered himself to the floor. He found an orange where he'd left it in the corner by the stove and began kicking it around the kitchen.

"And you try to resist seeing witchcraft?" I said. "You try to find other explanations? Is that what you mean by not going deeply into it?"

"Mmm. I try to undermine it so that I can keep on with my life. You see, if you start thinking deeply about this thing you can start thinking that everything that goes wrong is because of witchcraft. That can really mess up your life. Before you know it, you'll be living in another land, a world of your own, where you really won't be understood by other people. It messes up your mind."

"I think poor Madumo's already living in that land," I said.

"He can be," she replied, brushing crumbs from the tablecloth. "It's bad," she sighed. "It's bad. I don't really know how to explain it. Maybe let me put it this way: It starts from a kind of jealousy, jealousy of other people and a wanting to bring misfortune to others who are doing well and succeeding in life. Or it can come from the jealousy that comes when others are married and you don't get married, or your children don't get married or don't get jobs or whatever. It's the jealousy that comes from seeing the successful things that other people are doing and then you start having a hatred to those people. And when you start hating those people, you start thinking of bad things to do towards them. . . ."

"But even still," I said, "even if you do try to undermine it, witchcraft really happens? In reality, you say, it really does occur?"

"It does. But at my home, when we were growing up, my parents were not too much into this thing of witchcraft. We were Christians. Anglican and Methodist, even though my sister is Catholic since she was brought up by our aunt in Bloemfontein. Generally, we are not too much exposed to witchcraft. But the younger people, today, some of them they're very much concerned about witchcraft. So I can see how Madumo is affected."

"So that was the only time you were witched? When you heard them singing in your yard?"

"There *was* one other thing, though," MaMfete replied. "It was a while back, when I was working at the Carlton Hotel. Maybe ten, no fifteen years ago. It was before we extended this house. It was still a four-room house then, with that tall fence at the front. You remember I used to work afternoon shifts sometimes and knock off at twelve midnight. They used to provide transport to bring us home. So that fence, it was nice and secure. Nothing could get through it, not even a dog. I used to have the key. So that night when I got home I was thirsty, and I went to the bucket where we kept the water—we didn't have the tap inside by that stage—but the bucket was empty. So I decided to go outside and get water from the tap. Now, at my house the yard was very long and the tap was far from the door, down there by the toilet. So I went out to the tap. I got the water and was coming back to the house when I saw it. A strange animal! Right inside my yard!"

"A dog?" I asked.

"No. It wasn't a dog. It was like a bear. It was so pure white. But I couldn't see the head, and I couldn't see the back of it. But this thing was moving. Maybe it was my imagination, I don't know. It was slowly moving. Coming towards me. So then I ran back inside the house and locked the door. *Hhayi!* I was sweating. I nearly fainted." At the recollection of her terror, MaMfete burst out laughing, her laughter echoed by her grandson, who had found his way into a cupboard and was enjoying the clatter of pots and pans.

"Were you drunk?" I asked mischievously, knowing full well that MaMfete has never been a drinker.

"Adam!" she exclaimed, feigning indignation as she distracted the child from his noisy playthings and closed the cupboard door behind him.

"And then . . . ?" I pressed, urging her back into the story.

"And then I decided to go and peep through the window at the front. It took me really quite some time, though, before I got my breath back. I was so afraid. So, when I was peeping out of the window, there it comes. It was white, like a bear. But when it arrived at the gate it suddenly turned into a black dog, and it just went out through the gate. Just like that!"

My face must have been registering its usual doubt.

"Really!" she insisted. "I'm telling you the honest truth. The facts." We laughed. "I was terrified. I didn't sleep the whole night."

"So then what did you do? Did you go to the *inyangas?*"

"No, I went to MaMantsiwe, that prophet who stays in the second street—up there. You know her. She gave me some water to use in the yard, and since then I've never seen that thing again."

"So who d'you think sent it? What were they trying to do?"

"You know yourself who it was!" said MaMfete, mischievously alluding to an old woman in her eighties whom everyone in the area knows as a witch. We laughed again and paused to sip our tea. "In fact, one time that one was seen at our gate by our other neighbor."

"Really?"

"Yes."

"What was she doing?"

"It was after I returned from a funeral in Bloemfontein. Nobody had been at home at our place for the whole weekend. On Monday morning, when I came back, Mmaloto, she used to stay in that house back opposite, came over to my place. 'Hey!' she said. 'You know what? Last night I saw a terrible thing on your gate.' At that time we used to have two vicious dogs, and Mmaloto had been woken by the dogs barking. She said, 'I saw something on your gate. There was someone there, and she was wearing strange things, like a feather dress—a very strange dress. She was feathered all over, and the dogs were barking at her, and she was trying to give them something to quieten them but the dogs were really mad, and they were running around and barking all the time.' Mmaloto said she peeked through her window and she saw you-know-who."

"Really?"

"Yes."

"How did she recognize her?"

"In fact there was a noise coming from the next-door house, someone was shutting the toilet door. And that caused the one at our gate to turn around. So that's when Mmaloto saw who it was."

"And she was wearing feathers?"

"Feathers! Imagine." We burst out laughing.

A knock sounded at the kitchen door, and we both called out "Come in!" A neighbor entered looking to buy meat. We changed the subject. While MaMfete and her visitor talked about meat, I remembered Madumo and resolved to talk with him about seeking a cure. But I couldn't decide what I should say. Should I offer to subscribe to his feast for the ancestors? Should I offer pay a healer's fee? Or seek some other counsel with the clergy or the clinics? I had no idea.

As it turned out, my doubts proved unfounded. When we next discussed the matter of his curse, Madumo requested a minimal sum—a "reservation" as he put it—sufficient to buy a few groceries to tide him over and to pay for preliminary consultations with a sampling of local healers. We would see if he could find one who could help.

5

DIAGNOSIS

Madumo gathered up glasses from corners of his room and departed to rinse them at the tap outside near the toilet. Mpho and I, remaining behind in his room, looked at each other and smiled when we heard him bantering with BraJohnny, the shebeen-queen's consort, as he ordered our beers in the kitchen of the house across the yard. "It's been a long time," said Mpho. I knew what he meant. During the worst of Madumo's decline, Mpho had been his last remaining friend and, as in all such friendships strained by the weight of calamity, Mpho's patience had long been sorely frayed.

Mpho and Madumo had been friends since their schooldays. When Mpho first moved into Mapetla as a young teenager, he had been made to feel an outcast as a "Zulu" by the local Sotho-speaking boys (who cared little that his family was actually Swazi). Internalizing the ethnic divisions imposed on Soweto in the 1950s by the architect of apartheid, Dr. Verwoerd, they bullied him and made his life a misery until Madumo stepped forward to be his friend. Over the years these roles came to be reversed as Madumo became the outcast and Mpho served as his protector. The local guys used say Madumo's mother was a witch; Mpho would deny it. In the past year the two friends had almost drifted apart completely. Were it not for the fact that I am close to both of them and had drawn them together again, they would have little to do with each other now.

In the week since embarking upon his search for a cure, Madumo had been making rounds of various healers in our vicinity. There are two basic types of healers in these parts specializing in treating the woes of sufferers such as Madumo: the traditional healer and the Christian prophet. Traditional healers are also commonly known, in Zulu, the Sowetan lingua franca, as *inyangas* or *sangomas.* (The terms in Soweto these days, along with those from other regional languages, are mostly interchangeable, and whatever subtle distinction they may once have carried has been swamped in tides of innovation and ignorance.) They heal by virtue of their special calling from ancestral spirits, who empower them in the use of herbs and other substances. Prophets, authorized through their connection with the spirits of deceased ancestors mingled with those of church founders, ultimately find their calling through communion with the Holy Spirit. They heal by means of holy water or everyday commodities, such as tea, coffee, soap, or Vaseline, administered in procedures not dissimilar, from the perspective of an outsider, to those of traditional healers. In my experience, all healers, Christian and otherwise, whatever else they may do, claim to be able to read the past and divine the future of their patients in order to provide a much needed spiritual security in the present for people living in a world littered with evil supernatural forces they ignore at their own peril.

Although he had previously purchased herbal remedies from traditional healers, and encountered countless prophets in the Zion Christian Church into which he was born, Madumo had never before known an urgent need for help in overcoming a wholesale collapse of his life and fortunes such as now assailed him. Previously, like many who have escaped the need for counseling and succor, he'd had a certain disdain, not to say contempt, for the work of healers and the needs of their clients. Now he was less assured.

Madumo visited two prophets before consulting the *inyanga* upon whose diagnosis he was about to report. One of the prophets had been too busy to see him. The other, a woman by the name of MaRadebe, had given him a consultation in which she diagnosed that he had lost contact with his ancestors but could tell him little more. Madumo was not impressed. The *inyanga,* however, a man named Mr. Zondi, had impressed him deeply. On his first visit the *inyanga* agreed to consult with Madumo's ancestors and told him to return the next day with six candles—red, blue, white, yellow, green, and orange—and twenty rands to open the way. The next day, Madumo came with his candles and cash—the money serving, this first time, more as a formal expression of respect for the *inyanga*'s ancestors than as a payment for service. Mr. Zondi accepted the money and lit the six candles. Then he burnt some of the herb called *imphepho* in a saucer, called upon his ancestors, and revealed to Madumo the hidden dimensions of his sorry plight.

Mpho and I were summoned the next day.

"So what did he tell you, this *inyanga?*" I asked when Madumo returned with the bottles and glasses. Mpho popped the top of one bottle with another and filled his glass with Castle lager, passing the bottle to me next.

"He told me about fate," replied Madumo, tipping droplets of water from his glass to the floor in the manner of someone paying homage to unseen spirits before filling it with beer from the bottle I passed. "He told me about fate and misfortune and the lack of communication with my ancestors."

"Is that all?" said Mpho. Though pleased to see Madumo cheerful for a change, he was still feeling less than charitable towards our friend.

"And again, about that girlfriend that I'm having a kid with: He said she's very jealous and wants to be married by me."

"That's way off the mark," Mpho snorted. The proof of a healer's power to divine your future and remedy your present is the ability to accurately report your past. Mpho and I both knew well that the woman of whom Madumo spoke had no such desire for marriage. We'd seen ourselves how poorly she regarded Madumo, berating him mercilessly for visiting his daughter empty-handed to the point where he no longer felt he could see her at all. Theirs had been a brief encounter. The way Madumo tells it, she had been much taken by the fact that he was eating calamari a few years back when, along with Thabo, we had taken her and her friend to dinner in town. He attributed his erotic conquest that night to the exotic dish of squid. Anyone would assume that a man commanding such a plate must have prospects. She quickly discovered the limits of his prospects, though not quickly enough. When their daughter was born, Madumo nicknamed her the Calamari—Marie, for short. The child's mother knows her by another name. When a squad of emissary uncles called at Madumo's house on a mission seeking cash for *lobola,* bridewealth, or else "damages" and child support, Madumo, who had nothing, had no option but to run away. Once the girlfriend's family learnt his true circumstances, no one talked seriously about marriage, though they never made him welcome to visit his daughter nor ceased complaining about the extra mouth to feed.

"Yeah. So that one *is* off the mark, I suppose," said Madumo. He seemed to be getting nervous, agitated. "You know, when he was doing, like, the reading of my life, that *inyanga,* he asked: 'How's your social life?' So that was when he pinpointed the Calamari's mother. He said it's going to be a hell of a war there. He said: 'She's crossing her fingers to you and saying, "No one's going to get him."' So there's that. That's what he told me. She's jealous."

"What else?" asked Mpho drily.

"Well, he also said that, like, about my friends . . . he said: 'They are quite quick to become angry with you.' He saw that

I'm not on good terms with a lot of people. And that's true. You know that yourself, Mpho. And even you, Adam. You were too much angry with me when you came this side. Even before, when you didn't know the setup, like, with the drugs and what what . . ."

"But Madumo . . . ," said Mpho.

Madumo cut him off: "It's general, like. Generally just being an outcast to everybody. Chased from my home. Having nowhere to stay. It means something." His eyes fixed on Mpho's and mine in turn, and we both looked away. When I looked up again, they were still darting to and fro. I reached for the bottle at his feet.

"So did he tell you what it means?" I asked, pouring myself another glass.

"He did!" he exclaimed. "This one, Zondi, he's too powerful! He told me all about my life. He made me put my hands over the saucer with the *imphepho* and made me sniff the smoke through my nose. Hey, that smoke was too tough! I thought it was going right through my head. Then he talked again to the unseen powers. He began to talk in deep, deep Zulu, calling the surnames of his ancestors, begging his forefathers to give direction, to help me. Then he asked me for my surnames. After that, he told me many things, all my problems, like. And he told me how he could cure me."

Madumo seemed convinced that the *inyanga* was powerful, capable of solving all his problems, and this conviction was beginning to radiate through him. Since I had committed myself to aiding in his quest for a cure, his spirits had risen markedly. He no longer seemed so mournful, so flat and dejected as before when he spent whole days in bed, staring at the corrugated tin of his ceiling. His days now had purpose and he attacked his project with vigor. We spent hours discussing the types of healers available and their various reputations. In these endeavors of healing everything depends upon power. Without access to great power a healer is useless in the battle against the invisible forces of evil and misfortune. But for their hapless clients, gauging a healer's power is never simple. Madumo was beginning to invest himself with confidence in this healer's powers; I was beginning to overcome my habitual skepticism about all things spiritual and encourage him. But I wasn't convinced yet.

"So what is it about the diagnosis that gives you such confidence in this guy, Madumo?" I asked. "I mean, this talk about the Calamari's mother doesn't sound so special to me. If I was an *inyanga* and some Soweto guy like you came into my place looking for help, I'd know for sure that he has a kid somewhere and that he's having problems with its mother. I mean, it's obvious. Everyone has that problem. Even Mpho here, the honorable Mr. Mathebula, has a kid with a lady who thinks he should be marrying her. And the ancestor stuff, too. You told me that yourself. You don't need an *inyanga* to tell you you've been neglecting your ancestors. And besides, he could tell that just by the fact that you came to see him. I mean, who ever goes to an *inyanga* when everything's going well?"

"No, Adam. He told me certain things. The truth! I talked to the man for two hours. Even if he was talking deep Zulu and I couldn't understand everything. He was telling the truth. I'm positive."

Madumo may have been convinced, but he didn't seem eager to expose the details of the truth he'd heard at the *inyanga*'s place. He changed the subject.

"I could go to MaRadebe instead," he said, staring intently at the dregs in his glass. "She charges less."

"So how much will it cost with this guy?" I asked.

"Six fifty."

"Six *hundred* and fifty?" I asked. "Shit!" It was enough for six months' rent on the room for which he was already two months in arrears and a sum well in excess of what I could dispense without heed.

Madumo leant forward nervously. "First it's two fifty for *ukugezwa.* He will wash me with *muthi,* some kind of special herbs. Then I should vomit with some other herbs, use steam, and some *spuit.*"

"*Spuit?*"

Madumo shifted his weight and gestured as if inserting a spout into his rectum. I got the message. Mpho looked skeptical, silently studying our friend.

"Then there's *ukuqiniswa,* some kind of protection. He will cut me with a razor on the hands and legs. That's two hundred. Then the third stage is to be discharged. He says then we should communicate with the ancestors by means of a hen. A white hen. So he will slaughter it and communicate with my ancestors in a sort of mini feast, like. That will be two fifty. Usually it should be five hundred for discharge, but he's giving me a discount."

"Two hundred and fifty?" I asked. The sum was far more than the amounts people in this cash-strapped place would ever dream of paying doctors or hospitals. "So altogether the whole thing will be six hundred and fifty?"

"Yeah. That's what he's saying."

"They don't mess around, do they, these *inyangas,*" I said.

"They don't," agreed Mpho. He turned to our friend: "So, Madumo, why don't you go to that guy in Chiawelo, the one that Santu was talking about?" He pressed Madumo to consult this well-known *inyanga* in a nearby district of Soweto, who was reputed by another friend of ours to possess remarkable powers and who refused payment until his treatments were adjudged successful—even then only asking you to give what you could afford. But Madumo still insisted upon Zondi. Mpho pressed him to consider the ZCC, the Zion Christian Church, the church of his parents, where the treatment would be free. Prophets of the ZCC—the biggest church in southern Africa—are renowned for their work against witchcraft. But Madumo was adamant: his heart was set on Zondi.

Mpho was still skeptical: "So tell me, Madumo, how do you know this *inyanga?*"

"I've known him a long time . . . ," Madumo replied. He told us how, back in the eighties, some friends were afflicted by venereal disease and were recommended to Mr. Zondi at Merafe Hostel. He'd prescribed them bottles of *spuit.* They were pleased with the results. When I expressed doubts about the efficacy of herbal enemas for the sorts of conditions he was describing—which sounded to me like syphilis or gonorrhea, and which I doubted were the afflictions of "friends"—Madumo replied that they also went to the clinic for an injection. I doubted that, too. The *inyanga* was needed to treat the underlying cause of the disease—the curse that had brought on the bad luck opening the way for infection. Antibiotics might cure the illness, but unless the witchcraft that lays one open to illness is removed, and protection secured against whatever further affliction might be despatched by those responsible, curing the illness alone is merely treating the symptom, not the cause. Madumo's friends discovered Mr. Zondi to be not only effective, but reasonably priced, so they spread the word. A bottle of his *spuit* was only ten rands—about the cost of three bottles of beer at the time. After hearing of their treatment, he said, Madumo consulted the healer a number of times for his own ailments, though he never underwent a major treatment such as was now required. During the years of war around the hostel in the early nineties, Madumo told us, he'd lost contact with Mr. Zondi.

"So you really want to go through with this?" I asked.

Our friend took time to answer, turning to Mpho for a cigarette.

"Yeah," he said, drawing in the smoke. "Yeah. Because now I am being haunted by a nightmare. I'm frightened. I'm frightened. . . . I don't want to die." We sat in silence. Madumo passed back the cigarette.

Mpho broke the silence as he poured himself another glass of beer. "But, Madumo," he said, "I thought you wanted to commit suicide? What made you change your mind?"

"Basically, I failed. Because it's difficult to commit suicide. It's so difficult. . . ." He scratched his fingers through his uncombed hair. "It's difficult."

"With a gun it's easy," replied Mpho, pulling an imaginary trigger on an invisible gun cocked at his temple and teasing Madumo into laughter.

"Even if you're having a gun, it's not so easy," said Madumo.

"You also have to be drunk. You have to have a gun *and* be drunk. First you must drink, or else you won't do it. So, when you're planning this suicide you go to the shebeen to buy beer. You'll meet someone there at the shebeen. You'll talk. Drink. After a few beers life will be smooth; you'll be enjoying yourself in that shebeen. At the end of the day, you'll have enjoyed yourself, so you'll come home to sleep. Tomorrow, maybe you'll plan it again. You'll go and drink. Maybe this time you'll get a woman. Then you'll be at home in your room with a woman and you won't be thinking of killing yourself. No, it's difficult this suicide. I've tried. Many times, I've tried. But I didn't succeed. I've had no success at that, either. . . ."

Suddenly the mirth was gone, as if a briefly flaring match struck in a darkened room had flickered its last and died. From behind his laughter, clouding across his face in an instant, an image of his terror emerged. Last night he had dreamt that he was in a shebeen when a fight broke out. Everyone was fighting, as sometimes happens in such places. Suddenly, the chaotic brawl changed shape and the fighters turned into a mob united in rage against Madumo. He fled to the toilet outside, struggling to hold the door against a throng armed with knives and guns. They were shooting and kicking at the metal door with resounding booms, and his bowels turned to mud. His screaming as the dream reached its climax woke his neighbors in the next room. Their calls for quiet punctuated with angry thumps upon the wall roused him in time to escape the mob's wrath. For the rest of the night he dared not sleep for fear of the dream, while screwing his nerves to breaking point extracting its meaning. He was convinced the dream was yet another premonition. His mother had frequently dreamt premonitory dreams, for she was spiritually inclined. Madumo, too, had this capacity. Indeed, he had dreamt her death long before his mother died. Now, it seemed, he was witnessing his own.

"So, Madumo," I said, vainly trying to inject a positive note into this baleful scene, "what exactly do you hope to achieve through this treatment? What d'you expect to happen?"

"Ah," he sighed, "it's hard to explain. It's difficult. . . ." He turned to Mpho: "Can you explain, Mpho?"

"No, I can't. I can't . . . ," Mpho replied, drifting into his own reverie. I poured myself more beer. Mpho too had had his torments of witchcraft in recent years and his own struggles with *inyangas.* His child had been born sickly a couple of years ago, and the hospital could explain little with their batteries of expensive tests. Knowing about genetics and the mysteries of chance, he strove to keep things in perspective. But the child's mother's family knew better. They were convinced that the two elderly neighbor women, who had asked to use their toilet only days before the birth, must have been up to no good. They must have been the source of the witchcraft afflicting the infant; they must have placed herbs in the outhouse to attack the mother-to-be. Mpho was not convinced, but it would have been irresponsible, and the cause of endless recrimination, for him not to do everything possible to aid the infant. So there had been no avoiding *inyangas.* The child survived, but was still not well.

A clutch of drinkers spilled out of the shebeen, laughing and clattering across the darkening yard, calling out greetings to us as they passed.

"It's general," Madumo said when the commotion ceased, answering a question I'd forgotten had been asked. "A general improvement should happen. With this treatment, life should just come okay. No problems, like. Good fortune should come to me, instead of this suffering."

"But okay," interjected Mpho, "there's protection, too, you're going to be protected, among other things."

"Yeah. Protection."

"Protection from what?" I asked.

"From danger . . . "

"And from being arrested," added Mpho, a hint of resentment entering his voice, "since you're involved in crime."

"Just put those things aside," replied Madumo testily, butting out his cigarette. He was getting tired of Mpho's disapproval. "It's general, general protection. Like when someone comes to you in the street and says, 'Hey you! Come here! Where's the money?' And if you don't have money he just stabs you to pieces. That kind of thing. I'll be protected. And again, the problems that I'm having at home, being totally rejected by my family. So now I'm alone in the world. . . ."

"Do you think this *inyanga* can help with that?" I asked.

"Yeah, I do. And it's important to be in touch with your family. We should reconcile."

"So how can the *inyanga* help with that?"

"He's going to give me herbs that will take out bad luck, so when I go home there will be reconciliation."

I was skeptical: "How can herbs bring that about?"

Mpho was skeptical, too: "You should be sitting down with your family, Madumo, and having a round table," he said. "Maybe you should call on some elders to come, too. Settle this thing properly, in a procedural way."

"No," replied Madumo, "he said that with these herbs there would be an automatic reconciliation without needing a round table to solve those problems."

Madumo was convinced of the *inyanga*'s power. We quizzed him for awhile about the herbs to be used. I tried the blunt approach: "You know these herbs are all bullshit, Madumo, don't you? Most of these guys are just taking chances. Their 'herbs' are just lawn clippings and scrap."

Madumo laughed, but would not be induced to doubt. "You see, Adam," he said, "it all comes down to the science of that *inyanga.* If he's knowing the right herbs, then those herbs can do miracles. But it depends on the power of mind, too. My mind. These herbs are helped by my belief, by my faith in Mr. Zondi. I can use millions of herbs, but without any belief, they won't work out."

"Mind over matter," said Mpho.

"So did this Zondi say you'd been bewitched?" I asked, changing the subject but finally getting to the point. An uproar from the drinkers congregating in the yard distracted us for a moment.

Madumo paused. "Ya," he said. "He did. He said I *had* been witched." He paused again, slowly twirling his beer glass in one hand, studying the patterns of foamy dregs clinging to its sides. Suddenly he looked up at us, one after the other, fixing his gaze finally on a spot near the stove. We were bathed in silence. He lit another cigarette.

"Go on," I said.

"He said that they used the soil from my mother's grave. He said they took that soil soon after she was buried, and they mixed their herbs in with it. Maybe they put that mixture in a bottle and buried it in the yard. We don't know for sure. But that is what has caused me to be rejected by my family, for them to fight me, all of them. And even to be having problems with my friends, and girlfriends, like, that's the reason." He paused again. Mpho and I were silent and still. Madumo's voice was on the verge of breaking: "Because I've been rejected, too much. And it's all because of this witchcraft." Again he paused and still we were silent. He regained his composure: "So you see, Mpho," he continued, "a round table can't work in this setup, not when it's caused by witchcraft."

"Who did this?" I asked. Mpho drew deeply on his cigarette and let out a long slow whistle of smoke.

"He didn't say," replied Madumo. "He just said a 'relative.' Not immediate family, but a relative. A woman. He said it was a grown woman, a grown-up. Elderly, like. So there's a lot of women like that. It could be anyone. But truly, I know he's telling the truth. I know that someone has witched me."

"So in order to cure you, what has to be done?" asked Mpho.

"I have to go to my mother's grave and take some soil back to Mr. Zondi. Then he'll mix herbs with that soil and wash me with the mixture. Then that witchcraft will go back to that one who sent it. *They* will be the one suffering misfortunes."

Madumo's mother had been wise to the possibility of further attacks by witches at the time of her death compounding the damage they had already done by killing her. She told her children that they must not slaughter a beast for her funeral, as is the custom in these parts. She was afraid that certain relatives might take some of the half-digested grass from the intestines of the freshly slaughtered cow, mix it with their evil herbs, and hide the mixture inside the yard during the night of the vigil before the burial, with dire consequences for her family. Either that, she warned, or they would use some of the blood, which flows from the dying beast's throat into a pit in the yard. In that case, the witches would come back late at night, dig up the soil where the blood was buried, mix it with their herbs, and bewitch her family. Such dangers Madumo's mother foresaw. So she made her children promise that instead of slaughtering a cow to feed the mourners, they would buy "ready-made" food—chicken pieces and meat—and make do. She also enjoined them to offer mourners only bottled liquor in place of the customary home-brewed sorghum beer. On the day of her funeral, in the face of gossip and raised eyebrows, her requirements were fulfilled. Yet despite all her precautions, as Madumo was now discovering, the witches had found a way. No one had thought to mount guard over the grave, and now the consequences were being felt by all.

"Madumo," I said, after he'd recounted his *inyanga*'s diagnosis, "you don't really believe that story, do you? How can a handful of dirt and grass cause all this conflict and bitterness? Besides, didn't you tell me yourself that this whole conflict with your family had been caused by your brother trying to get control of the house after your mother passed away?" In 1994, the houses of Soweto—which had been built in the apartheid era by the white authorities as rental units under strictly controlled terms—were granted to tenants as freehold property under a deal struck between Nelson Mandela and F. W. de Klerk. Houses that had until recently been despised as apartheid's "matchboxes" were now valuable real estate, and nearly every family in Soweto was riven by conflicts over ownership. Even Winnie and Nelson Mandela, after their divorce, went to court over the ownership of their old matchbox. Madumo had told me he suspected that his younger brother, abetted by their sister and other relatives, was trying to sideline him and their eldest brother in order to preempt their claims to the property. "Where's the witchcraft in that?" I asked.

"You know, Adam," replied Madumo somberly, "sometimes I just try to push aside all this thinking about *inyangas* and witches and those supernatural powers and try to think in this world of living things alone. So that's why I said that my brother just wants to push me aside to get the house, that they were just accusing me for nothing. But then, you know, even if I am trying to keep my mind free of superstition, it's generally known that when the father or mother passes away in a family this side, things like this witchcraft *do* happen. You can try not to think about it, but you can't deny it. And I've seen it myself. Many times. And how else can you explain this situation that I'm in, this bad luck and misfortune that I'm having? And you know yourself, Adam, that I never used to be like this. So I just have to keep telling myself that I'm lucky. And I *am* lucky, in fact. I had to leave that place, it's true, but at least I'm still alive. Otherwise, I could have died in that house. This thing is serious, Adam. As serious as death."

"So, Madumo," said Mpho, standing to smooth his jeans over the corrugations impressed on his arse by the beer crate, "how do you know that this *inyanga* isn't a fake? How do you know he's not just taking chances to take your money?"

"No, I know. He told me things about my life. Things that nobody could know. I have one hundred percent faith in him."

"But you know yourself how these *inyangas* are," Mpho retorted.

"No, I have one hundred percent faith in him. One hundred percent!"

I made one final proposition: "Madumo, what if I get this six hundred and fifty from the bank and just say to you: 'Here's the money. Do whatever you want.' . . . Like, you could use it for school fees, a feast for the ancestors, give it to Mr. Zondi, or even pay your rent. . . . Or drink it. Whatever. What would you do?"

"No. I will go to that guy. Because I know he *will* help me.

And then, when things come good, I will be able, you know, to make more than that money. That is what I must do. And I have that faith." He tapped three times on the cabinet by his bed to drum home his point. "*One hun*dred per*cent.* Because there's no point in going through these things without faith. Without confidence. It would be just throwing money away."

I agreed to get the money. Before I did, however, I wanted to meet this Mr. Zondi. Madumo said he would arrange it after the weekend.

6

TALKING OF WITCHES

Monday morning. In the backyard of the house in Lekoka Street, piles of laundry waited alongside buckets of soaking whites for the mother of the house to return and begin scrubbing. Inside the house, in the red-and-white kitchen, MaMfete and I had finished breakfast and were dallying over tea. I'd just finished telling her about Madumo's visit to the *inyanga* and the diagnosis of witchcraft perpetrated by an elderly female relative.

MaMfete laughed a long, throaty ironical chuckle. "I'm not surprised," she said. "They're always blaming the old ladies."

"That's because they're too dangerous," I said. We laughed together.

A knock sounded and the kitchen door opened before we had time to reply. Modiehi, MaMfete's friend and neighbor from down the street, entered. "What's so funny?" she asked in greeting, sitting herself at the table, upon the low stool that hides the rubbish pail. Tall for these parts, Modiehi sports an unruly head of hair streaked a rakish grey in the middle of her forehead, above a handsome face with a strong square jaw.

"Witches," replied MaMfete, still chuckling. "Adam's telling me about this witchcraft."

"*Hawu!*" exclaimed Modiehi in mock horror, pursing her lips and jutting her jaw. "Why do you want to talk about such things?"

"Because it's interesting," I replied. Modiehi feigned more disapproval. "Besides, didn't you know it's increasing these days?"

"*Hawu,*" snorted Modiehi again. "How can you say such things?"

"Because it's true," I replied. "And another thing, did you hear about this Inkosi ya Manzi?"

"The snake?" said Modiehi.

"Yes," I said. "He's been threatening the people in those shacks on the other side of Dobsonville, the place they call Snake Park. He says if they don't move straight away, he's going to demolish all their shacks and dump them on the border of Swaziland."

"*Hawu!*" exclaimed Modiehi again while MaMfete chuckled some more. "Do you believe that?"

I laughed. "I don't know. That's what they're telling me. I was there yesterday. Last weekend someone was there passing out pamphlets saying that Inkosi ya Manzi was angry. The people have built their shacks next to the river where he stays, and they are disturbing him with their noise. So they must move or else he's going to punish them."

"Inkosi ya Manzi?" said Modiehi.

"Yes," I replied, "the King of the Water. They say he's a giant snake living in the river there."

"That's nonsense!" snorted Modiehi. "You don't believe that, do you?"

"No," I laughed. "Not really. But down there they do. They've been having meetings of the civic association, of the street committees, trying to decide what to do."

"Are they going to move?" asked MaMfete.

"Where can they go?" I replied. Most of the people I'd spoken to recently about the threat announced in the pamphlets were deeply concerned about the powers of this monster, but resigned to their fate. They couldn't move even if they wanted to. Most were only staying in the shacks in the first place because they had nowhere else to go.

"*Hawu,*" said Modiehi. "There's too much witchcraft in that place."

MaMfete burst out laughing again, joined by her friend. "You shouldn't waste your time with these funny things, Adam," she said, swinging her grandson onto her back and fixing him snug with a blanket fastened at her breast. He would soon be lolling into sleep. I offered our visitor a cup of tea.

While I refilled the kettle, MaMfete and her friend discussed the details of their business. Partners in a meat-selling venture, they buy chickens live from a farm on the outskirts of Soweto to slaughter and pluck in the backyard; beef offal they buy in bulk from an abattoir in Vereeniging, a town about forty miles from Soweto. Dressing the chickens is hard work and the profit margins are slender, but they can sell as many as they can pluck. The problem is their customers can't afford to pay, so the butchery business is also a credit provider—interest free, of course. (Unlike the moneylender down the street, who charges fifty percent per month.) MaMfete brings to the business a determination born of financial necessity. Modiehi has a car.

After a long career as a seamstress, domestic servant, and laundress in the five-star Carlton Hotel (where she once ironed Senator Kennedy's shirt), MaMfete was forced to retire in the early 1990s because of ill health. She suffers terribly from arthritis and high blood pressure. Her husband lost his job at the same time when the factory closed where he tended a machine that put glue on the back of paper for stamps. In the 1960s and '70s he'd been relatively prosperous as a carpet layer. Now he occasionally gets a "piece job" to pay for beer and cigarettes. For MaMfete, life in the "new" South Africa has been getting progressively harder. She ekes out her disability pension, depends upon her youngest daughter, Keitumetse, a schoolteacher, and struggles to build the business. She worries constantly about what the next month will bring. I help out when I can.

Modiehi retired from school teaching when the new government offered teachers retirement incentives designed to remove imbalances between overstaffed schools in the white suburbs and overcrowded black township schools, only to find that legions of experienced black teachers, like Modiehi, jumped at the opportunity to leave the system. Her husband owns and drives a minibus taxi. Their elder daughter, after a stint acting in a television soap opera, now serves as a flight attendant on South African Airways; their younger daughter is at the Technikon; their son is at boarding school. Such achievements tend to confirm the verdict of neighbors who adjudge the family "proud."

"Inkosi ya Manzi indeed!" chuckled Modiehi, half to herself, when I handed her a mug of tea, the business talk complete.

"So you don't believe in witchcraft?" I asked, half teasing.

"Well, witchcraft . . ." she replied, "it partly exists. That's true. But me, I don't believe."

"How can it partly exist?" I asked, swinging myself down from the countertop where I'd been perched and pulling up a chair to the kitchen table. "Either it exists or it doesn't, surely?"

"Well, I've never been witched," said Modiehi, sidestepping the problem. "Let me say, Adam, that I've never seen one, a witch. Because usually, when you are building a house people will say: 'Be careful! They'll do something, those witches, that will make this house never to be finished.' Or else, when the house is already finished, they'll say: 'Now that the house is finished, somebody must die.' But, oh well, I've never experienced that. We finished our house and, well, no problems."

Modiehi, like MaMfete, had extended and improved her house in Lekoka Street over the years. Of the thirty houses on the street, nine are remodeled for greater style and comfort, including indoor plumbing. The families with "big houses"—about the size of a small suburban bungalow—encounter a good deal of jealousy and resentment from their less successful neighbors. (And, although we didn't know it at the time, Modiehi and her family were busy building themselves a new house in the suburbs far from Soweto.)

"But still you partly believe?" I pressed.

"Yeah, I do—partly," she insisted, sustaining the vowel of "partly" as if to emphasize the possibilities of doubt. "Take for instance Martin's mother, my mother-in-law. That old lady was going along just alright until this woman opposite her gave her food. So she ate that food. The following day she was dead. You see? So that is why I say I partly believe. But only partly. . . . Hey, I don't know. Really. And don't tell me that the people who are doing these things are just ignorant people. Even educated ones, they do these things."

"What things?"

"Witching. You can tell yourself that educated people, they don't care about witchdoctors and witches, but then you see that these are the very people that care most about these things. They say they are educated, but they are dangerous."

"You know, Adam," said MaMfete, "this thing comes from a bitterness in somebody's heart, like a poison, causing jealousy and hatred. And you can never know what's inside someone's heart. Truly, you never know. You can think you know somebody, but you don't. And people who have this spirit of hatred, this bitterness, they can do anything."

"Anything," added Modiehi.

"So do you use *inyangas* to protect yourself?" I asked our neighbor.

"No, I don't. I don't like those people. But I once went to the prophet on the other street. With her you just put twenty cents on the table and she tells you this and that—what is wrong with your life. You can go to her now, Adam, if you want."

"Hey! What do I need a prophet for? I'm a white man."

"Don't think that just because you are white you are safe from the witches," said Modiehi, laughing.

"So why did *you* go there, then, to that prophet," I retorted, "if you don't believe in witches?"

MaMfete smiled and prepared her smoke of snuff. Suddenly her friend seemed in deadly earnest.

"You see, there was this lightning. I was rushing home from my sister's place one afternoon because it was going to rain. I got home and found the girls inside. Immediately I got into the house . . . Whaaaaaa!!!" She clapped her hands. "The lights went off. So we went outside, all of us. We looked at the other houses. They were all having lights. We went back into the house and we found candles. When we came to this side of the house, we found bricks fallen down from the chimney. Hey! They were fallen right down. 'What's happening?' we asked ourselves. We went to the main switch for the electricity and flicked it up. The lights came back on. After that the people around here started scaring me. 'That lightning is going to come back,' they said. 'The eggs are inside.'"

"The eggs?"

"Yeah, I don't know how to say it."

"Of the Lightning Bird?" I asked. I'd read about the Lightning Bird, Inyoni Yezulu, or the bird of the heavens, but I hadn't experienced much talk about it in Soweto. Perhaps because the high mast lighting serves as a lightning conductor and reduces the incidence of lightning strikes during the summer thunderstorms, people in Soweto don't seem to be as perturbed about the witchcraft of lightning as seems to be the case in rural areas.

"Hey!" Modiehi exclaimed, "I started panicking then. What if that thing did come back? We could easily be killed, the whole family. The people around said: 'You must go to see someone.' I said I don't know anybody. Then I remembered MaMantsiwe, the prophet. So I went to MaMantsiwe. I put my twenty cents on the table. She had another prophet there, an apprentice, like. So this apprentice didn't know me. And I didn't tell him anything. So he started talking. He says: 'There is lightning at your house. This lightning wanted to hit you.' '*Hawu!*' says I. 'Wanted to hit me?' 'Yes!' he says. They sent this to you. Says I: 'What must I do?' 'Get an *inyanga* to come and visit,' says he. But I don't like these *inyangas.* So, instead, I took incense, the same as we are using in church—the Anglican church—I took that incense and charcoal, I bought it in town, and I burnt it inside the house. I still have it. Now, whenever there's rain, I burn this incense and charcoal. It repels the evil spirits. So I still have it. I use it every time."

"And you never went to *inyangas* about these lightning eggs?"

"*Ha!* An *inyanga?*" Modiehi pretended to be affronted at the very notion.

"What's wrong with that? Or do you prefer strictly Anglican magic, huh?"

MaMfete laughed. "That's a good one! Anglican magic." Modiehi joined the merriment.

"So when the other prophet was telling you things, he was correct, huh? You believed him?"

"Partly." There was that word again. "Because I didn't tell them before about the lightning that struck my house. You see? So MaMantsiwe told me, 'You are fortunate. Your ancestors are very strong. Otherwise you would be long dead by now.'"

"Did she tell you who'd sent that lightning?" I asked.

"Ah," replied Modiehi, savoring the moment before adding in a conspiratorial whisper: "She said it was somebody from our street." MaMfete and I both roared with laughter.

"So didn't you suspect anybody?"

"I suspected this one," she said melodramatically, pointing at MaMfete as if condemning the witch to death.

"Did you do it? Huh?" I asked, peering at MaMfete over imaginary spectacles in the manner of a presiding judge of Salem. "Did you?"

"I did," she confessed, and we fell about laughing again. The child on her back stirred with all the laughter and glanced around bemused by the mirth. He curled his tiny fingers into MaMfete's hair and sucked on his silencer. We laughed long and heartily, but behind such laughter, even amongst close friends, suspicions can still remain.

"They never tell you the name, these people," said Modiehi

when the laughter died. So you just wonder: 'Who can it be?' They just tell you things like: 'That lady who has done this, she is short and stout, just about your color. She wears glasses. . . .' Obviously there's going to be somebody around who looks like that."

"So who did you suspect?"

"Well, I hear people saying, 'Ya, there's somebody on that other street who's a witch. . . .'" MaMfete and her friend burst again into peels of laughter.

"Don't mention any names!" I insisted, pretending to be affronted by this shameless gossip.

"They say: 'Ya, that one. She's a witch.' But I for one haven't seen her witchcraft. Maybe she's witched me already. I don't know."

"That's why you don't see her," teased MaMfete. We laughed again. MaMfete snorted her snuff and returned Modiehi to their discussion of business. I cleared the table of the breakfast dishes and set about washing up.

We can gossip and laugh about these things easily enough, but when it comes to witchcraft in this neighborhood, that old lady—the same one who was seen years ago dressed in feathers at MaMfete's gate in the dead of night—is no joke. An accounting of her handiwork as a witch in these parts would have to begin with the misfortunes of the family down the street, misfortunes affecting three generations over the past thirty years. The old woman from that family is mad. She shuffles about the streets in a daze mumbling to herself, never greeting anyone though she knows well enough who is who. If you greet her insistently she will mutter something that might be a greeting in return. Most people around here blame the witch for her condition. Thirty years or more ago the mad woman was not mad. This is what they say happened:

As a young woman in her twenties she married an old man twice her age with three grown children. The old man was working, so was able to support her. She didn't have to work. In fact, she has never worked in her life—a rare achievement for a woman of her generation who came of age in the early sixties when there were jobs to be had. Eventually the old man retired. Some time after his retirement, his pension was cut off. The Boers were like that in those days. They could just cut off your pension or cancel your pass for no reason. So the old man no longer had money. He was destitute. The mad woman, who wasn't yet mad, took another lover, a young man. The lover moved into the house with her, into her bed. The old husband was forced to sleep on the kitchen floor. The husband and wife fought constantly. The wife refused to feed the old fellow. If he wasn't able to cadge food from neighbors, he would sleep hungry. One day a neighbor found him collapsed on the open ground near where people used to dump their rubbish before the houses were built on the other side of the tar road. The neighbor ran back to alert his wife. But the wife couldn't be bothered coming to his aid. After a while she peered out of the house to see what was happening, as all the other neighbors had gathered in the street and there was quite a commotion. "Is he dead?" she asked. "No, just hungry," they replied. "Oh," she said. "I hoped he was dead." And she slammed the door shut. Sometime after that the old man's daughters, who were married and living in townships to the east of Johannesburg, came to take him away. There was a huge row in the house that day. When the daughters were leaving they flung their curses back at the old man's young wife: "You'll never find peace in this house!" a neighbor heard one say. A couple of months later the June Sixteenth Uprising began. Three days after that, on the day when the neighbor was supposed to be hosting a meeting of her Society, the old woman—who wasn't so old then—went mad. It was in the morning. The neighbor heard a noise coming from a yard. She went to investigate. The mad woman had climbed a tree, right up into the branches, and was singing hymns and praying in a loud voice. In between her hymns and prayers she would start cursing with horrible vulgar words. From that day on she has never been right in the head. People lost no time in blaming the witch, even though the neighbor insisted that the woman's madness was caused by a curse from the daughter of the old man. But the others didn't hear the daughter's curse, and the old lady was already well known as a witch.

This madness was just one of the afflictions to be heaped upon that house. About a decade after the woman went mad, she was raped by a young man from the other end of the street. She knew well who had raped her, but the young man escaped punishment because people thought the victim was mad and had invented the story. Then her niece married a man who came to live in the house and he went mad too. He used to have a shed in the backyard, where he repaired shoes. The shoemaker and his wife used to fight constantly: she in the kitchen yelling at him across the yard; he in his shed yelling back. One day he became so angry with her that he took a bottle of methylated spirits and flung the contents at his wife. But when he lit the match to burn her alive the fire flashed back at him, igniting the bottle which he was still holding. His coat caught fire and he ran screaming into the back fence, trying to climb away from the flames. Fortunately for him, the neighbor's son was watering their garden with a hose, so he doused the flaming man while a crowd of excited children made wailing noises like fire engines. The man was badly burnt but refused to go to the hospital. Eventually he recovered from the burns, but then he went mad and died. Before he died he contracted a terrible pain in his stomach they said was *isidliso*—witchcraft. His daughter, now a teenager, lives in terror every time her stomach pains her, becoming convinced that she too has been bewitched and that her time is nearly up.

The mad woman's nephew also went mad, shortly after her niece's husband died. He was a nice clean boy when he was young, but suddenly in his mid-twenties he started sleeping outside under a tree in the yard, even during heavy rainstorms. Sometimes he would sleep for days at a time. He would rave and shout in the street. Eventually he died, run over by a train as he was trying to take a shortcut across the line. Then the mad woman's other niece found she could never have children, just like her aunt. Now they say she is dying of AIDS. All of these troubles and more are the results of witchcraft, and everyone knows the witch. They even say that this witch destroyed her own son's wife in a car accident in Durban.

"So you're really interested in this witchcraft?" asked Modiehi when I returned to the table after washing the dishes.

"I am," I replied. "Especially since now it seems my friend has been bewitched."

"Shame," said Modiehi.

"But tell me," I said, "like, with that old lady you were talking about. Has anyone ever accused her of being a witch to her face?"

"Not face-to-face," replied Modiehi.

"Ya, they have," MaMfete interjected. "In fact, she knows it. Well, I don't know if someone went to her direct, but she knows that people around here say she is a witch. She's told me herself."

"Does it bother her?" I asked.

"She seems to be . . ." MaMfete paused, searching for the right word.

"Accepting?" I offered.

"No!" interjected Modiehi. "She's not accepting." She took me to be suggesting that the old lady admitted to being a witch.

"She's not accepting," added MaMfete, "but . . ."

Modiehi finished her friend's sentence: "She knows that people say she is a witch, but she's not agreeing with them that 'Yes, I *am* a witch.' She can never do that."

"But isn't she angry with the community for calling her a witch?" I asked.

"No, she's not angry with the community," replied Modiehi. "She greets us and everything. We are friendly to her. But it's that word. She can't accept that word."

"It hurts," added MaMfete. "That word is too much painful."

"So let me get this straight," I said. "Everyone knows that she's a witch, and she knows that they think so, but so long as nobody says anything to her, it's alright?"

"Ya," agreed MaMfete. "It's something like that."

"And she's the only one around here, the only witch?"

"The only one," affirmed MaMfete. "Okay, some times back there was another one also, but lately I don't hear about her." MaMfete turned to her friend: "Do you know her?" Modiehi knew only the one.

"So has anyone ever gone to that lady and said: 'You've witched me!'?" I asked.

"No," replied MaMfete. "It's very difficult to face someone like that."

"Even when an *inyanga* has pointed her out as the culprit?"

"Most of the time that sort of thing happens in Pietersburg," Modiehi said, referring to the region in the far north of South Africa, where hundreds of people, mostly old women, have been burnt as witches in recent years.

"But it also happens here," MaMfete added. "There was another lady who they accused . . ."

"And they burnt her house," said Modiehi.

"She was saved by the police," said MaMfete. "Then there was someone by the name of Majola in Orlando East. They said she had zombies in her house, and they said these zombies were going to be seen at Community Hall. They burnt her house down."

I told them the story of Chafunya's mother, who was hacked to death and her home destroyed by a mob of schoolchildren after her son, a notorious gangster, was killed in a shootout with a local schoolboy over a girl. The youths were convinced, along with everyone else, that the mother was a witch and had been giving her son herbs to make him more powerful and deadly.

"There was an incident here, too, a few years ago," recollected Modiehi. "It was when I was still teaching up there in Mapetla. There was a woman who was found naked early in the morning. She was just standing there in somebody's yard. You know we have this thing here that if someone has protected their house with strong *muthi,* and then a witch comes in the night to do whatever it is she wants to do, she will be trapped. She will be frozen, just standing there not able to move, until morning. And when you wake up inside the house, you aren't supposed to talk to her. So when I got to school that day, the children were running out of the schoolyard. 'We want to see the witch,' they were saying. '*Hhayi!*' I said, 'get into the yard.' But they wouldn't listen. 'We're going to see the witch,' they said. And they went."

"So there really was a naked woman?" I asked.

"There was. Afterwards I told the children that maybe that person was somehow mad, you know."

"Not normal," explained MaMfete.

"Yeah, not normal. But the children said she was busy witching. They would have killed her, but the police came and took her away."

"Was she an old lady?" I asked.

"I think so," said Modiehi. "But I didn't see her. You know, whenever you are old, this thing of being called a witch is an ongoing thing."

"Yeah," agreed MaMfete, "it's a risk for old ladies. When you are old they will say you are a witch. So you mustn't grow old as a black person. Because if you are very old, like that one in the other street, they will say: 'She's a witch!'"

"Why do they pick on old ladies so?" I asked. "I mean, anyone can do witchcraft, can't they? Even myself, I could go to an *inyanga* who is selling witchcraft herbs and buy some. . . ."

"You know why they pick on old people?" said MaMfete, another grin beginning to tug at the corners of her mouth. "It's because the poor old things don't have anything to do now. So people think that maybe it's their hobby to do witchcraft. They don't go to movies, they don't go anywhere . . ."

"Except to church," I said. We laughed.

"Even at church," rejoined MaMfete, "they can still do their witchcraft." She was only half joking.

"So how old must you be before you are at risk of being called a witch?" I asked.

"I can start witching now," replied MaMfete mischievously. "I'm a grandmother."

"No, No!" said Modiehi jumping to her feet. "When they see that you are starting to go like this . . ."—she shuffled around the kitchen as if hunched over a cane—"then they will say: 'No, why can't she die?'"

"And more especially," said MaMfete, "if your skin is very dark. Those ones are said to be witching the most."

"And widows?" I asked. "When your husband dies aren't you automatically accused of being a witch?"

"Definitely!" Modiehi replied, her jovial tone disappearing. I had clearly struck a nerve. "Husbands must not die. You can die as a wife. That's okay. Nothing will be said. But if a husband dies . . . Say if my husband died now, they are going to tell me that I witched him. Even if he dies outside the house . . ."

"In a car accident or something?" I offered.

"Yeah, in a car accident. They're still going to say that I caused that accident. That I have done that. That I've made it so that he must die. And at the funeral they will go to an extent of manhandling you, saying, 'What have you done to our brother?' I've seen it many times. Hey, it's dangerous to be a woman."

"Why is it like that?" I asked.

"It's always like that," said Modiehi.

"And it has always been like that," affirmed MaMfete. "You know, traditionally, those people used to be really oppressing the women."

"Anything that was said to you, you just had to accept it," said Modiehi.

"And as newlyweds," added MaMfete, "they made us work like slaves. Wake up in the morning and sweep the whole yard . . ."

"before six o'clock . . ."

"in the dark of the night . . ."

"and everyone in the house must have tea and breakfast . . ."

"and you must wash the whole family's washing . . ."

"clean the house, cook for them . . ."

"three meals: in the morning, at midday, and at night . . ."

"wash all the dishes, look after the children . . ."

"and the children's children."

"So if anything happens to the husband," said MaMfete with an air of resignation, "it's assumed . . ."

"that his wife has done something." Modiehi had the last word.

I interjected with the story of my friend Mr. Dladla, who was murdered a couple of years back, telling them how his friends insisted, against all available evidence, that the deed had been orchestrated by his common-law wife. She was then chased away from the home and business they had built together in their shack in Snake Park, leaving the property in the possession of his relatives.

"It's always the case!" cried Modiehi. "A man must not die."

7

THE HEALER AND HIS CRAFT

"There it is, over there . . . ," said Madumo, pointing to a shack in the distance, "that *mkhukhu* with the sign."

I steered the car, our clattering Dombolo, away from the gates of the hostel and over the ravines of the track leading down past its ominous red-brick facade towards the station. Above the small tin shack in the distance, on the open ground in front of the hostel amidst a cluster of similar constructions, I could see a sign wobbling in the breeze on two long, knobbly posts:

BROTHERS AND SISTERS
WE ARE ABEL TO CURE ANY SICK
PLEASE COME TO US

I parked the car.

"There he is," said Madumo, eagerly waving to a middle-aged man sitting in the window of the shack. "Mr. Zondi."

Outside the shack, on a table fashioned from an old packing crate, a collection of half-pint liquor bottles of the variety once favored for petrol bombs in these parts also announced with their murky brown liquids the presence of a healer within.

Township residents have always had an ambivalent relationship with the barrack-like hostel looming in the background of Mr. Zondi's shack. Like a fortress behind dark imposing walls, housing a population of several thousand single men, Merafe Hostel was built in 1972 amidst the family homes of Mapetla. In the seventies, before the wars began during the 1976 uprising, residents from the surrounding townships were not quite as wary of the hostels as they are today. They used to enjoy the performances of traditional dance mounted by the hostel dwellers on Sundays in the grounds outside the hostel. Men from all over South Africa lived in the hostel at that time, men with a lively sense of the traditions of their peoples. Their Sunday displays brought the air of a folk festival to the location. Local men in those days used to frequent hostel shebeens and occasionally use the showers there, as most of the township houses in those days had no bathrooms. Some local women, too, found profitable arrangements seeking boyfriends in the hostel, although more often women felt threatened by the enormous convocation of masculinity there. Young people like Madumo, however, born and bred in Soweto, disdained the hostel dwellers as backward and ignorant—especially when lowly paid migrant workers with dependants to feed at home in the country declined the invitation to join in the Struggle. Since 1976 periodic explosions of political conflict between hostel dwellers and surrounding residents have not helped relations. Hostel men that I have known consider local youths to be vicious and degenerate, lacking particularly the defining quality of African culture—respect for elders. In the days of Apartheid the police were happy to exploit these tensions.

In 1990, when I first encountered Merafe Hostel, there was a war in progress where Mr. Zondi's shack now stands. Like all the other hostels in Soweto, Merafe in that year became a stronghold for the Zulu-nationalist Inkatha Freedom Party and a base for sporadic armed attacks upon neighboring residents. This would not seem like an auspicious place to conduct business except for the fact that the rural areas—and, by extension, the hostels which are a rural enclave in the city—are considered to overwhelm anything the city can offer in the way of powerful witchdoctors. Rural areas are also home to the most fearsome of witches. That Mr. Zondi still works from the hostel speaks well for his powers, signifying rural roots in an urban domain. And although the hostels are no longer exclusively male, men predominate there still. From Madumo's perspective this gives Mr. Zondi's herbs an additional guarantee—they are unpolluted by the presence of women.

Madumo led the way, tapping lightly at the door before entering without pause for an answer. The healer's shack was divided into two rooms: an anteroom, where patients wait on coarse wooden benches, and an inner consulting room. Lining the far wall of the empty waiting room and imparting an earthy, cloying, bittersweet scent to the place was an apothecary of roots and bark piled loose on shelves and in assorted tins, jars, and recycled shopping bags.

The healer was waiting in the inner room, behind a folding card table carefully overlaid with a covering of newspaper and next to a window rescued from a wrecked Kombi. A new telephone sat on the window ledge at his elbow. He rose to greet us.

"Mr. Zondi," said Madumo.

Mr. Zondi, a solid man in his mid-fifties, had the look of a man who has known heavy labor, with a paunch suggesting he was now prosperous enough to have left such work behind him. He stretched out his hand and clasped mine in the powerful grip of someone accustomed to commanding respect. Somber in demeanor, though not to say stern, there seemed also something kindly, even gentle, in his disposition. His soft, round face would not have been out of place on a woman. Smiling as he answered our greeting, he turned to Madumo to say, "This white man knows Zulu well."

"No, Father," I interjected in the same language, "I speak Zulu only a little." Mr. Zondi seemed pleased with my efforts nonetheless.

After my brief exchange with Mr. Zondi, Madumo and his

healer conversed for a while in Zulu—"deep" Zulu of the sort not typically spoken by the youth of Soweto, even amongst those born into Zulu-speaking households. My grasp of the language these days is limited to little more than greetings. Several years ago, when I lived in Soweto full-time, I studied Mr. Zondi's language and gained some small proficiency in it. But the combination of forgetfulness during my life abroad and associating too much with the likes of Madumo—who usually speaks a mixture of several different languages in a distinctive Sowetan street argot known as *isicamtho,* or "talk"—has left me unable to comprehend more than the general drift of a conversation in "deep" or "pure" Zulu. Madumo himself is no master of this language. Linguistic purists, of whom there are many in the Zulu nation, would consider his speech hopelessly degenerate. Indeed, when he first suggested he wanted to consult Mr. Zondi—whom he described as a "typical Zulu from Mahlabatini"—Mpho and I both worried that his grasp of the language would be insufficient to enable him to follow the healer's instructions to the letter, as is usually required. Madumo assured us that he would have no problem, even though Zulu was not his mother tongue and he had never studied it at school. "And your ancestors?" I had asked. "How will they be able to communicate with a Zulu from Mahlabatini, like this Zondi, when they only speak Tswana?" Madumo insisted there would be no problem. He was sure, although he couldn't say why, that the ancestors could understand any language. I had sometimes had cause to wonder about that myself when called upon to say my piece to the ancestors during family rituals at home in Lekoka Street.

Madumo seemed relaxed and cheerful, proud to present his *inyanga* to me, and seemingly pleased, too, to be able to demonstrate to the older man his easy familiarity with this *umlungu* from overseas, his foreign white friend. He leant back comfortably on the old car seat that served as a sofa. I settled unsteadily on a red metal chair set at the table opposite Mr. Zondi.

Madumo explained, in Zulu, to Mr. Zondi that I was a professor from New York and that I had been staying in Soweto for many years. "He's wanting to know more about this witchcraft setup," he said. Mr. Zondi nodded sagely. Suddenly Madumo turned to me and said abruptly, in English: "So what do you want to ask Mr. Zondi?"

I was taken aback. Immersed as I was in the sounds and rhythms of their talk, I had lost touch, momentarily, with my own capacity for words. I mumbled something about witchcraft, about needing to understand it. I glanced at Mr. Zondi. He sat stock still across the table as if daring me to say more. I felt exposed. I didn't feel I could say that I was there to examine his credentials, to determine whether it was worthwhile investing in his services to heal my friend's malaise. Even less politic, I figured, would be to launch upon my usual disquisition about the necessity of distrusting all preachers, prophets, and priests—and witchdoctors. Madumo understood my ambivalence about purveyors of spiritual succor. He'd heard me rail against them a thousand times before. In the old days, he'd been cheerfully scornful, too. At first, when everything in Soweto had been strange and new to me, I'd suspended my habitual contempt for clerics and their ilk. Even back in '91, when a friend was dying from diseases the doctors couldn't name and we spent months traipsing from healer to prophet to priest and then back to the doctor in a sad, expensive, and dispiriting quest for cure, I kept my silence. After some years I learnt that in this priest-ridden place nearly everyone despises the other person's counselor, so my hostility to clerics and healers became a source of amusement to my friends. MaMfete, a woman whose generous piety suffuses every moment of her life, prefers to think that I couldn't be as irredeemable as I seem. As for me, while I sometimes believe my unbelief to be a limitation, it's not something I would want to change. So when Madumo turned and called on me to speak, I struggled for some serviceable words until I heard myself asking Mr. Zondi how it was that he'd become a healer. Madumo translated as Mr. Zondi gave me his story.

"I started in 1962 . . . ," he said, pausing to calculate how old he would have been in that year and deciding that he must have been about twenty. Like most rural people of his generation, Mr. Zondi has no record of his birthday. "That was when I was called." He had been afflicted with a mysterious illness causing pains in his chest and stomach. Shortly after the illness began, ancestors appeared to him in a dream and told him to go to the coast at Richards Bay to obtain water for healing. "They told me that I must go right into the water there. It was then that I knew I must *thwasa* to become an *inyanga*."

After obtaining the water from Richards Bay, Mr. Zondi was taken by his family to consult a well-known *inyanga* in the area to diagnose the true nature of his condition. This *inyanga* told him that his illness was indeed a call from the spirits to become a healer and that he would not be cured of his troublesome symptoms until he had answered that call and fulfilled the ancestors' requirements. In the process, he was told, the spirits that were now tormenting him would become his allies in the work of curing others. In the meantime the senior *inyanga*'s task would be to communicate with these spirits on his pupil's behalf. So Mr. Zondi followed the older man's lead and began learning about medicinal herbs and the rituals of healing. Every day, as is customary in such schools, the senior *inyanga* and his students would spend hours drumming and singing, calling down the spirits.

As Mr. Zondi described his days of drumming with the *inyangas,* I was reminded of the time, some years back, when a similar school was operating three doors down from our place in Lekoka Street. Every day the drumming would start shortly before nightfall. An insistent rhythm it was: steady triplets drummed out on the sun-cured skins of sacrificed goats stretched over the steel rims of discarded car wheels. Over and over and over again the distinctive da-da-dum da-da-dum da-da-dum would pulse through the neighborhood, signaling *inyangas* in training. In a call-and-response chant, Sifiso, our local *inyanga,* would urge his pupils to implore their spirits to listen. Children at play in the street, oblivious to these noisy interventions with the otherworld, would add a chorus of squealing from their games and their brawls. In the distance a stereo playing at full volume, as is the custom here, would be blaring disco against the noise of drums and brass coming from where the Mapetla Drum Majorettes were practicing their moves in the open space near the main road. Taxis hooting for passengers and trains rattling on the line to Naledi would round out the soundscape. Sundown would bring a slow transition to silence—and the antiphonal barking of guard dogs disturbing each other in waves across the townships of Soweto.

During his days of apprenticeship in 1962, the young Zondi would wake every morning at three and begin his drumming and singing. One night, before he awoke, his great-grandfather appeared to him in a dream and told him to sing no more. "The ancestors do not want you to sing," he was told. As proof of their powers, and testament of their intentions for him, he was given in the dream a recipe for herbs for protection from lightning strikes.

When Zondi awoke from his dream and told the senior *inyanga* that he would no longer be singing, the older man responsible for his training was furious. Zondi was supposed to be obeying the senior's instructions in every particular, not coming with funny stories about singing. But although the older man insisted upon following traditional practice, Zondi would not relent. He remained in the homestead in a state of disgrace. Relations with his senior soured completely. He could not leave before paying the older man the requisite cow in recompense for his services, but Zondi had no cow nor money to buy one. He did, however, mix the herbs prescribed by the ancestors to protect himself from lightning and was gratified to survive a storm when a tree nearby was struck.

Again his great-grandfather appeared in a dream, foretelling that a stranger from Inkandla—a district in KwaZulu—would soon appear at the *inyanga*'s house with the cow required by custom to pay for his discharge. Sure enough, in due course such a man appeared, and Zondi was released from his servitude. Thirty-five years later, recalling the incident in his surgery at

Merafe Hostel, Mr. Zondi laughed. "That *inyanga* gave up his herbs after that," he said. "He was no more trying to heal people after that. Instead, he went to get a job in town." Mr. Zondi didn't say outright that the man was a fraud, but a suspicion of chicanery clings to all involved in the business of divination.

Without completing his *ukuthwasa*—something like a final examination and graduation ceremony for *inyangas*—Mr. Zondi returned to his home and was taken under the direct tutelage of his ancestral spirit. He was told to find an *iswela* gourd—a calabash, which Madumo somewhat infelicitously translated as "bucket" when I asked the healer to clarify what he meant—and to adorn it with red and blue glass beads. The spirit told him to use this *iswela* for predicting the future and divining the nature of people's problems. His ancestors, he was told, would communicate with him through the empty *iswela*. By looking inside he would be able to read their intentions. And they would speak to him. They would transmit their instructions for treatments, prescribing whatever herbs or other substances were required and telling him where to find them. "Go to a certain mountain and dig up a certain root," they might say. After some time, Mr. Zondi's great-grandfather, the principal amongst his ancestors, commanded Mr. Zondi to also use *imphepho*—a sweet-smelling, everlasting flower that is widely used in Zulu rituals—in addition to the *iswela*. He was to burn the herb in a dish, and the ancestors would speak to him through the smoke. This became Zondi's main method of divination, an uncommon method in this region where diviners, numbering in the tens of thousands, typically use an assortment of astragalus "knuckle" bones, shells, and other small objects such as dominos, which they throw to the ground, reading the pattern of their fall as a revelation of the ancestors' will.

"Would you like to see?" Mr. Zondi asked when he'd finished explaining the *imphepho*.

"Yes," I replied.

He retrieved his briefcase from beneath the table. Opening the case, he removed a carefully folded red-and-black printed cotton cloth, placed it around his shoulders as a cape, and extracted from a clump in the case a handful of a dry herb resembling oregano, which he placed in a saucer on the table. The *imphepho* flared briefly when he put a match to it, then began to smoulder steadily, filling the room with smoke.

"Now the ancestors are coming," he said. "They are here with us and we can talk."

"You get power from these ancestors?" I asked.

"Yes," he replied.

We fell silent. The smoked plumed through pencil-thin shafts of sunlight streaming through old nail holes in the tin walls of the shack. Mr. Zondi sat with his eyes closed. Mine wandered and were stung by the smoke. I fought the urge to sneeze. Minutes that seemed like hours passed before Mr. Zondi opened his eyes and smiled. He said nothing about the ancestors and I didn't ask. It didn't occur to me as the smoke cut into my lungs that Mr. Zondi and his ancestors might be scrutinizing me to discover whether I came in good faith.

Madumo asked a question about the course of treatment they were soon to begin. As they talked I reflected upon the healer's tale. It was curious, I thought, that he should have chosen to introduce himself with a story of insubordination. From previous conversations with traditional healers and from my readings on the subject, I had learnt that apprentice diviners are supposed to subject themselves utterly to the will of their seniors, not only because obedience and service to the ancestors (mediated through the senior) is part of the spiritual discipline of the healer, but, more importantly, because during this time of spiritual excitation evil spirits—spirits bent upon their destruction—might attempt possession of them along with the empowering spirits of healing. Moreover, even the worthy spirits, which the healers seek to domesticate in the service of future healing, can cause a great deal of pain, discomfort, and turmoil in a novice's life if they have no way of making their intentions known. Accurate deciphering of such intentions requires the services of a powerful and experienced *inyanga.* By defying his senior *inyanga* when he was a young novice and placing his trust in his own ability to communicate with a single tutelary ancestor, Mr. Zondi had been taking serious risks. The fact that he had survived, indeed thrived, could only be interpreted as a sign of his power.

In the middle of pondering Mr. Zondi's powers, I noticed that Madumo had taken out his notebook and had begun confirming with Mr. Zondi his record of the costs for the various stages of treatment. When they first negotiated the prices Madumo had been pleased to be able to report that Mr. Zondi had offered to reduce the cost of the final "discharge" phase from five hundred to two hundred and fifty rands. He told me that Mr. Zondi knew he was short of money. He also knew that Madumo's *umlungu* friend was the person financing the treatment. I guessed that Madumo's recitation of prices was intended both to assure me that he would be scrupulous with my money and to assure Mr. Zondi that he would indeed have the wherewithal to continue with the treatment once they had begun. I was starting to feel more positive about Madumo's healing endeavor.

When their financial discussions were complete and the conversation had lapsed, Mr. Zondi gazed at me across the table. The *imphepho* had burnt out and the air was clearing. Our eyes connected for a moment before I looked away.

I coughed a little, awkwardly, to clear my throat. "So, Father," I said, "do you think you will be able to help this man?" I looked over to Madumo. He seemed to be studying something in his notebook. I found myself smoothing the newspapers over the edges of the table.

Mr. Zondi was clearing his throat in readiness for reply—we were all choking from the smoke it seemed—when the phone rang. He reached for the handset, greeted the caller, listened and grunted "yes" in Zulu half a dozen times, then hung up. "Ya," he said, turning back to me. "I can cure him. His case is not so difficult. Not at all. Because his ancestors are still with him. Even in these troubles he is having, they have not left him. No, we can beat this thing." He turned to Madumo with an avuncular grin: "We'll see this thing to finish, neh?"

I looked across to my friend, who was sitting forward on the couch, and caught the last traces of an attentive frown disappear in the face of a cheerful grin. "We will," he said. "We will."

Though I had my doubts about the nature of Madumo's afflictions and what to name them—psychological disturbance? distemper of the spirit? fraying of the soul? witchcraft?—I had no doubt that Mr. Zondi was sincere and skilled in whatever work it is that someone such as he does. He radiated confident authority. If I were Madumo and in search of a counselor or confessor, I thought, a man like this Zondi would do. And Madumo seemed at ease in his presence; indeed, under Mr. Zondi's influence, Madumo already seemed to be overcoming his morbid preoccupations. Whatever it was that the healer was proposing, I reasoned, it could hardly make matters worse for my friend.

Our interview was over. Clients were gathering in the waiting room. At this time of the afternoon, commuters start arriving by train from Johannesburg, and Mr. Zondi has many clients who stop by for a consultation on their way home. I wanted to talk more with Mr. Zondi, to know more about what it is that he calls "witchcraft," this thing that was afflicting my friend, to learn how it might relate to what I had learnt to call psychology. I wanted also to learn more from him about his work fighting witches, about the politics of witchcraft in Soweto. In recent weeks many people had told me that witchcraft was rampant and increasing since the end of apartheid. I was keen to discover why. But although I wanted to learn more from this *inyanga,* I could see that we would soon be outstaying our welcome. I asked if we could return another time to talk more about witchcraft. Mr. Zondi readily agreed. Madumo promised to return the following morning at dawn to begin his treatment. We bade the *inyanga* farewell and departed.

"D'you think it's too late for Jabulani?" I asked, starting the car. If Madumo was to begin his treatment at dawn, we needed to find the money—four hundred and fifty rands—for the first phase. A visit to a cash machine was required, and the closest banks were in Jabulani in the desolate fields of long dry grass adjacent to the Council offices, an area that was once designated the Central Business District of Soweto in the days when apartheid's planners were scheming to develop separate places for separated races. Business never took off in this district of Jabulani, but with the end of apartheid bringing an end to economic isolation in an era when the reach of modern banking networks stretched over planetary domains, the ATMs at the banks there were now happy to dispense cash for this *inyanga* directly from my bank account in New York.

Madumo paused to think. "Hey, I don't think we should go there this late," he said. "It's not safe." Cash machines in Soweto are also feeding troughs for criminals, and the Jabulani banks are dark and isolated, nicely situated for robbery.

"Southgate, then?" I suggested, thinking of the sparkling shopping mall on the highway between Soweto and Town situated in an area that the planners and politicians used to call the "buffer zone" between the "Black" townships and the "White" city. Now the area is a favored zone for building shopping centers catering to township consumers and to the new suburbs, where the black middle classes can separate themselves in comfort from their impoverished relatives in the townships.

"Yeah, Southgate is better. At least they have security there."

Dusk was settling on Merafe Hostel. The evening coal fires were attacking the thin, chilled air and my lungs were beginning to ache. The 5:15 train from the city had just arrived at Merafe Station. A tide of commuters was surging over the bridge into the smog, collars pulled close as they trudged past the hawkers packing their unsold wares at the hostel gates. A shebeen queen, potbellied and stonefaced, stood in attendance by her house of plastic and old canvas, while a gaggle of drinkers squatted on their haunches gulping Barberton from big tin cans. Brewed from bread, yeast, and sugar, Barberton is the cheapest drunk you can get, or so they say. I steered the rattling Dombolo back to the main road over the rutted track by the hostel, and we drove towards Southgate in search of cash.

8

A DELUGE OF WITCHCRAFT

As he began to glimpse the possibility of a passage through the torment he now knew to be wrought by witches, began to dare to hope, Madumo became convinced that he was not alone in falling victim to witchcraft in the new South Africa. All around he saw its evil presence. Every family seemed to be afflicted in some way, even those who appeared prosperous. Especially the prosperous! Stories circulated in whispers: this one is rich because he's made a deal with Mamlambo, the evil snake; he had to give Mamlambo his firstborn son so that Mamlambo would give him money. . . . Drawn by Madumo's growing obsessions, I too became steadily more aware of the fear of witchcraft lurking beneath the surface of everyday life. I would discreetly ask friends about their problems and learn that witchcraft was a worry to all. Madumo insisted that the "volume of witchcraft" was increasing enormously. I asked around. Most people agreed.

On our way back from the cash machine after visiting Mr. Zondi, we decided to make a closer study of this deluge of witchcraft. Madumo suggested that I tape an interview with him about his views on witchcraft in Soweto. We stopped at Lekoka Street to fetch my machine.

Over the years Madumo and I, along with Mpho, Thabo, and other friends, have recorded dozens of conversations about the situation in Soweto. When I was first here, in 1990, we used to gather with groups of comrades and talk about the Struggle; interview activists about their heroic deeds and analyze endlessly the possibilities for the future. South Africa in those days was a center of world attention, and Sowetans felt themselves to be at the center of South Africa. As an outsider, I was assumed to be telling their story to the world and "exposing the Government." At the time I thought I was gathering material for a study of political transition. We called it Research. Then the war with Inkatha began. You can hear it in the background of some of our tapes. In 1992, I bought a video camera and we began to document the everyday currents of life lived in the wake of History. We taped interminable talk about politics and violence and freedom and crime. We were always taping something: a chat after breakfast; a rally; a riot. The tape was rolling when the police began shooting at the crowds mourning Chris Hani in the streets outside Protea Police Station in '93. On that tape, the picture stays steady and zooms towards the gunmen as the volleys ring out, before tumbling skywards and then back to the ground amongst the feet pounding in flight from tear gas and bullets towards the shelter of a neighboring yard. (In the stampede away from the bullets one of the "comrades" had the presence of mind to try stealing Mpho's camera, but Mpho fought him off while they were scrambling over a fence.) After a while the video camera, and its "cameraman," were mostly pressed into service by the local kids in Lekoka Street to "televise" their impromptu talent shows, beauty pageants, and soccer matches. In '94, when the elections came, Madumo and I, along with our other friends, talked on tape about freedom and democracy and the prospect of a better life for all. We interviewed neighbors on their way to vote. We taped ourselves celebrating at parties and rallies. I took photographs, too. Thousands of them. They reside still in albums all over Soweto. I used to fantasize about "doing something" with all this stuff, but never got around to it. Though fragments have appeared here and there over the years, the mass of it is still waiting in boxes in my study.

So, when Madumo suggested we tape our conversations about witchcraft, it seemed an ordinary enough thing to do—just a way of telling ourselves we were being serious, doing research like in the old days. Madumo felt it was something he could offer me in return for helping him with the money for his healer. We fetched the tape recorder and stopped at Moloi's bottle store for refreshments before returning to Madumo's room.

I set up the recorder. "When would you say it started increasing?" I asked Madumo when the machine was ready. "I mean, I don't remember people being so much bothered by witchcraft before." I shifted my weight and Madumo's bed sagged. There was nowhere for me to put my glass. I couldn't get comfortable. My shoulder was cramping from sitting too long in the broken seat of the Dombolo while battling through throngs of commuters on the Old Potch Road from Southgate back to Soweto. I felt cramped, too, by the idea of being ON AIR and would much rather have stretched my legs out to where the microphone sat at the end of the bed and enjoyed my glass in peace.

Madumo, having organized the glasses and poured out two generous tumblers of whiskey, squatted in readiness on a beer crate beside the bed, focusing intently upon the microphone like a boxer in training setting up a rhythm on his speed ball. "This witchcraft?" he said. "I would reckon from '95 . . . January, January '95 . . . around that time . . . after the elections . . . That was when we Africans, South Africans, Black South Africans . . . we just thought . . . generally like, we thought that now we are free. Free at last. Free from the hands of the White Man. Everybody then just told himself that 'Oh, we don't have any grudges with Whites—they're our brothers and all—now we're going to face each other, black and white together, since now we are all free. We're going to face each other.'" He paused for a moment, studying his feet. "But instead, we found ourselves facing each other, black to black. . . ."

I found myself sitting upright, closely attentive.

"And one other thing that has caused this high volume of witchcraft," he continued, "is the lack of jobs. When other families are going well, their lives are compared. Then others become jealous of them and cause this harm. So it's lack of jobs."

"Let me get this straight," I said. "Freedom and democracy have caused the increased witchcraft because they've led to more jealousy. People are coming face-to-face with each other because they are no longer oppressed by the White Man. They are blaming each other now for their lack of success?"

"Ya," Madumo replied. "It's direct confrontation. Like, everyone is asking themselves: Who owns this? Who is having that? I don't know how to put it, really. Everything has changed. You know, in the past everyone was demanding their freedom. There was this slogan of 'We Want Freedom.' And everything was blamed on the National Party and the apartheid regime. Then the black leadership took over. So anybody with bad fates now, misfortunes like, is pointing the finger to someone else in a direct confrontation. There's no more of that old story of saying, 'I'm suffering because of apartheid, because of the White Man.' Now it's, 'I'm like this because of my neighbor.' It's all turned around."

While Madumo was speaking, his landlady's boyfriend, BraJohnny, appeared in the yard outside, stacking beer crates. A heavy-set man in his fifties with a light complexion and a clean-shaven skull, BraJohnny was dragging on a cigarette as he carried empty crates from the kitchen. Madumo greeted him and called him into the room. He showed him the bottle of Jameson Irish Whiskey I'd found in Moloi's. BraJohnny's eyes lit up. I switched off the tape and waited.

"It's special whiskey from overseas," said Madumo.

BraJohnny asked for a "tot" and Madumo said "sure." He filled a beer glass with whiskey. BraJohnny gulped a good mouthful and smacked his lips before exhaling a fiery gasp. "Phew!" he said. "That's hot stuff." Madumo laughed and drove the talk towards football, securing for himself thereby an invitation to the house to watch the big match between Kaiser Chiefs and Orlando Pirates on Sunday and the prospect of drinks in return. BraJohnny probably doesn't recognize Madumo as one of the crowd of faces on that day back in '86 when the young comrades disciplined him at a People's Court hearing. He'd been accused of mistreating his wife and taking up with a girlfriend—MaDudu. He was whipped almost insensate. While Madumo and BraJohnny speculated upon the outcome of Sunday's game and kicked about their memories of big matches past, I lost track of their talk and drifted into speculations of my own.

As Madumo says, habits of blaming apartheid were deeply ingrained here. And "Apartheid" named not just a government's policy or ideology but also the source and shape of a generalized misfortune: *Why are we suffering? Because of Apartheid.* The equation was too obvious to require elaboration. Even when unstated, as it mostly was, such an axiom could encompass in a solidarity of suffering the likes of BraJohnny and his estranged wife as well as the comrades like Madumo who had whipped him mercilessly in the righteousness of their "people's power." And it sometimes seemed as if misfortune became more bearable for having such a name. Suffering the afflictions of Apartheid was all the more noble for serving the cause of destiny: Freedom. At the same time, the motive force behind the suffering—the "racist regime"—seemed, paradoxically, all the more powerful for the invocation of that awful word naming its cause. There was so much suffering about. Who could doubt that *something* must be behind it? In the gigantic scale of its manifest evil effects, that powerful something towered over other agents of misfortune such as witches.

Then the politicians pronounced the death of apartheid and the Liberation Movement became the government. Freedom came and with it a chaos of possibility to fragment the meanings of misfortune. The solidarity of suffering was shattered as the question *Why are we suffering?* lost its distinctive hue. Blaming Apartheid and the White Man made less sense in an era of unparalleled social and economic advancement for black South Africans—*some* black South Africans. Cleaving to the old formulas would have made it imperative to ask: if the White Man is making our family suffer, why is he allowing another just down the street to prosper? And whereas in the old days the prosperous could be branded as "sellouts"—for no one prospered without the consent of the authorities—in the new South Africa everyone was supposed to be "progressing," and the purpose of political power was to make that happen. The image of power no longer represented the White Man. Institutions of government slowly took the form of ordinary black men and women struggling, and mostly failing, to do good things against overwhelming odds (with the exception of Mandela, who always carried some kind of saintly aura). The sense of the enormous evil potential of government gradually withered away. If there was no longer a monumental force of evil named Apartheid in the new South Africa, there was no massive countervailing force of the good, either. In such a field, the lesser agents of misfortune, the witches, could flourish.

Somebody, probably MaDudu, called from the kitchen door across the yard. BraJohnny answered the call and left, concealing his glass of whiskey in a hand crooked behind his sleeve.

Madumo returned his attention to the tape recorder. I flicked on the switch.

"What was I saying?" he asked.

"What were you saying? I don't know, something about witchcraft," I replied.

"About this witchcraft . . . ," he said, pausing for a moment, "oh yes, I remember. It's also about jobs. It's the lack of jobs that's contributed to the high volume of witchcraft. Because if someone is having a job, then his neighbors become jealous and will witch him so as to make him lose that job. That's why we're having so much high unemployment, because of this witchcraft."

"It's a vicious circle, then, this witchcraft business," I said, trying to gather my thoughts and return to the issue. "Witchcraft is causing people to lose their jobs, then the unemployment causes jealousy in those without jobs, so they then witch their neighbors who are more successful, causing them to lose their jobs, and that makes more unemployment, and then more jealousy. . . ."

Madumo paused for a moment. "Ya, it's like that."

"Yikes!" I said. We both laughed. "So nobody who loses his job thinks that it's just because of himself—he's lazy, say—or else because of the economy, or whatever? It always must be witchcraft?"

"No, not always. They're not always saying that. But it's difficult. If you lose your job, but then the other one doesn't, it's obvious you're going to suspect this thing. Obvious."

"So what is to be done?"

"Hey, we must ask Mr. Zondi. He can tell us that for sure. But the way I'm seeing it, I think these traditional healers must play a part. They're the ones who should be solving this thing. I mean, if we've got so many traditional healers, why do we have to suffer by becoming victims of evil forces?" Madumo remembered that at the inauguration of President Mandela in 1994 there had been hundreds of traditional healers massed at the Union Buildings at Pretoria to bless the new regime: "Who paid those thousands of healers at the Union Buildings? Why can't these healers protect our communities voluntarily? They can't just let our community be destroyed by this evil monster that is not seen, since they are in a position of curing it. They should form a club, like when they went to the Union Buildings for Mandela's inauguration and danced and burnt all the herbs for all South Africans—for Blacks, Whites, Indians, and all. They should go from location to location and pour herbs on the boundaries to keep out the witches. They should make rallies in the locations to sniff witches out. They should drive them out! They should protect the community by pouring their herbs in the street. We've got trucks and all. They should load in drums and drums of those herbs and pour them in the street. Sniff these people out. Definitely. I'm sure if they are going to protect us, witches won't be strong. If they just burn their substances, witches won't be strong." As a child of the era of mass action, Madumo thought it obvious that the healers should combine their efforts to struggle for the common good. "They should make rallies," he insisted again.

"But Madumo," I said, "I didn't think it worked like that. I mean, remember what Mr. Zondi said about his great-grandfather being the main man of his ancestors, the one from whom all his powers come? Wouldn't it be useless for Zondi to make a rally with other *inyangas* unless his great-grandfather approved? And who's going to organize all those dead ancestors? Hey, you'll have to wait until Mandela dies, then he can get together with Oliver Tambo and Slovo and organize the ancestors properly."

"And Hani! Don't forget Comrade Chris!" said Madumo, laughing.

"Yeah, of course Hani. They can build a nation of ancestors." I was joking, but the point was serious. In the past, ancestors of great chiefs and kings became ancestors of the whole nation, guiding and protecting their collective destiny. Not any longer. The casualties of colonialism in this part of the world had been felt not only amongst the living. Nowadays you are lucky if you know the name of your own father, let alone the ancestors of old.

"And another thing," said Madumo, returning to his theme with quiet intensity, "these *inyangas* are too jealous. That's why they don't organize. They're just in business for themselves; they don't care about anyone else. Why can't these people help with foreign investment? They've got the power to help with high escalating crime, help the police. Help the miners to produce more gold and prevent mines collapsing. And help fishermen down in wild seas. Help wineries in the Cape. Help with the different types of sickness that are found in the whole African continent. Sniff all the witches and destroy them from the society, since those witches are really cruel and destructive. And most important of all, they should stop supplying herbs to political organizations to strengthen them in fighting."

"But Madumo," I said, mischievously seeking to undermine

his confidence in the enterprise of divination, "if these *inyangas* are so powerful, why couldn't they find that little girl in the East Rand?"

The seven-year-old child disappeared on the day before she was due to appear in court to testify against the man accused of raping her. Four months later, as a result of the usual police incompetence, the child had still not been found and the case became a cause célèbre in the Johannesburg press. The girl's mother, with financial assistance of the congress of civic associations, hired a *sangoma,* a diviner, to help find her. Diviners are supposed to be skilled at finding things. Indeed, one of the tests they are given before graduating through their *ukuthwasa* involves finding a hidden object. No luck. A reward of ten thousand rands was posted by the police, but still the girl was missing. Shortly afterwards, the investigating officer convened a rally of diviners in a stadium near the child's home to determine her whereabouts. They were to become eligible for the reward. Few black South Africans would deny that the officer was acting responsibly. The diviners came in scores, with thousands of onlookers. They threw their bones, burnt their herbs, and communed with their ancestors. Then they sent the police off to the places pinpointed by the spirits. For the next week members of the South African Police Service searched houses, rivers, and swamps in diverse parts of the country in quest of the little girl.

The press reported the diviners' work with a mixture of irony and detachment. Black journalists are particularly skilled at striking a note in their writing that allows the believers to believe and the scoffers to scoff while preserving their own dignity as hard-nosed reporters amongst their white colleagues. My friends in Soweto especially enjoyed the coverage of the story of a diviner from the east of Johannesburg who made himself a laughing stock before a crowd of five thousand when he insisted that the girl was in a river nearby despite the failure of police divers to locate her. His spirits had told him she was there. The crowd insisted that he enter the water himself and retrieve the girl, but he was afraid of the snake. Bodies of water such as that river are widely believed to be the sanctuaries of magical snakes, and the diviner was terrified that if he entered the water without appeasing the snake he would be in peril of his life. The crowd had no sympathy, less patience. The very least he should do before entering the water, he insisted, was slaughter a goat to appease the snake. But there was no goat, nor time to delay. For even if under the water, the girl could still be alive. Most people here are convinced that the snake can keep people under water, alive, for years at a time. Indeed, many diviners insist upon having survived such an experience as a way of demonstrating their astonishing powers. The crowd at the river in Nyoni Park had no time for his fears. The diviner tossed a fifty-cent coin into the water in lieu of a sacrificial goat and began his search. A few seconds later he leapt from the water. The snake was after him, he shrieked. The police divers, burly Afrikaners, re-entered the water. They fished out a rusty exhaust pipe: the diviner's snake. The crowd was merciless; the diviner was miffed. "We do not need white people to interfere with this," he is reported to have said. "This is a black thing and needs the support of our people. All *inyangas* must come and coax the *mamba* so that we can take the child."

Reports of the divination fiasco occasioned much mirth amongst my friends in Soweto at the time, especially the story of the hapless diviner with his exhaust pipe. I wasn't surprised. People here tend to combine a deep faith in the general possibility of the divinatory enterprise with a hearty skepticism about particular diviners. Most people have received, or know someone who has received, false divination from these people. A granny I know, when her firstborn was an infant, discovered one of the baby's diapers to be missing—a potentially serious situation as witches could use the soiled nappy to perform their evil work on the child. She went to a diviner, who threw her bones and saw that the diaper had been taken by a woman neighbor to bewitch the child. After a terror-stricken week, during which she harbored all manner of plans for revenge should the infant die while she was trying to figure out how to pay for the treatment to protect the baby, the granny went to visit her sister and discovered the missing diaper safe and sound.

A couple of weeks after the spectacle of public divination in search of the child, the man accused of raping the child—whose trial had been aborted for want of a witness—was rearrested. Under the impression that he could apply to the Truth and Reconciliation Commission for amnesty, he confessed to murdering the girl and led the investigators to a grave miles from anywhere pinpointed by the diviners. The first official joint effort of police and diviners thus ended in a flop. But the failure of divination was not generally seen as proof of the futility of the whole enterprise of divination. All it proved was that the particular diviners who turned out to chase the reward money were phonies.

"No," said Madumo in reply to my question about diviners and the missing girl, "some of these people are just taking chances. You can't just trust them at all except if they prove their powers to you. That's why I trust Mr. Zondi. One hundred percent."

9

THE HEALING BEGINS

In Mr. Zondi's view, Madumo was a fortunate man. Despite his recent unhappiness and bad luck, his ancestors had not abandoned him entirely. Although Madumo had failed to consult them regularly and had neglected their needs, thus denying them the respect to which they were entitled, they were still watching over him. Were they not still in attendance, he would be dead by now. As Mr. Zondi explained it to us, his primary task in the healing would be to enlist these ancestors in repelling the evil forces that now had Madumo in thrall. Because Madumo had left his family home, however, these ancestors were unsure of his whereabouts. They were thus limited in their ability to protect him. The healer's principal task was to restore the connection between his client and the ancestors. Before he could begin on that, however, he had to repel the witchcraft.

Rising before dawn on the day assigned for the healing to begin, Madumo dressed quickly and hurried through the dark down Pilane Street to the hostel. Soweto was coming to life, straggling towards work and school. Commuters in long silent lines at the main road shuffled their feet against the morning's chill, awaiting taxis to town. Boxy grey PUTCO buses clattered past in roaring belches of black diesel smoke. Madumo turned down the path to the hostel gate. In the distance he could see the outline of Mr. Zondi's shack. As he approached he could just make out the rancid butter glow of candlelight staining the window and seeping underneath the door. He knocked quietly. Inside, in the waiting room, the *inyanga* was sifting through small pieces of ground bark. He looked up from his work as Madumo opened the door, answering the young man's greeting with a sonorous "*Yebo*"—Yes. Madumo handed him the four hundred and fifty rands. He started to complain about the cold weather but something in the *inyanga*'s face caused him to be quiet. Mr. Zondi pocketed the money without a word. Folding a small parcel of bark in newspaper, he placed it in the pocket of his grey tweed jacket and said quietly, "Come."

Madumo followed Mr. Zondi from the shack. Many times in the past few days he had reminded himself of his complete faith in this *inyanga.* Every day, in anticipation, he'd quietly rehearsed Mr. Zondi's accounting of the origins of his troubles, imagining the procedures prescribed for the cure. Yet entering the gates of Merafe Hostel in the company of this silent Zulu whom, he suddenly realized, he hardly knew, Madumo's faith began to falter. All the terrors of a collective nightmare descended upon him. He remembered the local stories of corpses found in fields nearby, stripped of genitals by hostel-dwelling witchdoctors; legends of Inkatha warriors guzzling bucketfuls of *intelezi* dispensed by *inyangas* like Zondi to make them fearless and invincible before rampaging from the hostel to attack residents; stories of captives seized in the vicinity of the hostel to till the fields of far off Natal. . . . I have one hundred percent faith in this *inyanga,* Madumo told himself again. He followed Mr. Zondi through the gates.

Shadowy figures floated through the smoke billowing from braziers near the gate. In the middle of the main drive, two men struggled with the engine of an ailing Kombi, cursing as it coughed and coughed again without sputtering to life. A woman swaddled in a sad pink dressing gown flung a basin of soapy water from her doorway while a loose-necked baby, secured to her back by a bath towel pinned across her chest, lolled this way and that. The stench of stagnant urine assailed his nostrils as they passed a wall that served as a latrine. The first smear of dawn stirred through the winter morning sky. Madumo followed his *inyanga* deep into the maze of barracks that is Merafe Hostel. Neither of them spoke. Turning the corner by a long low red-brick building, Mr. Zondi pushed open a door without knocking, startling a young man pumping a Primus stove on the floor. The youth looked up silently at Madumo for a moment before turning back to his work. Against the wall, half a dozen mattresses still in their plastic wrapping leant beside a tower of beer crates and two large freezers, suggesting that spiritual healing was not the only business conducted here. Madumo followed the *inyanga* into the interior room.

The room was bare except for a couple of battered old steel lockers, remnants of the days when these rooms were home to sixteen migrants sleeping four to a section on either side of the central kitchen. Mr. Zondi lit a fistful of *imphepho* in a saucer and placed it on top of a locker. He directed his patient to undress. Madumo slipped from his jeans and sweatshirt and stood shivering in his faded red underpants. Mr. Zondi opened his briefcase and removed his cape and instruments along with the six colored candles Madumo had brought to their first consultation. He lit the candles and stood them on top of a locker. A shaft of new morning light cut obliquely to a peeling patch of pale green wall. Sweet cloying vapors of *imphepho* plumed through the sharp morning air, expelling the scent of ghostly legions of sweat-drenched working men and their lingering residues of smoke, dust, and beer. Mr. Zondi approached his bone-thin patient, eyes impassive behind his full dark face. He carried a bundle of porcupine quills in one hand, the *imphepho* in the other. Setting the smoking saucer at Madumo's feet, the *inyanga* went to work. With a switch of quills in each hand, Mr. Zondi began jabbing and stabbing his patient in a staccato counterpoint across the back, chest, legs, arms, and head—even the soles of his feet—until Madumo was peppered with punctures.

"By this I am chasing away those evil spirits," Mr. Zondi explained, "and restoring good fortune." His words of deep Zulu dissolved into a sea of reassuring rhythm as Madumo closed his eyes against the stinging of the quills.

When little specks of blood covered his patient's whole body, Mr. Zondi gave two consummatory jabs to Madumo's breastbone and wafted the smoke of *imphepho* all around him.

"This is so that whatever you will do in the future will not be disturbed by witches, or by jealousy," he said. "People will appreciate your presence. They will not be short-tempered, or angry, or bored with you." He told Madumo to get dressed and go.

Madumo was delighted with this beginning of the treatment: "It itched like hell, man," he told me later, "but I could tell that it was powerful. No, that guy is too much powerful!"

The pricking with porcupine quills, however, was only a prelude. The real work of healing was just beginning. When Madumo returned to his *inyanga* the next day, Mr. Zondi laid down a strict regimen to be followed each and every day without exception. The first phase was to last fourteen days. Madumo was given two packages of herbs. One, a reddish tree root, was to be ground up and boiled. Madumo was instructed to steam himself under a blanket over the boiling mixture, breathing the vapors and making himself sweat. The other herbs, whitish stems of sundry indeterminate plants, had to be left soaking in a bucket of cold water. Every morning, before dawn, Madumo was to mix more water in the bucket, drink the mixture down, and then induce vomiting and purge himself of the brew.

So for the next fourteen days, roused each morning by the noise of his neighbor preparing herself for work, Madumo would rise, fix his *muthi,* steam himself, and vomit: Vomit, vomit, vomit . . . The evil inside had to be expelled. It was not easy work. The herbs made him feel tired, he told me; sometimes dizzy and lightheaded. "Mr. Zondi's herbs are too strong," he would say.

But he was determined. He didn't miss a day of that vomiting. Up before dawn, he would drink from the bucket of cold foul murky fluid, stick a finger down his throat, and heave, heave, heave until the retch became a spasm, and the spasms became uncontrollable, and the cramps began that forced him to the cold concrete floor in a fetal curl with half the bucket still undrunk. Then he would finish the rest of the bucket, add water for the next day's installment, and hit the road for a five-mile run before returning to bed, where, wrapped in his blankets, he would wait. On most days I would find him there when I passed by after breakfast. Day after day for fourteen days.

Madumo followed Mr. Zondi's instructions religiously. Every three or four days he would call by the shack outside Merafe Hostel to discuss his progress. He was dizzy and tired. Mr. Zondi was pleased. Everything was as it should be, and the witchcraft was being driven from his body. As a result of this treatment, Mr. Zondi said, the curse would leave Madumo and affix itself to the one who had sent it. Mr. Zondi was quietly confident, as ever. Sometimes I would accompany Madumo to the healer's shack, and we would spend the afternoon in Mr. Zondi's consulting room talking about witchcraft. Mr. Zondi spoke in the manner of a man with a message. His life had been devoted to fighting witchcraft, and the sum of his stories was the tale of a man who found himself losing but was determined never to give in. Yet although the witches were winning the struggle of good against evil in this new South Africa, business for Mr. Zondi had never been better.

After Madumo's first fourteen days were done, phase two began. Known as *ukuqiniswa,* the treatment was designed to protect him from further evil. More vomiting would be required, but first, the patient must be bathed. Again Madumo was led into the depths of the hostel before dawn. Mr. Zondi draped himself with the red-and-black cloth of his office and lit the saucer of *imphepho.* He lifted down a large tin bath from a hook on the wall and placed it in the center of the room. In the corner of the gloomy dormitory, on a well-worn board atop a green enamel basin, a chicken lay with its severed neck dangling above a dark pool of blood. From the inside pocket of his tweed jacket the *inyanga* removed a newspaper package, carefully unfolding it on top of one of the steel lockers. Madumo handed the healer a bag of his own.

The previous afternoon Madumo had made an excursion to his mother's grave at the Roodeport cemetery on the northwestern edge of Soweto. Smaller and better presented than the other cemeteries of Soweto, the place where Madumo's mother lies was originally reserved for white people alone, residents of the mostly Afrikaner town of Roodeport on the other side of the hill. Their graves were once in the middle of farmlands. Over the decades Soweto has swallowed the farmlands. The ancestors of Roodeport Boers now sleep surrounded by the houses and shacks of the Blacks, and the cemetery is open to all.

At the grave, Madumo had sat and talked with his mother awhile, telling her of the troubles he was healing and of the power of Mr. Zondi. He picked out the odd weed from around the grave and raked the bluestone gravel with which he had covered her mound some weeks before. When everything was tidy he surveyed his surroundings. The cemetery was deserted. Kneeling beside the grave he carefully scraped some of the gravel aside and prized loose some soil with the aid of a twig, scooping it into a grey plastic shopping bag. Quickly placing the bag in the pocket of his heavy woolen coat, he riffled the surrounding gravel over his traces. Nobody should suspect that the grave had been tampered with. The sun was already setting behind the avenue of whitegums at the edge of the graveyard when Madumo said farewell to his mother. He felt confident of her approval and hopeful for his future. To complete his mission he had to hurry back to Mapetla to buy two white hens for Mr. Zondi.

Mr. Zondi took Madumo's bag. A nod from the healer towards the tin bath on the floor reminded Madumo that he must undress. Gauging the contents of his client's offering on the palm of one hand while testing the knot about its plastic neck with the other, Mr. Zondi squeezed the soil from Madumo's mother's grave into a protuberant teat which he tweaked off in a spurt of dust and soil onto the mixture of herbs cradled in the unfurled newsprint sachet. From a pile of gizzards spread upon another newspaper the *inyanga* extracted a slimy sack, the gall bladder, and squeezed the greenish bile known in Zulu as *inyongo* onto his mixture of herbs and dirt. After kneading the mix with both hands, Mr. Zondi sprinkled the whole packet into the basin of blood, mixing it thoroughly with his soil-speckled fingers. He then carefully poured the basin into a large plastic bucket of water at his feet.

Another nod from the *inyanga* prompted Madumo to step naked into the bath. Mr. Zondi scooped up a jarful of his brew and, addressing the ancestors all the while, poured it over his patient's head. Madumo sputtered. Another scoop, and another, and then another poured down him until he was soaked and shivering and his feet were swamped to the ankles in a cold gritty soup. When the bucket was empty, the *inyanga* turned away from his patient to fix more herbs. He returned with a small pot of sap from a tree and smeared it across Madumo's torso. Madumo winced as the sap stung into his skin. When the work was complete Mr. Zondi instructed his patient not to wash for three days and to return at dawn the next day for the "operation."

The prohibition on washing was not unwelcome to Madumo, for the power supply in his room had failed and he had no access to warm water. When MaDudu, the landlady, had built the two-room-and-garage in the yard behind her house in the mid-eighties—the middle room of which Madumo now occupied—electricity was considered a luxury. The authorities were slow in electrifying the townships. When the boycotts started in '86, wires for lights were strung from the house to the outside rooms and along the beams from one room to the other. Sometime later someone spliced wire for a power outlet into the string for the lights. In the garage room, the largest of the three and occupied by the most prosperous tenants, they did the same to run a fridge, a stove, and a stereo. Downstream, the juice flowed through another set of lights and a cooker. Those were the days of boycott and struggle when no one paid for electricity in Soweto. "In Soweto we stay for free," the comrades sang. The government owned all the houses, but dared not evict their nonpaying tenants. They dared not disconnect the power, either, for fear of sparking another revolt. Subtenants, however, never enjoyed the luxury of staying in Soweto for free. By the time Madumo moved into his room, a new government was in office, a government of the people—a government that had granted the former tenants free title to their houses and was desperately trying to induce them to pay for services. The electricity supply commission installed meters in every house and started sending out bills. Householders like MaDudu began squeezing their subtenants for their share of the bill and another, silent struggle began. It had been Madumo's two-ring stove—"running night and day," as the landlady constantly reminded him—that caused the sparking of wires and fraying of tempers in MaDudu's yard. Madumo, beset by his own turmoil, was able to do nothing but shiver in the dark and wash in cold water.

On Friday morning, the day of the operation, Madumo was awakened before dawn by the angry clatter of his neighbor's tin door as she left for work. The only one in the yard with a job to go to, the lady next door was, to say the least, inconsiderate. Somehow, though, it never woke her husband, who always managed to sleep through till noon. Madumo pulled the blankets to his chin. Through the orange mesh curtain the yellow glow of the high mast floodlamp on the opposite street showed no sign of fading with the dawn. On the cabinet at the end of the bed he found a packet of cigarettes. As he lit a cigarette, he caught a whiff of Mr. Zondi's bath mixture and was relieved when the tobacco sizzled and fumed and cleared the air with smoke. His head ached from a late night of drinking. He pulled on his cigarette and studied the corroded corrugations of the tin roof, following their ripples to the line of electric wires leading to the dangling globe. His mother would not have approved. He closed his eyes and drew the cigarette to its end upon the filter. Move! he told himself. Mr. Zondi would be waiting. He lay still. He wondered whether this treatment was really working. What if it failed? Would he have the stamina to go through with it again? A thousand different things could go wrong. The herbs might not be appropriate for the task; or they might not have been mixed right. Or perhaps the witch responsible for the curse has discovered Mr. Zondi's treatments and was redoubling her spells. *It can become a hell of a war if that witch finds out,* Mr. Zondi had warned. Or, supposing that the herbs *are* doing their job, the ancestors might be displeased about something else. . . . How could this misfortune end? Anything could go wrong. He dragged himself out of bed and tried to expel these thoughts from his mind. Today's operation would be crucial.

Mr. Zondi, his shoulders draped with a leopard-print cloth, was waiting in his consulting room, shrouded in a haze of *imphepho* smoke, when Madumo tapped gently at his door. He packed away his briefcase and they departed for his surgery inside the hostel. In the hostel room, Mr. Zondi lit Madumo's candles once more and put a match to a fistful of *imphepho.* While the smoke billowed through the room he mixed his herbs on another saucer. Onto a teaspoonful of finely ground dark brown powder he poured three small pearl drops of mercury, mashing the mix until the mercury was dispersed in tiny droplets through the dusty herbs.

"We are going to make the operation just now," Mr. Zondi said as he scraped the mixture against the saucer with his spoon, jangling poor Madumo's nerves in the process. "You have come with the blade?"

Madumo handed him a razor blade wrapped in waxed paper. "Do I have to take off my clothes?" he asked, and was relieved to hear that the answer was no.

Madumo knew the procedure. The healer would make small incisions on his temples, the back of his neck, elbows, wrists, knees, and ankles—eleven points in all. Into the incisions he would rub his special mixture of herbs, vouchsafed by the ancestors, to protect the patient from future attacks by witches.

Mr. Zondi took Madumo's right hand. Holding it firmly, he cut two lines about a quarter of an inch long and an eighth of an inch apart into the wrist. Madumo winced. Taking a pinch of *muthi,* the healer rubbed the mixture into the wounds. Madumo grimaced as the mercury stung into the cuts. The procedure was then repeated on the left wrist, then the knees and ankles. Then the razor began to approach his patient's cheek.

"*Hhayi,* man! No!" exclaimed Madumo, stepping back. "Not on my face."

Mr. Zondi laughed. "Are you afraid? This thing of the face can make you more powerful."

"Sorry, *Baba* . . . ," replied Madumo.

The older man laughed again. Knowing the urban life as he did, he hadn't really expected Madumo to consent to having his face cut. But he enjoyed teasing this boy.

"No," he said, pointing to the diagonal lines intersecting the crease of his own smile, "you must have big ones, like this. Then you can be too much powerful."

"Sorry, *Baba,*" said Madumo again, half apologetically, contemplating the effect such scars would have on his life in the townships, how the evidence of his struggle against witchcraft would be read in the streets and shebeens of his world. Most people here have tiny discreet scars on their joints from these "operations," and if you know them well enough you might ask them why, to hear their stories of troubles past—perhaps it was lightning striking near the family home, or fears of a *tokoloshe.* But a Soweto guy sporting long cuts on his cheeks would give everyone cause for pause, especially a woman who might otherwise consider sharing his bed.

Mr. Zondi was not perturbed. He made his incisions behind Madumo's ears, close to the hairline. Then he made two final cuts to his patient's breastbone. When his work was done he gave Madumo another packet of herbs to boil and vomit for the next fourteen days.

After the operation Madumo felt strangely invigorated.

"Wild," he told me later when we met for drinks. "Serious, Adam," he said, "I felt like *fighting* because of that stuff. Even now, I just feel like . . . I don't know. I feel bossy. And I'm not used to that, picking fights with somebody. But it's what I want to do. It must have been some kind of *intelezi,* that *muthi* that he is using."

During the wars with Inkatha around the hostel I had heard endless disquisitions on the properties of *intelezi.* Comrades I talked to were convinced that the Inkatha men were dosed with the stuff and that it gave them superhuman power.

"I thought he was just protecting you generally from witchcraft," I said.

"Yeah, he is. But it feels like this herb needs something to boost it, like blood. Yeah. Blood! Once you have been given *intelezi* you should do some killings, or assault. Then you will have boosted that *intelezi.*"

I didn't like the sound of that. Madumo was not lying when he said he wasn't in the habit of picking fights. He did, however, have a penchant for provoking others—sometimes deliberately—with his sharp and irreverent tongue.

"You mean through fighting someone you can make the herbs stronger to protect you from witches?"

"Yeah. You get more and more power. And it's easy to assault someone when you have this *intelezi.* When we were fighting Inkatha, everyone had *intelezi.* And Mr. Zondi, he must have been making gallons and gallons of *intelezi* for Inkatha at the hostel."

We reminisced for a while about the wars with Inkatha. Our talk of the war was picked up and amplified by the other drinkers around the crowded table. Each had a story to tell, funnier and more hair-raising than the last. Suddenly Madumo turned to me, confidentially, and changed the subject: "Mr. Zondi said he wanted to give you a treatment."

"What?"

"He said that he should treat you with *muthi.*"

"Why?"

"He said that when you're around, the people who are witching me are quite aware that you are with me. So now, I'm taking a treatment to protect myself. But you, you won't be taking that treatment to protect yourself. So all my bad things, all those bad things that Mr. Zondi is taking out of me, will just fall over to you. The witches will start attacking you. That's how these witches work. That's what Mr. Zondi said."

I laughed. "Now you tell me."

"It will all fall to you," said Madumo, laughing too.

"Jesus!"

"So he doesn't want you to be messed up. They should leave us both, these witches. Go somewhere else. So, even now, I'm quite aware that my misfortunes are becoming . . ."

"Coming to me?"

"Yeah."

"Shit! Thanks a lot."

"But he was talking generally," said Madumo. "Like, I mean, it's not that you are going to get sick, or die. He just feels he should give you something. And it's not just him. In fact, this idea is coming direct from his ancestors."

"So what would it be? What does he want to give me?"

"He says power. He's talking about power—*amandla.* He wants to give you power, so that when you go back to America you should be liked by your seniors and have success in your life—personally, socially, financially . . . just generally. So that you get what you want out of life in fact."

"Thanks, but no thanks," I replied. Then I paused, tempted by the memory of encounters with other African healers in the course of a generally fortunate life. "So what would he do to me, anyway?"

"Maybe there'll be some herbs. You can put them in your wallet. These *inyangas* have got special recipes for Whites. I don't know what kind of *muthi* he's going to give you, but I think he's going to give you one of the best *muthis.* But I don't think he's going to apply the razor."

"Shit! I'd hope not. Not with the mercury. I don't want to become wild with *intelezi* too."

“Hey, that stuff, it stings. And it was itching like hell afterwards. And you know, when he was doing that operation, he sort of closed the curtain there and the mercury sort of lit up. You could see a blue light, something like a blue flame.”

“I’ll think about it,” I said.

10

OF WITCHES AND THEIR CRAFT

During my first visit to Mr. Zondi our conversation had been cut short by clients seeking consultations, so I prevailed upon Madumo to accompany me to the hostel early one Friday afternoon during the week after his treatment began to visit his healer again. Madumo was feeling drowsy and dizzy from all the vomiting of herbs. "Maybe I should have a checkup as well," he said. Despite feeling shaky and unwell, he was eager to hear more from Mr. Zondi about witchcraft. I suggested we should tape an interview. Madumo said he wanted to ask his healer about the history of witchcraft, about when it all started and where it came from.

We found the healer at his post in his shack by the hostel. He was alone and seemed pleased to see us. The aromas of an *inyanga's* earthy apothecary met us at the door. After the usual greetings Madumo was despatched by the older man to a shack nearby for a bottle of Coke. We slaked our thirst from the one available glass and settled down to talking. Madumo explained that we wanted to tape an interview. Mr. Zondi agreed. I set up the recorder on the card table serving as his desk and took a seat on the rickety red chair opposite. Madumo settled back on one of the car-seat couches. He had brought his notebook.

"So why did you come to Johannesburg, Mr. Zondi?" I asked, opening our interview.

The healer paused for a moment to button his grey pin-striped jacket.

"Well, I first came to Johannesburg, to Merafe Hostel in fact, in 1981," he said. A when is as good as a why, I thought, so I didn't interrupt and listened to his story.

Despite the strict regulations of "Influx Control," regulations devised by the apartheid authorities to prevent migration from rural areas into cities (long denominated the "White man's creation"), which were still on the statute books at that time, Mr. Zondi never worried himself about permits. He didn't bother with the details of documentation because he had no intention of getting a job. Instead, he pursued business for himself as an *inyanga* at the hostel. Hostels like Merafe were built by the white authorities to house single men coming to the city with temporary labor contracts, men who had left their families behind in the impoverished rural homelands. Hostels were a fertile field for healers like Mr. Zondi in the business of sowing the seeds of hope in the furrows of misfortune. Occasionally he had to pay bribes to the hostel management to secure his place, but he had influential friends in Merafe from his home place in KwaZulu who helped him out. During his early years in Soweto, Mr. Zondi operated out of his room in Merafe, the room he shared with fifteen other migrants. Then he built a shack outside the hostel to make his practice more accessible to local residents.

"So tell me, *Baba*," I asked when his portrait of the healer as a young man was complete, "are the problems you were seeing then, when you first came to Soweto, the same as you're seeing today?"

"It's getting worse," he replied. "Worse."

"Witchcraft?" I asked.

"Too much. Too much! This witchcraft, it's increasing. And these witches are becoming too clever. They're becoming too much professional."

"So they're causing new problems?"

"No, the problems are the same as before, but now they're more difficult to cure. Too much difficult. They're too much clever. And another thing: these witches, they are having many assistants. When one witch dies, there is always an assistant to take over. They study hard. Always they are studying and learning new things."

"So how do they learn their witchcraft?" I asked. Madumo had his notebook open on his knee and was scribbling furiously.

"Sometimes that witch will hand on the secret knowledge to the son or else the daughter, down through families."

"Are they always related?" I asked. "The witches?"

"No, not always. Other times the assistant is not related."

"So are there those who are born witches?"

"Some are, yes. Some are born with this witchcraft spirit, but most they learn it from their relatives."

"So their secret is in their knowledge?" I posited. "In their knowledge of herbs?"

"Always!" replied Mr. Zondi enthusiastically, slapping the flimsy table with a solid thump and making me feel as if I'd been deemed a worthy interlocutor. "Definitely, the secret to their power is in their herbs."

I asked him how he kept up with these diligent witches, and he told me that keeping up with the innovations of witchcraft is always difficult for a healer like him, no matter how energetic he might try to be as a student. For his powers derive from the ancestors, and they are set in their ways. To make matters worse, the "professional" witches against whom bona fide healers struggle are virtually indistinguishable from legitimate *inyangas.* Although their work is evil, these witches can pose as healers and anyone can go to them, if they know where to go, and purchase herbs to use as weapons against their neighbors, relatives, former friends, workmates, or lovers—against anyone who might be close to them. Though they keep their practice totally secret, those with evil in their hearts can find them.

"And these are the ones that are doing *muthi* murders, too," interjected Madumo, regarding his senior with an expectant look.

Mr. Zondi nodded.

"What are they about?" I asked.

"I don't know these things," replied Mr. Zondi coyly, "but I have heard that there are some who are using this human flesh for their witchcraft. They kill people and take some few parts, maybe the liver, the private parts, or the heart, windpipe. . . . A person who does this is trying to uplift his witchcraft. It is very much calculated. So they mix that flesh with their herbs and that is their witchcraft. Sometimes it's to make luck for business. Sometimes it destroys the luck of other people. It's too much powerful. And they can dig those bodies up from the graves."

"Most of those who are doing business this side," added Madumo insistently from the sidelines, "they're using this *muthi* with body parts. Maybe they're having a grocery or a bottle store, so they'll use this *muthi* to boost them, to bring customers."

I was skeptical about that. I doubt that *most* of the businesses use human body parts. I would say it's only some of them. I've heard countless stories over the years about these so-called *muthi* murders, the killing of people for body parts to use in magic medicines. Most of these I tend to discount as urban legends, although periodically the local press will carry reports of court cases involving the procurement and sale of human body parts or else report the discovery of mutilated corpses. I imagine the commerce in body parts by Mr. Zondi's professional witches to be analogous to that of illicit drug dealers. Every city in the world has a shadowy underground market in illicit drugs, a market that most citizens imagine to be more extensive that it is. But if one of the honest citizens decided suddenly to purchase a kilogram of cocaine, say, they would find it extremely difficult and dangerous to do so. Yet, miraculously almost, the illicit trade persists, and those who desire the drugs seem to be able to find those who are willing to sell despite, or because of, the best efforts of police. Something similar probably happens with Mr. Zondi's professional witches and their clients in Soweto, except in one regard: while I have heard many people described as "witches" and have sat in on countless speculative discussions of the probable source of apparent witchcraft, I have never heard anyone recommend the services of a reliable witch with a high quality product. Nobody advertises services as a witch, and I've never heard of people announcing they are in the market to buy *muthi* for witchcraft, certainly not if it involves body parts.

"So, Mr. Zondi," I asked, "do people ever come to you looking for herbs for witchcraft?"

He laughed a hearty, throaty laugh, and his face lit up for a moment before settling into a mask of solemnity. "Many times. It is often that I'm being asked for these things."

"How do they ask? I mean, if I wanted some herbs for witchcraft, what would I say to you?"

"No, they will come maybe and say, 'I want to see so and so dead by sundown.' Or they will be telling me about their sister-in-law or someone and say, 'No, that one is a witch, you must give me something to take care of her.'"

"So do you?"

"*Hhayi!* I don't practice this witching. But many, they do. . . ." He chuckled quietly to himself, pondering his next words. "One day a man came to me looking for these herbs of witchcraft. I said, 'No, I don't have those things. You must go somewhere else.' But he kept on asking. So I said, 'Okay, I can find you those herbs, but they are expensive. Five thousand rands.' After three days he came back. He had three thousand. Of course I didn't have his herbs. I said to him, 'That one who is promising me this herb is still busy. You must come back tomorrow, with the full five thousand.'" According to Mr. Zondi, when the man finally returned with the correct money, he told him that the specialist he'd engaged to prepare the herbs was no longer available, so he couldn't help.

I didn't ask whether he kept the five thousand rands. Looking over to Madumo and wondering what I should ask next, I saw he was still writing in his notebook.

"So, *Baba*," I said, "what is witchcraft, really? How does it work?"

Madumo looked up from his book. Before Mr. Zondi could reply, he added: "In general, like, where does it come from?"

"Ah," the *inyanga* replied, "this thing is something that erupted long ago, some kind of evil spirit that has been carried down through the generations. No one knows how it started, but since long, long ago it's been carried from generation to generation. People have adopted this evil spirit and turned it to make it work for them."

"So what is it that witches do?" I asked. "How does this thing really work?"

"I am not a witch," exclaimed Mr. Zondi, feigning indignation with a furrowed brow but with laughter in his eyes, "so how would I know that thing? What I know is that they are capable of anything, these witches. When the evil is in them, they can do *anything*. Sometimes they can put their *muthi* in your food. Or they can bury it in your yard. They can make it in a line so that when you walk on it, it can kill you. And you won't see it, that *muthi*. They can make a powder and then blow it, like this. . . ." He held an upturned palm in front of him and blew an imaginary puff of herbs into the air. "That *muthi* will then travel to wherever you are and kill you."

"And then there is the *tokoloshe*," added Madumo, putting his notebook down. Mr. Zondi nodded. "That one is too much dangerous."

"Ya," said Mr. Zondi. "The *tokoloshe* can drive you mad."

I had heard many times about the *tokoloshe*, a marvel of laughter and dread. Sometimes the victim merely dreams she sleeps with the *tokoloshe*, but still the damage is done. Even children can be afflicted. Mr. Zondi told us the story of a woman who brought her five-year-old child to be treated. The boy had taken to wandering in the yard naked at night and was becoming disturbed. Mr. Zondi diagnosed the evil work of the *tokoloshe* and prescribed herbs to rectify the situation.

"Even other animals, they can be used for witchcraft," said Mr. Zondi, reciting the catalog of witches' familiars: "Cats, baboons, snakes—even a chicken. They can be used by these witches to do their work."

"So does everyone have the power to be a witch," I asked, "or is it only some?" Madumo began writing again.

"No," he replied, "not everyone. Not everyone. Although in my opinion I can see that the majority of people, they do have that thing. Because to be a witch doesn't start only from the herbs. It starts from jealousy. Once a person doesn't like his neighbors, or any person near him, he creates his witchcraft spirit. And then tomorrow he can visit one of those professional witches who has a business of herbs to act on what he's got in his spirit, in his heart. And the majority of people, they don't love each other. So that is where it starts."

"So can people use these powers for good as well as evil?" Though I've never heard of someone in Soweto bolstering their reputation for healing by alluding to their capacity to kill, in other parts of Africa this is sometimes said to be a way of enhancing the healing mystique.

"*Hhayi!* This witchcraft power is for evil only. They never use it for good. And God doesn't like it, witchcraft. Even the Bible says that witches, like all the people who kill—hooligans, criminals—they will never enter the gates of God. The Bible says that the witches must be killed: *Suffer you not a witch to live. . . .*"

I have many times heard similar declamations. Though I still, perhaps naively, imagine there can be little difference between the supernatural powers activated by a healer in the course of healing work and the powers despatched by a witch using similar herbs, those who claim to know about such matters here are appalled by the suggestion. Sometimes, in discussions like this, I've suggested that the invisible powers accessed through ancestors for the purposes of healing might be akin in nature to those orchestrated by witchcraft. The idea has seemed positively blasphemous. Mpho deems me willfully blind on this point. For although occult forces can be manipulated for a variety of purposes, the moral nature of the power is inseparable from its efficacy.

"So Mr. Zondi, is it really true that witchcraft is increasing nowadays?" I asked.

"Yes," he answered. "It is."

"Why?" I asked.

"Jealousy," he replied. "There's too much jealousy." But he was puzzled about the recent increase in jealousy. "The way things are now," he said, "when a person buys furniture, the other one gets jealous and wants to destroy him. You've got cows? They'll kill you. You can't buy a car. You can't even buy a pair of trousers. You can't do anything with your life. They don't want any progress. This jealousy is too high, and it causes the witches to be more active." Mr. Zondi's view was that jealousy was running out of control in recent years, since there has been freedom.

Certainly the objective conditions for an increase in jealousy are everywhere present in Soweto these days. Some people are prospering conspicuously while others are not. Most families are in the same sort of financial position that they were before the end of apartheid. At the same time a quickened pulse of consumer desire is palpable and everyone seems struck by an intense drive to mark status through the acquisition of desirable commodities. And everyone seems dissatisfied with their lives.

"So what should be done about this increase in witchcraft and jealousy?" I asked Mr. Zondi.

"The witches must be eliminated from the community," he replied gravely, pausing for his audience to measure the weight of his words: "Eliminated." I looked up, shifting uncomfortably on the hard metal chair. Madumo was no longer writing. "The problem is," the healer added, "these witches are getting too clever. Too much clever. They're protecting themselves against us, we *inyangas.* Even if we can cure one person, that witch is still free to strike again. No, this problem of witches is a problem for the whole community."

To my ears, the problem of witchcraft sounded akin to the

problem of crime, and just as intractable. "So how would the witches be identified?" I asked.

"If someone is a powerful witch around the community," Mr. Zondi replied, "the community knows it. They *know* that person. They know that he's a witch and he's the one that's giving them troubles. There are many people who keep *muthi* in their houses. What do they need this *muthi* for? They are not *inyangas.* They are not healing people. But still they are having too much *muthi.* No, they are doing witchcraft. So the community must set up a forum, they must elect their own *inyangas* to that forum. Then the police should round up these people and force them to drink their own *muthi.* If really they are healers, they will be fine. That *muthi* will not affect them. But if they are witches, that *muthi* will kill them."

"What if they refuse to drink it?" I asked.

"If someone is refusing to eat his own *muthi,* then it means he is a witch. He should be punished." He paused for a moment as if pondering his words. "In Shaka's day," he added, "they didn't have this problem. They were just killing those witches. But now they have these human rights, so you can't just kill them."

"But I thought that in the olden days they didn't just kill witches," I said. "Didn't they go to the chief and call the *inyangas* to have a trial?"

"You are right," he replied. "It was like that, but no more. In those days, if someone was suspecting somebody of being a witch, they would go to the chief or the headman in the village. Maybe they would say: 'Now we've got a trouble in the village. We don't sleep well at night. We often get some illness. Our children don't enjoy the life.' That sort of thing. Then they would point to the one that they say is causing their troubles. Maybe his name is . . . Adams." Mr. Zondi's eyes twinkled as he hit upon the name. "So then, that one, Adams, would come to the chief and say: 'Mr. So-and-so has said I'm a witch. Myself, I don't know that thing. So look, I've brought my cattle to the court. Let us go to the *inyanga* and find out who is really the witch.' Then the person who has accused him will also bring his cattle. They will go with some relatives and maybe two or three elders from the chief's council and go to the *inyanga.* And they will be going far from the village, so that the *inyanga* must be independent. So that *inyanga* will throw his bones, and he will look at his bones, and if he is powerful he will identify the whole problem. He will tell them why have they come. Maybe he will say: 'Mr. So-and-so has said to Adams that he's a witch, and Adams took the matter to the chief, and you have left some cattle with the chief, and now you've come to me to identify the witch.' All the delegates will agree. Then he will continue to say: 'Now, Adams, you know that in your area most of the people are having a suspicion of you.' You will say: 'No! It's not like that.' Then the *inyanga* will say: 'Don't you remember in such-and-such a year it happened that so-and-so died in your area, and that death was unexpected?' You will say: 'Okay, ya, it happened like that. I know that person.' Then he will say: 'You know, Mr. Adams, at your place, right in your family, there's something wrong, a quarrel, and there's too much bitterness. And they are accusing you, they suspect that you are no good.' You say: 'Maybe, ya . . . ya . . . ya . . . they used to say that. But it's not true! I don't know nothing about this witchcraft.'" Mr. Zondi was animating the parts of this hypothetical exchange with such gusto that I felt sure he had participated in such a scene before. "Then that *inyanga* keeps on reading his bones and telling you things, making it clear that he knows what is what until finally he says: 'You know yourself, Adams, that you are having a friend on the north side of the village where you once went to buy a certain herb. And that herb you've kept in a bottle or in a horn of a goat or a cow. Why? And you don't put that herb inside your house, or even inside your yard.' Then you will admit: 'Yes, it's true. I *am* having that thing.' And he will ask: 'What kind of medicine is it that you have to keep outside? If it was a good medicine, a worthy medicine, you should keep it right inside the house. No! That's a poisonous something! That thing, it turns into a snake at night! Or a dog! Or a baboon! It turns into many types of wild animals. It changes all the time. No! That is the thing that causes trouble amongst the people in the village where you stay. I can see that really you are a witch.' And all the witnesses will be there listening, and they will see that the *inyanga* has proved the case, that he has the evidence. Then they will go back to the village and give the chief the results. And the chief will say: 'Now, Adams, you have been arguing for quite some time and yet you know yourself that you are a witch. As from today we don't want to hear about unnecessary illness or death in this place. We want silence. We want peace. Once we hear anything that will worry us, you must know that we are going to kill you. Or else we will banish you from this area.' Then Adams, who is proved to be the witch, will lose those cattle he brought to the chief's kraal."

"Then what will he do?" I asked, full of concern for my namesake. "Surely it's too dangerous for him to stay?" A client entering the waiting room interrupted us for a moment. Mr. Zondi bade him to wait and be patient.

"No," he continued, "if that person is not really a true witch—if he's just bought something that was poisonous by mistake—he will leave the area straightaway. He'll be too afraid. But if he *is* really a witch, he will never leave. That witchcraft thing pinches him all the time. He will stay and cause troubles and more troubles until we move him from the area. Or until he is killed." Mr. Zondi paused for a moment. Madumo and I were riveted to our seats. "So that," he concluded with a satisfied smile, "is the procedural way to deal with witches. But today, they just point to somebody and say: 'You are wasting our bloody time for nothing.' And then they kill him straightaway. They don't follow procedures. They don't wait for proof. And mainly it is the youth who are doing this thing. And that is not correct."

"So what should be done to them, Mr. Zondi," I asked, "these witches, once the forum of *inyangas* sniffs them out, what happens then? You can't kill them." The new constitution had abolished the death penalty.

"Life sentence," the healer replied firmly. "They should be in jail for life, locked up far from the other prisoners where they cannot get their hands on *muthi*."

Under the law as it stands, not only are the police not likely to arrest witches, but accusing someone of practicing witchcraft is itself a crime. The Suppression of Witchcraft Act is still on the books and little changed from colonial times, when the people writing laws probably believed that witches didn't exist. Under this act, someone accused of being a witch can take his or her accuser to court. The police are then faced with the dilemma of seeming to protect witches from punishment; torn between the need to uphold a system of law premised upon modernist notions of human rights and the worry of being seen to be in league with enemies of the community. As another healer once told me, "People, they know that there *is* witchcraft. So if the government says, 'There is no witch,' this means that they are protecting this witchcraft so that it must grow, grow, grow. . . ." The problem with witches, like all forms of radical evil, is that you are either for them or against them. In these parts it's no use pretending they don't exist or seeking some ground of neutrality.

A murmur arose from the waiting room as more clients arrived and were informed about the white man with the healer. I still had many questions for Mr. Zondi, but time was running out. Madumo said we should be leaving, but Mr. Zondi waved his concerns away. I asked him about the role of the local council in containing witchcraft. In November of 1995, local council elections were held in South Africa, with Soweto being divided between two jurisdictions of the Greater Johannesburg Metropolitan region. Each location of Soweto now has its own ward councillor. If witchcraft was as big a problem as Mr. Zondi insisted it was, surely these people, sworn to serve the community's interests, should be doing something about it? I put this proposition to Mr. Zondi.

"It's a good suggestion," he said. "A good suggestion. They *must* do something. But they must be procedural. They should elect a council of traditional healers to deal with this thing. Otherwise," he paused to emphasize his point, "people will just point out anybody, such as neighbors or anyone that they hate, and accuse them of being witches." For even if the community does in fact know when there is a real witch in its midst causing real harm, false accusation can easily be fabricated. Anyone in these parts who was around during the political struggles of the 1980s knows how easy it is for innocents to be targeted as enemies of the community.

By now the afternoon throng was spilling in waves from the station once again, and the waiting room was beginning to get crowded. I thanked Mr. Zondi for his time and we rose to leave. Madumo made an appointment to return the next week for further treatment. At the door I paused to ask about the Council of Traditional Healers membership certificate hanging on the wall. Mr. Zondi took down the framed certificate and handed it to me with evident pride. He had told us before about this organization, whose leaders have the power to intuit whether a diviner is genuine (thus obviating the need for examinations or other professional credentials). Having such a certificate, he'd told us, might prove valuable were a patient to die while under his care. "You see," he said, smiling broadly, "I am not a witch."

11

A WITCH'S BREW?

From a hinterland between waking and sleep, the steady whooshing of MaMfete's tap in the yard outside slowly flooded my dreams. Muffled for a while by the lathering of suds in the concrete washtub, the gushing stream of water soon started beating an insistent tattoo on the tin bath as MaMfete rinsed the clothes she had already scrubbed. Occasionally, the solid splosh of another sodden garment dropping into the bath would counterpoint the rhythm of her brush on the clothes in the tub. Monday morning; washing day. I rolled over, again, reluctant to greet the working week after another weekend of the Sowetan party life.

Arising from beneath the washing day chorus, the whisking beat of Keitumetse's short straw broom reached me in my bed in steady crescendo as she approached. I could picture her, bent double with one arm behind her back, driving the dust towards my room in the far corner of the yard. I turned again to the wall, searching in vain for the remnants of dreams. A hail of gravel rattling against the thin pine boards of the door shattered my reverie. The sweeper had arrived. Another flick sent a shower of grit under the door.

"Hey you!" I grumbled. "Somebody's sleeping in here." A muffled giggle preceded the third wave. I pulled on my jeans and opened the door to a blinding African morning and the sparkling smile of MaMfete's younger daughter, my "sister." With a scarf tied neatly over newly permed hair and a blue towel girding her waist over a long brown sweater, she stood on the threshold of my room waggling her switch at me like an accusatory finger.

"Morning," she said, putting her hands to her hips and pretending to frown while struggling to suppress a grin. "How's the morning, my brother? Not feeling so great, huh? I heard you come in last night. Very late. Where were you from?"

"Why do you make all this noise then," I said, "when somebody's trying to sleep?"

"Somebody?" she quizzed.

"Me," I said.

"Sorry," she said, her grin pealing into laughter. "But we must do our work. Anyway, I thought you were awake already." She peered into the room. "Or are you having somebody inside? Hmmm?" she demanded, scanning the room again and laughing. "Maybe you've got that 'Somebody' you were talking about?" She laughed again, a light sparkling ripple of laughter that made me smile too. Keitumetse can rarely finish a sentence without a solid burst of laughter. "Hey! Just look at this room. When are you going to let me clean it?"

My room was in its usual state, strewn with papers and books and dust and empty bottles from yesterday's visitors. A couple of itinerants from the mountains of Lesotho, whom MaMfete hired by the day a couple of years after I arrived, built this room. Before that, I shared Thabo's bed. It's a comfortable room, with doors on either end and a window. At the corners of the window the walls are singed from the arc of the welding machine Mpho's uncle borrowed to install the burglar bars, an arc so powerful we had to tape the recalcitrant trip-switch down in the front room while the weld sizzled and hissed and the lights of the house flickered fit to burst. Uncle's bars are sheer artistry, fashioned from lengths of steel reinforcement rod, with rows of jailhouse verticals surrounding a central secure diamond. MaMfete uses my room for her ironing and sewing while I'm away. Then her friends gather here in the afternoons to talk and laugh, especially when Nono, our sardonic neighbor from two streets away, calls by with her mordant stories. On the wall, above the fold-away table I use for a desk, is a large hand-colored woodcut of the Provost's lodgings at Worcester College in Oxford, etched by an old friend and identical to the one presented to the Provost on his retirement a few years back, except for the addition of a huge villainous rat, a sorcerer's baboon, and an inky old witch. The children here love it. I try in vain to explain that it's not a photograph.

"And you?" I grumbled, sinking back on the bed to pull on my sneakers. "What's with you, anyway? Always working: cooking and cleaning . . . sweeping and polishing without end. Don't you ever get tired of it?"

"I don't," she replied. "I like to clean the house."

"Why?"

"It must be clean," she said.

"Well the house is one thing," I said, "but sweeping the yard and polishing the stoep is another. And polishing the taps? That's nonsense."

"No," she said. "It must be clean. The whole house. Inside and out." She turned on her heel and headed for the front of the house to polish the stoep. "At least we don't shine up the rubbish bins," she called back, pausing for effect before laughing, "like they do in Alexandra." I followed her to the front of the house, remembering the brightly polished garbage cans we'd seen in her aunt's flat in Alexandra.

It is Sisyphean labor, the polishing of stoeps in Soweto. Many of the streets here are unsealed, the open spaces dustbowls, especially in the dry season of winter. When the wind blows, as it does, the whole place lives and breathes in a fog of fine brown dust. In summer, when it rains, the dust turns to mud. Yet every morning, early, the stoep must be polished. It is work deemed fit for daughters. I tried it once, to the merriment of the Lekoka Street girls who gathered to watch and criticize. My back ached for days.

I stood back, leaning on the wall, as Keitumetse sank to her knees onto a piece of old sackcloth. She circled her brush on the concrete. "This is just a waste of time," I said, breathing the scent of paraffin wax. "You do all this work and five minutes later it's dusty again. Or someone will come. They'll walk all over it."

"I don't worry about that," she said. "I can't avoid it. I can't prevent it. I'll clean it again tomorrow. I'm going to clean the stoep again tomorrow."

"And the day after?"

"Every day. Every morning." She looked up at me, sidelong, laughing again. The wiping continued.

"Why?" I asked.

"To keep it clean, of course. When someone comes through the gate they must see that this house is clean. If you find the front being clean, then you know that the house inside is also clean. You can eat there."

"Hah!" I replied. "You want to know the real reason why you have to polish the stoep?"

"What is it?" she asked, giving the floor a final swipe and rising from her knees. She stood back to inspect the deep black waxen luster that shone on the concrete. "So what is the real reason then? Because we're afraid of what the neighbors will say if they are seeing our house dirty?"

"No," I replied. "Well, yes, that too, I suppose. But the real reason is advertising. It's for advertising the young daughters of a house. I learnt about it from a nurse we met in the shebeen last night."

"The shebeen?" said Keitumetse, raising a disdainful eyebrow.

"Yeah, Sister M she calls herself. So, the thing with this polishing is to get the girl outside early in the morning, when everyone else is asleep or gone to work. Then the young men walking down the street can see her on her hands and knees and see she's a good worker with nice round buttocks. . . . That's what it's really for. At least, that's what Sister M told me. Then the boys can propose love to the girls polishing the stoep, and the girls end up married. So you'd better be careful. . . ."

"You're not serious," said Keitumetse with a laugh.

"Serious!" I said. "I just thought you should know."

"Well," she said, "thanks for that. Now, what's for breakfast? Do you think we can wait all day for you to get the breakfast?" Finding fault with a patch of her polishing, Keitumetse returned to her knees and removed the imperfection, swirling her bundle of old pantyhose across the gloss. She rose again, the job finished. Stepping back onto the pebble pathway running across the front of the house, she chuckled and said, "Do you want to know what happened to that *mqomboti?*"

"What?" I replied, knowing already what had happened to the big pot of *mqomboti,* sorghum beer, which neighbors had sent over for me on Sunday morning. Naome had told me that she and the other women in our house had tipped it out because they suspected it had been doctored with *muthi.* Later, when I asked MaMfete and Keitumetse about the beer, they became evasive. I was curious about why Keitumetse was raising the subject now. "So what happened to the *mqomboti?*" I asked on cue.

Keitumetse replied with a story about her sister finding cockroaches in the beer. She didn't know that Naome had already told me about the *muthi.*

I pressed her for the truth: "What about the *muthi?*" I asked.

"What *muthi?*" she replied, taken aback.

"I heard there was *muthi* in the *mqomboti.*"

Keitumetse looked up, startled. "Who told you that?"

"Naome," I said. "She told me everything. So what's your story?"

We walked slowly down the side of the house to the living-room window. She began polishing the black concrete ledge, slowly rubbing the cloth up and down. "Okay," she said eventually, "you want to know what happened?"

"Yes. Everything." I could understand their reticence about talking of witchcraft, but if, as I suspected, they thought they were protecting me, I wanted to know exactly what it was that I was being protected from.

"It was on Sunday morning," she said. "I told you about the . . . was it the mud or maybe it was shit . . . I don't know. When we woke up on Sunday morning after that party there was mud, or something funny, rubbed on the wall there by the side gate. While Mummy was busy cleaning the wall, this girl came from that other street and said her granny was asking for Daddy. So we said, 'No, he's at home. He's inside.' And she said that her granny wants him to come there. She's made some *mqomboti,* and he must come and drink it."

"So," I interjected, "what's wrong with that?"

"Now," Keitumetse explained, "in the African culture, you don't have to call somebody if you've done *mqomboti.* They just come. If you've done a feast for the ancestors, people just come." She began polishing the window sill again. "So we were suspicious." She spoke softly; seriously. "You don't have to call people or invite them. Even your next door neighbors, you don't have to invite them. So we said to that girl, 'No, we'll tell him.' After five minutes, her granny came. 'Oh, what does the granny want now?' we thought. She was asking for Daddy. Then she talked to Daddy and they went out together. So then Daddy came home with the pot of *mqomboti* and said it was for you. He said that granny told him he must come back to their place and drink some more. So we said: 'Uh-uh, this is nonsense.'"

Suddenly, she began to laugh and fell back from her work, shading her eyes from the sun as we stood together in the pathway. I looked at her, puzzled. I didn't see what was so funny.

"I still don't see why you had to throw it out," I said, kicking at a tuft of dead grass by the fence.

Keitumetse reviewed the situation: "We just thought, 'Uh!

uh! Why should that granny do this? She wanted to make sure he comes and drinks the *mqomboti.* Ah no! He was going to have stomach cramps . . . and get sick . . . even die!'"

"Why?" I asked. "How was the *mqomboti* going to do that?"

"We thought there was something fishy in that *mqomboti,*" she replied, returning to her work on the window sill. "Maybe they had put herbs in it."

"And why would they do that," I asked.

"Because we are thinking . . . that the old lady . . ." Keitumetse paused for a moment to consider the import of what she was about to say. "In fact," she continued, "we all *know.*" She stopped polishing and moved back against the high chain link, grasping a strand of barbed wire behind her and stretching out into a cruciform to ease the strain on her shoulders. "You can ask anybody you know around here about that granny. They will tell you: 'No! That one, she's a witch.'"

She dropped an arm from the fence in a graceful sweep and paused for a moment as the terrible name settled between us. Raising a hand to shield her eyes from the bright sun behind me, she studied my face, mask of perplexity that it was, and laughed again. "Serious, Adam. I'm serious," she insisted. "She's a witch."

"So, why do you think your father was supposed to be the victim?" I asked.

"Ah," she replied, her tone quiet, resigned, "we've always been the victims here at home. And what made us more suspicious is the mud we found on the wall. Seipati said it was shit, but I think it was mud. What do you think about that?"

"I don't know," I replied. "It's all pretty strange. I don't see why . . ."

I ran out of things to say. I couldn't begin to understand the depths of enmity coursing beneath the placid surface of life in Lekoka Street. Knowing not to believe in witches, and preferring not to believe in malice, I knew not how to read the signs. I found it especially hard to believe that the same community of women I'd seen come together in adversity and grief could be plotting to kill and destroy each other by means of witchcraft. Yet it was true that the previous morning there had been a strange smear on the side wall by the gate. It was no accident that it was there, but I couldn't begin to interpret what it might have meant. Perhaps it had been connected with the party we'd had on Saturday night, a party to which, unlike the ancestral feast in the next street, few of our neighbors had been invited. Perhaps someone had been resentful about that.

"You don't think that there was *muthi?*" Keitumetse asked.

—

"Huh?" she said. "Don't you think there was?"

—

"No!" she insisted. "Say something! Yes or no!" Her smile was still broad beneath raised eyebrows.

I tried to remember if I'd ever seen signs of animosity between the family of the witch and our household. I had not. Certainly nothing to warrant an attempt at murder. "I'd be surprised if . . . ," I said.

"If?" she snapped. "How would you know?"

"By tasting it . . . ," I said.

"Oh," she said, looking at me with a condescending smile, chuckling softly. "You wouldn't taste anything."

She stopped talking. In the harsh sunlight of a winter's morning, she straightened her sweater, pulling it over her hips and rolling down the sleeves. Leaning against the wall, taking an occasional swipe at the windowsill with her cloth, her eyes issued a challenge.

I responded: "Don't you think that it was *me* that was supposed to be the victim?"

"Yes," she said, continuing to flick the cloth idly at the sill. "In fact you *and* Father, you were both going to drink that *mqomboti.* Because that granny also told Daddy: 'You will give this to Adam.'" Keitumetse began to laugh again, gesturing first with one, then two fingers. "So both of you, you and Daddy, were going to be the victims." A car struggled noisily down Lekoka

Street and back again, leaving us swaddled in silence in its wake. "Maybe you would have died."

"Why?" I asked. "Why would they want me to be a victim?" It didn't make sense.

"I don't know," she said. "But it was going to work, even on you. Don't you think the *muthi* would work on you?"

"But what if they were just being friendly?" I said. "Everybody knows I like to drink *mqomboti.* Whenever there's a party around here, they call me to come for *mqomboti.* MaDooka sends me a pot every time she brews." I wanted to refuse this lesson my sister was teaching: that you must presume malice in community life despite all appearances to the contrary.

"Ha!" she retorted, breaking into sarcastic laughter. "That one knows that you like *mqomboti?*"

"Everybody knows that," I replied. "When they had the party at their place last year, that old lady made *mqomboti* and kept some specially for me."

"And then?"

"And there was no *muthi* in it."

"Oh, really?" she said. She took a few more desultory swipes at the sill.

"None at all."

"Anyway," she concluded, "we thought that there might be witchcraft, and you think the other way round. I think there *was muthi,* and you are lucky we caught it." We both laughed.

"I must go and see my *inyanga* anyway," I said.

Keitumetse laughed again at my mention of the diviner. Standing with hands on hips, looking up at me, challenging, her eyebrows raised, she said, "Why do you have to go to the witch-doctor if you don't believe the *muthi* was going to work on you? Mm? *Why?*"

She leant towards me. I shrugged.

"You know, Adam," she said, "with people around here, if you are an enemy to somebody, if they are jealous, and they know that you like liquor or *mqomboti,* they usually get you with that liquor or *mqomboti.* They say *muthi* works faster in alcohol."

"So why would they consider me an enemy?"

Again she stepped back to the fence and raised both arms to support herself with the wire: "They are jealous of us," she said. "You are part of our family. So why wouldn't you be an enemy if we are?"

12

CHURCH

"No," said Madumo, "we must go inside." I was reluctant. Churches always unnerve me. "Just drive in," he said. "There's nothing to worry about. This is my church. I know these people." We were parked in the street outside the high grey cinder-block walls of the Zion Christian Church in Phiri, a neighborhood adjacent to Mapetla.

"Straight through the gates?" I asked, starting the engine.

"Yes."

Inside the compound nobody seemed to notice the self-conscious white man parking his battered Dombolo in the middle of their churchyard. They were too absorbed in their work of healing and being healed. The compound encompassed about half an acre of dusty ground, most of it open and uncovered. Along the eastern wall, a lean-to roofed with rusting sheets of corrugated tin supported on beams wired to rough-hewn poles sheltered fifty or more rows of smooth-worn wooden benches. Over the years the structure had settled and sagged and was now propped up here and wired up there. Along the northern wall a variety of sheds, shacks, and lean-tos housed the church's office and workshops. Scattered groups of congregants sat huddled over fruit tins, sipping their contents in silence.

"I'll wait here," I said when Madumo opened his door.

"No. Come with me," he commanded. I followed him across the compound to a group of men at the far side, near the sheds. He smoothed his jacket down and ran his hands over his hair as we walked. A tall, thin man, very dark in complexion with closely cropped hair—evidently the custodian—watched our progress. As we neared, he rose from the group of men sitting at the door of a tin shed and approached us, an empty jam tin in one hand.

"*Khotso!*" said Madumo, using the distinctive greeting of the ZCC meaning "Peace."

The custodian stood staring at us for a moment but said nothing. He gestured to us to follow him. Reaching deep into a water barrel with the jam tin, he scooped out a canful of water, dipped his hand into it, and splashed water at Madumo's face and over his body. Three times he splashed. Then he dipped and splashed three times at me. Madumo turned his back. I followed suit. The custodian splashed our backs three times each. Madumo turned again. I turned, too. He held his hands out cupped before him. I followed. The custodian dripped water on our hands and offered us the tin from which to drink. Drenched and purified, we were allowed to state our business.

Madumo introduced me to the custodian: "Mr. Mnyama," he said. Later we speculated that the name, meaning "black," must surely be a nickname prompted by his blue-black hue. Madumo explained that I was a professor from New York and was interested in studying the church. He said I wanted to interview people about witchcraft. I remained silent, trying to look humble and friendly like the sort of white man I imagined they might be happy to talk to. Mr. Mnyama remained silent, hardly even nodding as Madumo spoke. Then he tilted his head a bit in my direction and studied me from beneath drooping eyelids.

The way I saw it, a good part of Madumo's problem stemmed from the fact that his brother had heard some nonsense about

Madumo killing their mother from someone in this same Zion Christian Church. He'd been told by a prophet here that their mother's death had been an "inside job." The brother assumed this meant Madumo was the culprit and presumed he'd killed their mother with witchcraft. So Madumo was chased away from his home. This didn't seem very Christian to me. I wanted to know more about these people who, in the name of Christianity, could condemn a man to a perdition of social death as a perpetrator of witchcraft.

Mr. Mnyama listened politely to Madumo's story, then told us he could not help: "You must come on Saturday," he said, "between four and five in the afternoon, or on Sunday, at two or maybe three to past three. You must talk to the chairman. There's nothing I can do." Mr. Mnyama spoke *Sepedi,* or Northern Sotho as it is sometimes called. Madumo replied in *Sesotho,* or Southern Sotho. My teeth were chattering as the holy water soaked through my clothes. Under the long lean-to a solitary figure in a heavy overcoat sitting with a five-liter can at his feet stared at us sidelong for a moment before lifting his tin to take a weary sip of the contents. We agreed to return on the weekend.

On Saturday we returned to the ZCC compound at the appointed hour of four. Mpho was with us. We dallied outside in the dusty street while the voices of the women's choir soared over the high wall of the compound, unnerving me once more with the presence of their piety. I didn't feel we could just barge into the middle of a service, so I prevailed upon Madumo to go ahead into the church to see if our visit would be welcome. He returned and beckoned us to enter. Mr. Mnyama was at his post with his can of water when I parked the car. He drenched us once more. His job, as Madumo explains it, is to prevent evil spirits from entering the church's yard. Under the lean-to a circle of some forty or fifty women were singing and stamping their feet in the dust.

Mr. Mnyama, recognizing us from our last visit and seeming, marginally, less impassive although not exactly friendly, explained that the man to whom we must speak had not yet arrived.

No sooner had he said this than his attention shifted to a red Mercedes Benz pulling into the compound. A man in his mid-thirties jumped out. Mr. Mnyama did not throw water at him. Instead, he drew the man aside and spoke to him in a low voice. The newcomer was a small man, trim, wearing a suit and tie and displaying a brisk energetic manner. He dismissed Mr. Mnyama and introduced himself. I assumed he was the chairman of whom Mr. Mnyama had spoken.

"Ernest Mabitsela," he said, his welcoming smile failing to conceal the peremptory spirit of his inquiry. "What is it that you want?" When I later learnt that he was the deputy principal of a local high school, I was not at all surprised. Though he studied both of my companions in turn, his question was spoken in English, fluent English, and addressed directly to me.

Madumo began to answer, but before he could intervene, I tried to explain the purpose of our visit: "We came here the other day," I said, "hoping to talk to people." Mr. Mabitsela said nothing. I couldn't tell whether he was pleased to see visitors to his church or not. "You see," I continued, "I've been staying in Soweto, on and off, since 1990, in Mapetla Extension. I'm writing a book. I'm writing about the changes in life here since the end of apartheid."

"You're from New York?" he asked.

"Yes," I replied. "I teach at a university in New York, but I've been coming here since 1990." Mr. Mabitsela nodded. "And one of the things I've noticed since then is that people are less concerned now about politics than about spiritual insecurity. People are telling me that witchcraft has become a big problem lately. And I've heard that this church is very important in the community. So I'm interested in talking to people in the church about problems in the community, especially to learn more about the work of the church in fighting things like witchcraft. Because I've heard that the ZCC is the biggest and fastest growing church in the country. I want to get a firsthand account."

Mr. Mabitsela, who had been nodding politely during my speech, replied: "New York, is it?" I nodded. "Well, I'm sorry, but I can't help you. You see, I have to talk to the elders of the church. In fact, they are waiting for me right now. If you won't mind, please let me go and talk to them." He led us to a table in the far corner of the big lean-to adjacent to the office and disappeared into the shed.

We looked at each other and shrugged. None could say what lay in store. The women were still singing. Though there was nothing lovely about the surroundings, rudimentary and rough-hewn as they were, the steady rhythmic singing of the Saturday afternoon women's choir—their spirited elaborations of elemental harmonies interlaced with a soloist's plangent threads of counterpoint in a minor key—suffused the place with such enchantment that the plumes of Soweto dust stamped up by the choristers' feet and rising into the sharp beams of late afternoon sun seemed unutterably beautiful.

We waited in uncomfortable silence listening to the choir. In the far corner of the yard half a dozen prophets were at work. Periodically one of them would approach the choir, single out a member, and signal to her with a clapping of the hands that she must come and hear the words of the spirits. It was during a similar session that a prophet told Madumo's brother that someone inside their house was responsible for their mother's death. I assumed that as visitors we would be spared intercourse with the spirits, but we had hardly been sitting there for five minutes before a prophet approached. She was a short stout woman. The buttons of her khaki uniform strained over her belly, and her bottle green beret sat like a toadstool above a face that looked like nothing so much as a potato. She came towards us, bending slightly from the waist and clapped sharply twice, gesturing for Madumo to follow her. Madumo pretended not to notice her. She clapped sharply again.

"Shit," muttered Madumo under his breath. "I'm not here to be prophetized. These people can harass you to the amen." He rose reluctantly, clenching his fists in the pockets of his peacoat, and followed the prophet to the far side of the yard. Madumo hadn't been "propheted" for years.

When he returned, Madumo was sullen and uncommunicative. Before we could ask why, Mr. Mabitsela emerged from the office accompanied by two elders of the church. Mr. Mabitsela introduced the younger of the two, a fit-looking man in his mid-forties, as the chairman. Madumo introduced himself as the son of his father, and it turned out the older man knew the family. We took our places at the table and the chairman convened the meeting. Mr. Mabitsela asked me to explain to his colleagues the purpose of my visit. I repeated my earlier presentation, adding, on the advice of Mpho, that I had been hearing many bad things in Soweto about the ZCC but wanted to learn the truth for myself.

In fact, before I had begun these inquiries at the ZCC I had heard nothing out of the ordinary about this church, whose members are ubiquitous in the townships and rural areas of black South Africa. But as soon as I started visiting the church, friends in Soweto began to warn me in earnest about becoming involved with the ZCC, for it is widely believed that the reason for the ZCC's success derives from their use of human body parts in magical *muthi.* "Under no circumstances must you go to Moria," I was told—Moria being the headquarters of the church in the Northern Province. For in Moria, it was insisted, I would be killed and my body stripped of its vital organs. Just last Easter, when more than a million Zionists from around southern Africa converged on Moria, a chief from a village in North-West Province made the pilgrimage and never returned home. Villagers, incensed by the thought that their chief had been killed for body parts, stormed the local ZCC church and drove the Zionists out of town. The ZCC retaliated with a lawsuit. Mr. Zondi, amongst others, told me in deadly earnest about a storeroom in the bishop's palace at Moria stocked full of body parts from which the *muthi* is made to draw members to the church. Rumor has it that Mandela, after having entertained the bishop at his presidential mansion in Cape Town, went to visit the palace in Moria. The bishop returned Mandela's hospitality by showing him around his house, just as Mandela had done in the president's house.

They looked in all the rooms but one. "What's in that room?" Mandela asked. "You can't go in there," he was told. Mandela was furious and ordered the police to storm the secret room. Inside was a store of body parts: from Whites, Blacks, Coloureds, everyone. . . . As to why this was never publicized, there are two basic stories: one has it that Mandela was bribed to keep quiet; the other has it that Mandela appointed a secret truth commission of powerful witchdoctors to investigate and counteract the powers of the ZCC.

At the conclusion of my presentation, the three gentlemen of the Zions nodded sagely but said nothing. I wondered whether I should say more, tell them that all I had in mind was to have a chat with a few people around here, nothing very taxing. I just wanted to get some sense of their theology in practice, some sense of what witchcraft means to ordinary members and how they use the church to fight it. Before I could say anything, however, the chairman began to speak.

"What you have to understand," he said, his words slow and careful, "is that we are a centrally controlled church. So we here at the Moroka branch are not in a position to grant your request. Before we can talk to you, we will have to get permission from headquarters."

I nodded in agreement, assuming all was lost. It seemed that the chairman, a major in the South African National Defense Force, was politely dismissing me. Then, to my surprise, he outlined the procedure they would follow: First, the elders of the branch here would draft a letter to the regional headquarters in Alexandra township (the black ghetto in the northern suburbs of Johannesburg). After consideration by the regional secretariat, the letter would be forwarded to the headquarters of the church in Moria. "If the response from Moria is positive," the chairman concluded, "they will send a letter and the way will be clear."

It all seemed rather complicated to me, as if I was being vetted for a major research project. But I nodded in agreement as the chairman spoke. If permission was required, permission would be sought. Why not?

The elders rose from the table and we all shook hands before they retired to the office to draft their letter. It turned out, Mr. Mabitsela explained, that regional headquarters was holding a convention that very day, so if we were able to take the letter to Alexandra township straight away, the process would be expedited. We waited at our table. In the background the choir was still singing. A young girl in a khaki uniform dandled an infant on her knee. Prophets prowled the periphery.

"Don't be surprised if they come and prophet you," said Madumo after the elders left. No sooner had he spoken than a prophet approached and summoned him for a hearing. "*Hhayi!*" he exclaimed. "Not again." He followed obediently, nonetheless.

When the prophet had done with him, Madumo was summoned into the meeting of the elders. He told the elders again that he was a member of the church and, after they had satisfied themselves about his identity by cross-examining him on his family background, he was delegated as our guide in the church. A few minutes later he returned.

"They want your ID book," he said.

"I don't have one," I replied. The ID book, which had replaced the hated passbook of apartheid, is a diminutive passport that includes all the bearer's particulars with pages inside for recording driver's and firearms licences. I fished in my pocket for my Australian driver's licence: "Will this do?"

"Sure," he replied. "They are just being procedural." He disappeared back into the office.

The prophets were still busy summoning women from the choir.

"What if a prophet calls you and you refuse?" I asked Mpho. I could tell he was feeling edgy and in need of a cigarette.

"I wonder," he replied. Mpho is not a member of the ZCC. In fact, he has little time for these khaki-clad worshipers with their five-pointed star badges, whom he derides, in the manner of many young Sowetans, as "sheriffs." "You have your constitutional rights," he added. "Freedom of religion and all that. They can't force you."

No sooner had he spoken than another prophet approached us. I had not expected this, assuming that a white man, especially a stranger, would be immune from the inner spiritual dealings of the church. But the woman faced me and clapped twice. Insistently. Then she turned to Mpho and clapped at him. We hesitated a moment, looking at each other in puzzlement, then rose and followed the woman across the yard to the area behind the cars. An old man in a grey suit shadowed us. He must have come from the elders' office. When she reached her position our prophet sank to her knees. We followed her example. Our shadow joined the circle. Another elderly man, appearing out of nowhere, joined us.

Crouched on all fours on a hard patch of Soweto ground in the fading light of a winter's evening, I listened as our prophet began to chant in a language I could not understand, and I began to have serious doubts about what I was doing there. Her incantation began to warm up. One of the elders produced a large notebook. He asked about for a pen while the prophet ranted. I handed him mine. The prophet's chant was becoming ever more intense. Carefully opening his notebook, the elder began to transcribe the words of the spirits issuing from the prophet's mouth. From the torrent of language surging above him bearing messages from unseen domains, the old man distilled two lines of laboriously penned words: *Barnabas has sent this white man. He must be made welcome in the church.*

At the close of her encounter with the spirits, the prophet announced that the visitors should each contribute a sum of three cents to the church and that a ritual of welcome should be performed for us.

I felt strangely elated by this news that I had been endorsed by the spirits. Madumo was terribly impressed by the fact that this prophecy had been recorded in the Book: "It means that prophet wasn't just messing with you," he said, "not like the one that prophetized my brother that time." I wondered why, if the spirits had already spoken, it was necessary to get a letter from headquarters. "What happens to the prophecy if the answer from headquarters comes back as no?" I asked Madumo later. He did not think it possible.

While Mpho and I were being "prophetized," Madumo was being appointed by the elders as our guardian and guide for the mission to regional headquarters in Alexandra township. Before we left with their letter, they poured holy water on him in order to purge him of evil sprits. They gave him the letter, addressed to the regional secretary, and urged us to travel immediately to Alexandra so that we might catch the church officials visiting from Moria.

I had only been to Alexandra once before, to visit MaMfete's cousin on the day of our trek to the *inyangas.* Likewise, Mpho had only been here once in his life. Madumo, newly inspired by his appointment as custodian of our fortunes, claimed to know the place well. Alexandra is a black suburb, predating the forced segregation of the 1950s, that had survived the National Party's program of eliminating what they termed "black spots" from the otherwise exclusively White suburban areas. It is a completely different place from Soweto, which was a product of the state's drive for "properly planned Native townships" and still bears the hallmarks of the regulating hand of officialdom on every structure and street. Alexandra is an overcrowded ramshackle slum and is reputed to be the most crime-infested area in a crime-infested country. Occupying about a square mile of ground divided in a typical North American grid of rectangular blocks, the place is composed mostly of good-sized suburban blocks with a principal dwelling surrounded by shacks and rooms divided and subdivided into next to nothingness and crowded in upon by shanty stalls of tin and cardboard lining the streets. It has a crowded, teeming, ominous feel about it—quite unlike the Soweto we had just left and which we know so well, especially at dusk on a Saturday winter's evening. Needless to say, Alexandrans visiting Soweto find that place monstrous and intimidating.

We found Alexandra, and found that despite his bravado Madumo had no idea how to get to the headquarters of the Zion Christian Church. Steering the Dombolo down the narrow streets was giving me a headache. Knowing that a single mistake—such as crunching someone's fender or running over a child—could prove fatal to a white man and two Sowetans was making it worse.

"Stop and ask one of these deputies," said Mpho as we came abreast of a pair of men in the uniforms of the ZCC. Madumo climbed out of the car as I tried to maneuver it onto the pavement and out of the path of the continual procession of hooting taxi vans.

"They're lying, man," Madumo said when he returned to the car. "They say we must turn right down there and then it's right, and right again. . . . They don't trust us. 'Why do you want that place?' that one said. He didn't believe I had a letter." We drove on.

Five minutes later, we pulled up beside another pair of ZCC men. They gave us a different direction, but by this time I was beginning to get a feel for the geometry of the Alexandran grid. Confident that the 19th Avenue we sought was probably the seventh street from the 12th Avenue we were blocking with our inquiries, I continued in the way pointed by the first guides. Before long the streams of men in khaki threading their ways home through the dusk thickened and we knew we were on the right track. Turning right into a dark deserted street we began to hear the distinctive singing of the Zionist congregation. I parked the car and struggled with the length of chain and steel that our friend Bheki had devised for locking the steering wheel to the clutch pedal.

We entered the gates of the Zion Christian Church Regional Headquarters. The yard was in darkness. In the distance, a service was still in progress—men grouped on one side, women on the other. Suddenly the yard was flooded with light and a pair of young men approached us in the manner of sentries demanding to know our business. On our way to Alexandra we had decided that as we were entering strange territory, I should take over the presentation of our case and milk the slender advantage a lone white man has. The elders back in Phiri had warned Madumo:

"You know these Pedis," they had said, referring to the dominant ethnic group in the northern region of the country where the ZCC is headquartered and thereby preparing him not to expect a warm welcome.

"We have come with a letter for the regional secretary," I said in response to one of our inquisitors. I held out the letter for him to see. He inspected it without touching it. I noticed another young man in khaki hurry away to summon superiors from their offices at the far corner of the compound. Before long he reappeared with three older men. These men did not wear the khaki uniform of the rank-and-file but were dressed in respectable grey business suits and ties. On their lapels they had pinned the signature five-pointed star badge on the bottle green ribbon of the faithful.

I presented my case as I had done earlier in Phiri, told my story about my book, and presented the sealed letter from the elders of the branch in Soweto. The three listened quietly. Then, without so much as a word of acknowledgment to me, they turned to my friends and grilled them peremptorily in *Sepedi*—the language of the people about whom Madumo had been warned. My friends elaborated upon my tale. Eventually, the man who appeared to be the most senior of our three interrogators, and whom I took to be the secretary of the branch, returned his attention to me. Speaking in English, he explained that permission for my research would have to be granted by "Moria," the ultimate headquarters.

"You are lucky," he said, "because tonight we are having a convention and some of the elders from Moria are here. So we will take this letter and read it now. At least that way, if the answer is 'no' you will hear it straight away." With that the elders departed, leaving us in the custody of a junior man, who guided us to benches in the rear of the assembly area.

After about ten minutes the elders returned. Our original troika was accompanied by seven or eight additional gentlemen in suits, presumably the elders from Moria.

"No," said the secretary in affirmation, smiling and nodding his head, "the letter is very good. It is correct. Very procedural. They have done the right thing there in Phiri. Now we will take this letter to Moria and get clearance. I'm sure you can expect an answer soon." When I pressed him about when "soon" might be, he suggested a matter of a few days, perhaps the following Wednesday. "Don't worry," he said. "You will have a reply soon."

With the business concluded, the group of elders pressed in upon us, greeting me effusively and teasing my friends for going about in the dark with a white man. They were curious to know more about the white man who had lived so long in Mapetla. When they heard that Madumo had been a member of the church since birth, they chided him jokingly for not wearing his badge.

"Hah!" exclaimed Madumo, when Mpho and I took up the chastisement again in the car on our way home. "They were just appetizing themselves at my expense—taking a nibble for the sake of a laugh. They know I can still be a member and not wear a badge."

We returned to Soweto to await our call.

13

MADUMO'S ADVICE TO THE LOVELORN

On my way to Madumo's place one afternoon I passed my old friend Nono on the street near Moloi's bottle store, and she insisted that I buy her a beer. So I bade her accompany me to Madumo's with the inducement that he lives behind a shebeen. When we arrived, my friend was on his hands and knees scrubbing the floor.

"That's beautiful," said Nono. "Look at that. *Hhayi wena,* you must polish too!" She squealed with joy to see a man on his knees.

"Of course," said Madumo. "Look, I've even polished all the doors in this yard. I told these others, 'You don't respect yourself.' I told them, 'Me, I respect myself. Even my door must shine.'" Each of the red metal doors lining the bare concrete yard was carrying a deep ochre luster over its chipped red paint.

"No, my girl," Nono said, "you will make a good husband. You must marry me." Nono, a neighbor of mine from the other side of Mapetla, is a maverick grandmother going on sixty, a dedicated and unapologetic drinker and smoker, and a woman with no intention of ever marrying again since her husband departed for another woman some twenty years ago, taking their two children with him.

Madumo was in good spirits. His day had begun early with the vomiting of Mr. Zondi's herbs. He followed that with a five-mile run to the police station and back, and a breakfast of chicken scraps left over from our lunch the day before. Mine had started with a long breakfast and chat with MaMfete followed by a couple of desultory hours trying to work in my room before the Lekoka Street children returned from school demanding attention.

While Nono bantered with Madumo about his housekeeping skills, I called for two beers from BraJohnny, who was running the shebeen in MaDudu's absence. With two cold Castles between us, Nono and I perched ourselves on beer crates outside Madumo's door and watched the man scrub.

"Yes, Madumo," said Nono, savoring her beer. "You'll make a good wife. An *excellent* wife." She swallowed the rest of her glass in one draught. "You'd make a good wife, but look at you. All alone in this room without a woman. Why?"

"Who says I don't have a woman?" replied Madumo, sweeping his floor cloth behind him over the white vinyl tiles in an insolently graceful and athletic gesture.

"*I* say you don't have a woman," retorted Nono, "because you wouldn't be there on your knees if you did." She turned to me: "I know these Soweto boys. You can't tell me about Soweto boys. They're too much lazy if there's a woman around."

"Maybe my wife's made me drink *korobela*," said Madumo mischievously, referring to the potion for securing a lover's obedience, "so that's why I'm being her slave."

"Ha!" snorted Nono. "That's a good one. *Korobela!* He's drunk *korobela?* He's lying. He just doesn't have a woman, that's all."

It's a matter of some dispute, this *korobela.* Men will generally take the sort of view that Madumo was expressing, seeing *korobela* as an infringement of their autonomy. They see it as a form of witchcraft. But women are more likely to think of it as a legitimate, albeit lamentable, medicinal assistant for securing the attentions of the wayward fathers of their children. *Inyangas* will openly advertise their ability to provide a *muthi* capable of returning an absent father to his duties. And lovers in love will underline their excessive devotion by joking to each other that their beloved must have fed them *korobela.* Underlying all this talk, however, is the very real fear of a capacity for someone to remove your ability to choose and act freely without your ever realizing it. For the jealousy that motivates witchcraft is not only the resentment of the envious but the bitter desires of the sexually jealous as well.

"So answer her question, Madumo," I said. "Why don't you have a woman?"

"Why don't you ask why *he* doesn't have a woman?" said Madumo, settling on his haunches and jutting his chin towards me.

"This one?" she said. "He's mine. To hell with the Mixed Marriages Act. Apartheid is finished."

"Some wife you are, Nono," I said, "and just a minute ago you were busy proposing this man."

"Hah!" Madumo exclaimed, turning to Nono, "this white man wants to be in love, but he won't admit it." He picked up his rag and darted to a spot on the floor he had missed. "What he doesn't understand," he said, turning again to Nono and wringing his washrag into the bucket, "is how to propose ladies this side. He doesn't understand that women this side are exposed to TV soaps—*Dallas, Bold and the Beautiful. . . .*"

"Bold and the *Bloody Fools,*" grunted Nono, pouring herself another glass and fossicking in the pocket of her pink floral apron for the remains of a cigarette.

"Bold and the bloody fools," agreed Madumo. "And they normally practice their sex lives like what's on TV. But when they feel in love, emotionally and sentimentally really in love, then they'll behave just like African women." He settled to his haunches and leant back against the wall. "So this one is too much Western, he'll never understand."

"And how is that, Mr. Loverman?" I asked. "How is it when the African woman is in love?"

"She'll become quiet. I don't know how to put it exactly. It's like she's cold. She'll just become cold to you. All that charmingness is gone. Smiling to you? No. Not at all. Am I wrong, Nono?"

"I don't know," said Nono, somewhat sullenly. I could see she didn't like the turn this talk was taking. A clanking of chain and clattering of a closing door sounded from the toilet in the corner of the yard.

"What do you mean, 'cold'?" I asked, my interest piqued.

"In fact, she won't show whether she really has that love or not. The warmth of that love. She will wait for you to come to her. You won't find her open, flexible to you. Caressing? No. She will just be cold. She'll react slowly, very slowly. All of them, they're like that—neh, Nono?" Nono just grunted and pulled on her cigarette. "Even our girlfriends, when they're really in love, when they love you for true, when they're not just playing, they become very cold. Cold, cold, cold . . ."

"Why?" I asked. "Surely they'll give a sign that they're interested?"

"Generally, I think it's an African thing. You see, you are too much of a Westerner. You're expecting her to give you a sign. But an African woman is going to think—No, I must respect him. To give you that sign, if she really loves you, is to say she's a bitch, that she knows well this thing of sex. So her reputation will go down. Her status will be less. So instead she becomes cold, because really she's in love. It's part and parcel of defending herself as if she's innocent in this sexual life."

"Is that true, Nono?" I asked.

"Ya," she said, reluctantly. "What he's saying is true. But you know these Soweto girls, Adam," she said. "They're none of them any good. You can't trust any of them. You must get one fresh from the box. And then take her away from this place. It's no good here."

"How can you say that, Nono," I replied. "You know it's you I'm saving myself for."

"*Voetsek!*" she snarled, grinning.

Madumo, having lost interest in cleaning his room, picked up his cloth again and began wiping the floor near our feet in a slow superfluous arc. "Have you noticed, Adam," he said, glancing up slyly at Nono, "how these women hate each other? More especially the older ones—stalwarts, like. That's why they're always making trouble with witchcraft."

I looked at Nono. "He's talking shit," she said, her eyes following the sweep of Madumo's lazy cloth.

Madumo rose to toss the water from his bucket into the yard.

"So why does a woman go cold if she loves you, Madumo?" I asked, trying to return him to his theme.

"You know, with an African woman," he said, "she'll never admit to having had more than two other boyfriends. She'll say, 'Look, in my sexual life I've met with only three men. The one is that one I had a kid with. The other one, I used to be in love with him, but now we're no more on good terms. So you are the third.' And they'll say, 'I'm not used to men.' So it's part and parcel of her defense." He settled himself onto the end of his bed and tossed the cloth over the upturned bucket.

"Protecting her virtue?"

"Yeah. With Africans, I'm telling you. They'll limit it to three. Well, if it's not two, it'll be three. Have you realized that? They'll never admit to more than three."

"Nono?" I asked.

"*Ag,* man," she replied. "You people are talking too much. Buy me another beer." As I rose with the empty bottles she began humming her favorite ditty: "Don't worry, be happy . . ."

When I returned from the kitchen with the beers, Nono and Madumo were deep in a conversation about *fahfee,* the Chinese numbers game.

"And I was having a dream last night," Nono said, turning to me. "You were in it, Adam, and there was a white dove, too. That's number 16. But what does that bloody China call? *Makaka.* Shit. Number 24."

"That was me," I said, opening the bottle. "So what was I doing in your dream anyway, Nono?"

Nono didn't pause to answer. She was too preoccupied with her story about the *fahfee* runner who had profited at her expense. For thirty years Mr. Lee has been coming to Lekoka Street to collect the bets, twice a day. The whole of Soweto is a patchwork of *fahfee* runners and collection points. Everyone knows a system for beating the odds and choosing the winning number. There are thirty-six possibilities for each fifty-cent bet, each one with its own symbolic equivalent, like Nono's dove. And everyone has their own way of reading the signs to predict the winning *fahfee* numbers. For Nono, who is deadly serious about the *fahfee* business, the whole world is a huge compendium of signs and omens bespeaking the forthcoming *fahfee* number. Only she lacks to tools to decode it correctly.

"So yesterday the police caught that bloody Chinaman," said Nono. *Fahfee* collectors are involved in a ceaseless game of hide-and-seek, or bribe-and-seek, with the police. One of the many mysteries of apartheid in Soweto was how the Chinese number runners survived in the black township during the racial madness of that police state. "You should have seen them," said Nono. "As soon as that bag was given to the China, they pounced. They made him pay fifty rands for bribe." She clapped her hands and grinned. In the next instant the smile vanished. "Did you hear about MaParaffin?" she asked. We were given news of a neighbor, a grandmother, recently admitted to the hospital. "Nobody comes out of there alive," said Nono gloomily. She wiped a hand across her face as if drawing down a new expression. "God is great," she said. If MaParaffin doesn't make it back from the hospital, Nono will be there with the family during the vigil for the deceased, as she always is, chopping vegetables, stirring the pots, and helping with the sorghum beer, helping brew the beer and helping drink it. "And that China . . . Tomorrow . . . ," she said and returned to her beer.

"So, Madumo," I said, grasping the opportunity to return to our previous line of talk, "if I was in love with an African woman, how could I tell if she's interested? Just because she's gone cold? She might just be cold because she doesn't like me. . . ."

"Well, basically, I would say you have to try your hand. Like kissing her. If she responds positively, then, basically, she loves you. But if she doesn't respond, then it means she doesn't want you at all. But, *hhayi!* it's confusing. Like with us guys from the urban areas, when we go to the rural areas, we're in the exact same situation as you. In the rural areas you might meet a woman who's never been caressed or stimulated. Some of them, they've made love before, but in a different way. Up there you don't kiss, you don't do nothing. You just put the dick on and go. So to us urban guys, it becomes too difficult. She'll tell you, 'No, I'm not used to that. I'm not used to being kissed. I don't know that.' So, if she loves you she'll just react positively and be quiet and look at you. Just look at you. You'll do whatever you want to do. She'll just look at you. Even in the urban areas they're like that sometimes. Particularly if a woman loves you, really loves you. She'll react like that. Up until when, maybe after some times when now she's used to you, or maybe if you have bought something, or if you're buying her some drinks at least. Then she'll not be shy. But in soberness? No. It's difficult."

"And even if she likes you, she's supposed to refuse?"

"Yeah. Generally, it's like some kind of cross-examination, testing whether you are really up to that or if you're just testing her. Because they are concerned about their virginity. Even if that's finished, they still have that concept. Though not when there's money there. You pop out money; the virginity status goes to hell. They'll give you whatever service you want."

"So that's why he doesn't have a woman, Nono," I said, trying to engage her in a conversation that was going nowhere. "Because he doesn't have money."

Nono again went fishing in the pocket of her apron for a cigarette, her silence betraying not so much boredom with this chatter of young men, but the general contempt of older women for all such nonsense.

"So really, Adam," said Madumo, lighting his own cigarette, "I'm telling you, it's really very hard to fall in love with African women." He passed his cigarette to Nono.

"Thanks for the advice," I said.

"You know, Adam," said Nono suddenly. "What this boy is saying is the truth. If a lady is loving you, don't be so cruel."

"Who said anyone was in love with me?" I interjected, to no avail.

"Don't be so cruel, man," continued Nono. "Propose her. Tell her, 'I love you, my darling.' You know, if you don't propose her, she will end up hating you, neh Madumo? She'll think you are playing with her."

"Ya!" replied Madumo. "If she's expecting that proposal, and she wants that thing, you'd better be careful."

"Propose who?" I said wanly.

"Because these women can witch you," chimed in Nono. "They can make you drink *korobela* and you won't even know it. Then, before you know it, you're a slave to that lady."

"A slave?"

"She's right, Adam," said Madumo. "That thing can happen. You know yourself how women will give a man *korobela* so that he must be tame. After work, he must come straight home. He shouldn't fall in love with any other woman. So that *muthi* really condemns a man. It goes beyond making him into a good husband; it turns him into a fool. Really. In fact, it makes his senses to be dying. He becomes a Stupid, in fact. And then, even the woman who has applied this *korobela* to her man becomes bored. Sexually . . . socially . . . bored! Their life together becomes really boring. Now that he's there every day, she doesn't want him anymore. So she goes out to find someone else to be in love with. So it destroys. This *korobela* penetrates more and more and more until in the end it destroys him. I am wrong, Nono? . . . Am I wrong Nono?" Madumo insisted.

Nono was quietly pondering her beer. "No, you're right. But if you men weren't all useless, we wouldn't need *korobela*."

It was getting dark. Nono announced that I must drive her home, so I did.

"Hey, that one!" said Nono as the Dombolo rattled down Rakuba Street. "He's mad."

"Not completely," I replied, struggling with the gears. "Even when he's talking nonsense, there's always something there."

"Ha!" she snorted and began to hum her tune. A loving parody: Don't worry, be happy. "Korobela," she said, and returned to her song.

The darkening roads were crammed. I wove a way between stop-and-go Kombis and turned off the main road to cut around by the hostel. Don't worry, be happy. . . . As Nono hummed away beside me, my mind drifted back to our talk of love and magic. Korobela. Where's the witchcraft in that? I wondered. Would it work on me? How would I know? What if the witch's brew, from which my sisters had spared me, had been a potion brewed for love, not for death? Who could say? Maybe that granny, whom we all knew as the witch, had stirred out of kindness her *muthi* into the beer to salve a lovelorn girl's desire? I wondered whether I'd mind.

"Stop!" cried Nono. I'd passed her house. She disappeared into the darkness, and the car was suddenly full of local guys, jubilant at the prospect of a quick ride home.

14

ISIDLISO NIGHTS

One morning, a Tuesday late in July, I knocked on Madumo's door and heard no answer. I pushed open the door and found him huddling fully clothed under the blankets on his bed. The room smelled sour and musty. I left the door open.

"Are you okay?" I asked. He looked up at me and said nothing. I sat on the end of his bed. "What's wrong?" I asked. He struggled into a sitting position. "Can I get you anything?" He shook his head. My friend looked terrible. His hair was matted, his skin a sallow greyish color. "Are you okay?" I asked again.

His voice was weak and weary. "No man, I am not. I'm not okay. I nearly died. I very nearly died. I am lucky to be alive. . . ." He labored over every word.

"What's wrong?" I asked.

"Isidliso," he said, collapsing back onto his stained green pillow.

"*Isidliso?*"

"Yeah, *isidliso.* I'm scared, man. I'm really scared. This *isidliso* is killing me. I've been fighting this thing the whole night. I didn't sleep. Not at all. Because this thing was scrubbing me, like. Inside. Going up and down here, in my chest."

Isidliso is one of the most common afflictions of the witch's craft. It takes the form of a small creature lodged in the gullet. Sometimes it resembles the shape of a crab, other times a frog or small animal, a lizard, say. It can even take a man's form and devour a person from the inside out. Most commonly sent by the witch through *muthi* adulterating food or drink, the *isidliso* slowly consumes its victim, creating all manner of hardship and pain along the way, such as friendships breaking, lovers leaving, or jobs disappearing. *Isidliso* is greatly feared. It can even enter the victim while he sleeps; the witch places the *muthi* in his mouth. In exceptional cases, Mr. Zondi had told us, the *isidliso* can even enter its sleeping victim through food consumed in a dream. The *muthi* is placed in the food and the food sent into the dream through witchcraft. Once inside its victim, the *isidliso* is in a battle to the death and the victim must engage a powerful healer to repel it. Unless it is fought and destroyed, it will destroy the victim. For one who is not strong, however, the battle itself can kill. As an epidemic of AIDS sweeps through this part of Africa, *isidliso* is the name that springs to mind amongst many in the HIV's path. Madumo's terror was heightened by the fact that he had fought with *isidliso* before. At that time, however, his mother was still alive. And she was "spiritually inclined," so she knew what to do. The battle had taken three or four days until the *isidliso* was broken into pieces resembling mushrooms and expelled from his arse in a foul-smelling fury. This time Madumo was on his own. . . .

"How do you know it's *isidliso?*" I asked.

"I know," he said. "I know." He began to suspect *isidliso* the previous week when he found a dark grainy substance like coffee grounds in the refuse of his morning vomiting, but he hadn't wanted to mention it. "Yeagh!" he said. "That kind of stuff. Like coffee mixed with some thickish stuff. It's like this thing we get on top of the river, the greenish stuff."

I asked him again if I could get him anything, and though he declined food, and antacids, he agreed to some cold drink, so I went down to the shop and bought a liter of soda water. It was the closest thing I could think of to an anti-*isidliso* remedy. After drinking deeply he seemed to recover a little life. He sat up in bed and arranged the pillow behind his back for support.

"So what d'you think provoked it last night?" I asked.

"You know," said Madumo, "I think it was that spiritual prophet at the ZCC. You know, that last one, when he hit me that time on the chest, he hit me right on the target. Already that target was moving, but he noticed it. You heard it yourself. It was, boom, in my chest. He must have seen that creature, the *isidliso*."

Last night, Madumo and I had returned to the ZCC church in Phiri to see if there had been any response to the letter. We'd passed by the compound several times since the despatch of the letter, always to no avail. Last night we arrived shortly before the seven o'clock Monday service was to begin. Mr. Mnyama greeted us with his jam tin and drove the evil spirits away with the usual three splashes on the back, three on the front, and a sip from the can before telling us that the people we wanted would be there shortly.

"Is this any way to treat a white man?" I grumbled when we returned dripping to the car. It was going to be a bitterly cold night.

"Perhaps they're aware that you're staying in Mapetla Extension," Madumo said. "They could be aware of the evil things you're exposed to there in Mapetla. Or maybe it can be because of being with me, too. It could be that evil things are coming against you because of helping me. Or else the neighbors there in Lekoka Street. They know that this white man is helping us. Because whenever you're around they see that those guys, your friends, we are getting fat. We have nice jackets, shirts, whatever. So that guy with the water, he won't tell you what he's driving away. But he sees something, for sure. Though it's not good to ask. Because if you ask questions he'll think you're undermining his authority."

While we waited in the car a circle of the faithful formed in the church's yard and began a chant known in *Sepedi* as *mpogo,* a rhythmic calling down of the spirits of the ancestors accompanied by steady hand clapping. A young man, despatched by Mr. Mnyama, approached the car and cautiously tapped at Madumo's window. He told us we must join the circle. Madumo acceded to the instruction but was irritated as we walked towards the circle. "No, man!" he snarled in a stage whisper, "this is totally out. Totally out!" I didn't wait for his explanation.

In the past weeks I had discovered that Madumo took his status as a life-long (albeit lapsed) member of the church very seriously, holding strong views about correct procedures in the church and disdainful of irregular behavior by the congregations towards visitors, especially a white visitor. Later he explained: "That guy should have called me alone. Telling you, a White, that you should pray is totally out. Whom will you pray to? Lekganyane? It's one thing if you go voluntarily. No one can complain. But they shouldn't summon you. I know this church very well. *Very* well." Madumo was also, in his words, paranoid about the church—as well he might be given his recent history. My curiosity, idle as it had been, had brought us here in the first place, but when the business about the letter and permission from Moria set us on the road to a full-scale investigation, Madumo took control and became deeply interested in the outcome.

"No," Madumo continued, "some of these people they just want to call the white man so that they can boast of their powers. It's just harassment."

We joined the circle for *mpogo* and for fifteen or twenty minutes we chanted the same humming line over and over and over, clapping the rhythm until my palms felt fit to bleed. Then, at a signal from an elder, the chanting ceased and we took seats on the benches—men on the right, women to the left. The service began. No sooner had the first hymn begun when we were called by a prophet, a solid short woman clad in khaki.

"Oh boy!" said Madumo under his breath as we followed her

from the shelter to the corner of the yard. We knelt together with the prophet and she began "propheting," shouting and growling in deep idiomatic *Sepedi.* Her propheting was directed at me.

"You have high blood pressure," Madumo said, translating for the prophet. Then he turned to me: "Answer her," he whispered. "Is it true?"

"No," I replied.

"Your stomach, it is paining," she said, through Madumo, after a long inspired rant.

"No," I replied.

"You are having pains in your hands," she pronounced; this after another lengthy interview with the spirits.

"No," I replied. By this time I was beginning to feel sorry for her. I was in excellent health and her diagnosis was getting nowhere. I wasn't giving her a chance.

After a long ejaculation of grunts and phrases, the prophet concluded. Madumo translated: "Your ancestors are worried about you. Your family feels abandoned. You must contact them at home."

"Okay," I said. "That's probably true. I'll phone my mother tomorrow."

We returned to the benches under the lean-to. Mr. Mabitsela, with whom we had become quite friendly since our first visit, had arrived and taken over the service. He introduced me to the congregation as someone who had come from America and was staying in Mapetla Extension. He told them that I had heard that the ZCC was the most powerful church in South Africa and that I wanted to learn more about it. He said that the elders had written to headquarters in Moria about me. He told the congregation they should make me welcome. Then he read from the Gospel according to John: "I am the door: by me if any man enter in, he shall be saved, and shall go in and out, and find pasture." His gloss on the text for the congregation at the Moroka branch of the Zion Christian Church that cold Monday evening in July was that it meant they must have faith in Jesus and make this white man welcome. Switching to English, for my benefit, he explained how the signature five-pointed star of the church, worn by all members, symbolized the star that guided the three wise men to the crib of Jesus in Bethlehem. Before he could complete his homily, however, another prophet clapped her hands at us.

"Oh no!" Madumo whispered as we followed her across the yard to the place of prophecy, "this is harassment. They're going to prophet you to the amen. They're too excited to get hold of a white man."

Our new prophet was another stout woman of late middle-age accompanied by an older man serving as interpreter. Older men of his generation frequently take ready exception to township boys like Madumo. He asked Madumo whether he preferred Zulu or Tswana as the language of translation. . . . "Or Afrikaans maybe?" Madumo replied that he should give it to us in English. The prophet began to growl with the words of the ancestors as we huddled in a group on our knees. She told Madumo that his ancestors had taken him out of the mud that he had been in. "They will give you their blessing," she told him. "And this White man, the ancestors of this church are going to give him more power."

"More power," Madumo repeated later when we were enjoying the warmth of Ncane's shebeen. "Did you hear that? More power. Those prophets have given you more power. And they can do that, you know. They can. When you go back to overseas you'll be untouchable. I mean, your seniors there at work, or maybe that foundation where you are asking for funds. . . . Everything's going to get the green light. And the ancestors of this church are happy to get somebody who will expose the powers of the church in other countries." I can't say I was convinced.

Then there was the small matter of the car. Our prophet diagnosed that someone had bewitched the twenty-year-old Mazda. "You are going to have problems with that car," she told us. That was something I didn't want to hear. Only a week earlier I'd had to have the engine rebuilt after the head gasket blew. It still needed a tune-up, but was running well enough. I told her the car was okay, but our prophet was adamant: the congregation must pray for the car, and one of the elders must burn two papers for it and pour holy water on it. We must also secure a bottle of holy water in a transparent bottle to keep in the car at all times to protect the vehicle from evil spirits.

Madumo and I also needed protection, she told us. We were told to ask the church to pray for us three times. In addition we were to buy a special bar of Sunlight soap and a bottle of Vaseline each—yellow for Madumo, white for me—which should be blessed by the church and used exclusively in our daily baths. We were also told to vomit with "FG coffee"—"Fine Ground," I presume— an execrable local mix of ground coffee and chicory. When I expressed my distaste for this particular brew, Madumo told me I could substitute for the contents some decent beans once the container had been blessed.

Madumo was greatly impressed with this second prophet. He quickly arranged for one of the elders to burn the papers—two strips torn from the local newspaper—and to pour water on the car. Before the papers were burnt to drive away evil spirits, the appointed elder tapped us each in turn on the head, breast, belly, and joints with a green paper covered with sacred writing, praying in *Sepedi* all the while. At the conclusion of the ritual, Madumo enthusiastically agreed to purchase the Sunlight, Vaseline, and FG as soon as we left the church. A bucket of water was sprinkled over the car, inside and out—including the trunk and under the hood. We then returned to the body of the church for the prayers to be said. No sooner had we resumed our seats with the rest of the congregation than another prophet appeared and summoned us to follow.

"Oh no!" Madumo muttered again. "This is too much harassment." But we couldn't complain. As Madumo explains it, we must follow the "spiritual clause." This is the principal clause in the constitution of the church, he says. When a prophet is "spiritually inclined" and feels the call to summon someone for a consultation with the ancestors, that person must follow, no matter what.

Our third prophet was a barrel-chested man in his mid-forties who barked incomprehensible words in a loud honking voice as we followed him across the yard. To me the words sounded like obtuse Biblical references—"Paul Four, Paul Four. . . ." Madumo thought he was speaking Portuguese. Whatever it was, it was clearly not for our ears. He strode across the yard and we scurried to catch up. Again we crouched on hands and knees while the ancestors spoke. This time they brought bad news.

The prophet reported that we must be careful: "Do not trust anyone," he said, delivering the words of the ancestors to our interpreter, a young man this time. The ancestors of the church, he told us, have given us their blessing, that was good, but we must still be careful. He told us that when we come into the church the ancestors will see to it that no one will disturb us. But he warned us not to trust too easily. "Don't be worried when the prophets call," he said. "But if they scold you, do not trust them too easily." Then he thumped Madumo on the chest. My friend suddenly turned deathly grey in the dim light of the church yard. I heard the dreaded word: "*Isidliso*."

Again we were prescribed a brew of FG coffee along with Vaseline and Sunlight soap. Papers were to be burnt as well.

When our prophet had finished and disappeared in search of new victims, the interpreter, who introduced himself as "Charles," took me by the hand. Night had fallen; the service under the lean-to had concluded. The compound was now abustle with people completing their treatments for ailments the prophets had uncovered, hurrying to finish before the streets leading home became too deserted and dangerous.

"He's right," said Charles, upon completion of the introductory pleasantries.

"Who is?" I asked.

"That one, the prophet. He's right when he said you can't trust anyone. Even here, inside the church. There are still witches. Even here, in the house of God . . ."

Charles told me his story. He had become a member of the church some two or three years earlier. Prior to that he had been suffering from a mysterious stomach complaint. The doctors at the clinic couldn't help him. He went from *sangoma* to *sangoma,* spending all his money. Still he remained sick. *Isidliso.* Then he came to the ZCC. Here he was welcomed. Without being asked to pay money, a prophet diagnosed his complaint. He was told that the illness, the terrible pain in his stomach, was being caused by his deceased grandmother. Although this grandmother was in the realms of the ancestors and charged with the task of looking out for the interests of her descendants, she was instead evil and bent upon destroying her own family. She was a witch. And a witch whose work did not cease with death. Charles had dreamt that he saw her dancing. He should have dreamt her watching over him, not dancing. "Dancing!" he exclaimed, marveling still at his lucky escape. "I could have died." After being cured of his affliction, Charles considered the ZCC to be truly the church of God. "Every time I saw a person with that five-pointed star," he said, "I called him my brother. I thought they must be children of God. Never did I believe that evil could be here inside the church. Never!" He soon found out, however, how naive he was. For witchcraft is everywhere, even inside the church. Charles told me stories of the witches that had been discovered inside the church. "I truly believe still that this is God's church," he said. "But the devil is here, too. And there are plenty people doing the devil's work here. Every day." He told me that there are people inside the church practicing witchcraft by prescribing "dirty" treatments, adulterated doses of the coffee and tea that is regularly dispensed in the healing routine. "They can tell you to drink that coffee or tea and then they can put something in it. You can die."

As a solitary white man in this place fashioned for apartheid, I've often been overwhelmed by the generosity of Sowetans. Here in the ZCC in Phiri, despite all the earlier dithering about securing official permission by letter from Moria, I found myself being welcomed into the congregation with open arms. Indeed, in typical Sowetan fashion, the welcome was excessive. Being propheted three times in one night was some kind of record in

Madumo's experience at the church. Yet just as the welcome was being extended, so was I being warned. As I listened to Charles's story of the evil lurking beneath the facade of piety, I reflected upon Mr. Mabitsela's earnest endeavor to present the church to me as a church of peace in the image of the Christian Gospels. I shouldn't have been surprised. I've heard the same dual message countless times before: "We're not as bad as people say," and "Trust no one." Whether the community into which I was being welcomed was the neighborhood, the comrades, the hostel, or a confraternity of criminals, I've always encountered someone striving to present their world in a favorable light and someone else offering the advice: Trust no one! It's a standard theme of life in this place that beneath the appearance of love and togetherness lies a reality of jealousy and hatred that must be guarded against at all times. I am generally of an unsuspicious disposition, so I mostly ignore the advice. Perhaps because of this, I am rarely troubled by the undercurrents.

While I was talking with Charles, the circle formed again to sing the *mpogo* chant that opens and closes the service. Madumo was there chanting with the rest. In a burst of enthusiasm, he stepped into the circle and danced. It was his way of telling all that he was a genuine moZion.

On the way home we stopped to pick up the Vaseline, Sunlight soap, and FG coffee. Madumo promised to take them to be blessed later in the week. I told him I'd call by in the morning. Thus began Madumo's *isidliso* nights.

"*Hhayi!* man," he said. "When that prophet hit me in the chest—did you see that?—then all of a sudden I became sick. I mean, I'm *sick,* Adam. Seriously sick. I could feel this thing moving up and down inside. But I didn't know this thing was going to give me such a serious fight. The whole night I've been fighting it. But now I have a problem. . . ." He slumped back onto his pillow.

Madumo's problem was that he was already undergoing treatment with *muthi* provided by the *inyanga,* Mr. Zondi. It was

Mr. Zondi's duty to heal him in all regards. If the ZCC prophet was speaking the truth, and Mr. Zondi had not spotted the *isidliso,* then Madumo should follow the prescriptions of the prophet and drink the FG coffee. He was supposed to boil the whole half-pound packet in a saucepan of water—"boil it to the amen," he said—and then drink it down while it cooled. Then vomit. But this entailed a major risk. For the medicine of the ZCC might clash with the medicine of the traditional healer, the *inyanga.* The spirits of the church (which empower the coffee) are totally opposed to the spirits of the *inyangas.* "It can kill me," Madumo said, his face bearing the strain of his terror. "Do you see that?" Whichever way he turned, there would be nothing but trouble. "This thing is going to give me a hell of a problem. Because it's man-made. And the one who created it is quite aware that I'm fighting this thing off. And he's going to put more effort, or she, whoever it is, is going to put more effort in, just to make this thing kill me."

"Who do you think is behind it, then?" I asked.

"In fact, the way I see it," he replied, "it's a conspiracy. A large crowd. There is that one who has taken the soil from the grave, and . . ."

"There's more than one?"

"Yeah. More than one. Many more than one."

"Who told you that?"

"No. I just know it. It can't be just one alone. It's a conspiracy. A whole family. And when you are bewitched by a family, it's even more difficult to be cured."

Though the door was still open, a sour stench still permeated the room. I peered behind the door, only to find the dregs of a night's regurgitation in a yellow plastic bucket. With a wordless gesture, I offered to take it out. Wordlessly, he assented. I flushed the stinking mess down the toilet and rinsed the bucket. This was going to prove to be a major test for Mr. Zondi, for if he turns out not to be a powerful healer, a genuine *inyanga,* he will fail to cure my friend. Madumo was frantic. Returning to the room, I offered again to buy him food but he refused. Fighting the *isidliso* meant, amongst other things, starving it. He'd not been eating for days, and drinking little.

"So they've turned my mother against me," he said.

"Your mother? How can that be?"

"With the soil. And they know the whole story of my family, all the names. They know how to call the names. Then they are using the soil from the grave. So they know how to call up my mother. That's how I know it must be inside the family. Lucky for me, they don't know my whereabouts. They've lost my trail since I left home."

"I don't understand," I said.

"When they did that thing with the soil, my mother just slipped off. She was no more a barrier to protect me from them. She became like a bad ancestor to me. They turned her against me with that soil. But then it wasn't totally, like. Because it was she who drove me away from that house. So the ancestors, generally, are still with me. Because although I'm away from home and struggling, I didn't have any direct confrontation, like. I wasn't stabbed, run over, or arrested. So somewhere, somehow, she and those other ancestors, even those ones from my father's side, they are still here to protect me. But this *isidliso.* This is a real problem. They can get a printout from this thing. That's how they control it. Remote control."

"So who is behind this then, Madumo. Who is the witch?" I asked.

"I know who it is," he replied. "I know well who is responsible for this, and for all my misfortunes. . . ."

The culprit, he suspected, was a cousin of his mother, also a ZCC member, living in a nearby district of Soweto. She was the one who came to the house when his mother died to preside over the mourning. During the days before a funeral in Soweto, the bedroom of the deceased is cleared of furniture and a mattress is set upon the floor. A candle is kept burning at all times. An elder of the family, a female elder, is supposed to stay upon the mattress until after the funeral, sitting quietly while visitors stream through the house offering condolences, praying, and singing hymns. The mourner is supposed to cover her head with a scarf, wrap herself in a blanket, and stay quiet and still until the funeral is over.

"So that cousin of my mother's," said Madumo, "she was the one sitting on the mattress. So while you are sitting on the mattress you're not supposed to be moving around the house. You should only go out either late at night or early in the morning. And you should balance your diet so as not to be pressed to go to the loo. Well what made me suspicious was that she said she wanted to vomit with some stuff while she was there, to clean her stomach. She asked me to buy some baking soda. She wanted to vomit outside the house; outside the house, but next to the door."

Madumo refused to buy her the soda. "You'll vomit after the funeral," he told her. When he asked some other elders of the family about this request, they were shocked. He became convinced that the aunt was up to witchcraft.

"So she was going to mix that soda with *muthi.* If we'd let her do that vomiting, it was going to be witchcraft to the first degree. It would not take long. After two or three days—before the funeral in fact—we were going to do something like take axes and chase each other. Me, my two brothers, even my sister. We would all have been dead. Fighting to death, in fact. So now this *isidliso,* in fact this curse generally, is because we stopped her then."

"So why would she be doing that?" I asked.

"Jealousy. Jealousy. She's not supposed to do such a thing, but jealousy can make a person do anything."

"Why would she be jealous of you? Your mother's just died, you've got no money. . . ."

"I don't know. I really don't know. Because we used to go to her place and visit all the time. Maybe it's because we didn't ask anything from her. Because with we Africans, if you don't ask anything, they say you've got pride. Like, maybe you've already had lunch somewhere and they offer you food when you visit. So if you say thanks, but I've eaten already, they will think that you are undermining their food. Maybe that's what happened and she thought we were undermining her food. Being suspicious, like. Because we didn't used to ask favors of that aunt."

Madumo was also suspicious of the fact that, as well as wanting to vomit, the aunt helped herself to some of his mother's clothes before the period of ritual mourning was complete and the ceremony of washing had taken place. He was particularly bitter about a pair of slippers—"big ones, made of fur, perfectly designed, like a duck"—that his sister had allowed the aunt to take. "Because it's dangerous for someone to get shoes of a person who has passed away," he said. "Shoes and underwear. It's too dangerous. They can do witchcraft with those things."

Shortly before Madumo began his treatment with Mr. Zondi, he dreamt of this aunt. He dreamt that he was fighting with her. "No," Mr. Zondi told him when Madumo recounted the dream, "you are fighting with her. But you have defeated her. That dream simply means that you have won the war." Then they began their treatment of the witchcraft and the aunt was forgotten until suddenly this *isidliso* arose to torment him. If it was indeed directed by this aunt and backed by a conspiracy reaching into his own family through his brother and sister as he suspected, even to the spirit of his late mother, the *isidliso* was sure to pose an enormous problem.

"So that's why I'm scared," he said, pausing to run his hand back and forth over his thinning disheveled hair and search on the cabinet for a lost cigarette. "I'm so scared. Because I know that to fight these things depends a lot on luck. If I'm lucky I can maybe break it down in days, the days to come. Otherwise, it can stay here for years. Ten years or more. This is a scary situation. A very scary situation."

Adding to his fear was the fact that he was faced with a decision between following the path of Mr. Zondi or returning to the ZCC. Mr. Zondi had not mentioned the *isidliso.* Perhaps he did not even realize its presence. Perhaps this healer was not as powerful as Madumo had led himself to believe, as he so desperately needed to believe. On the other hand, Madumo reasoned, if the ZCC prophet *was* speaking the truth he should join the ZCC at once and throw himself into their treatments full-time. He should place all his trust in the Zionist way, enlisting the power of the ancestors of the church, his own ancestors, Jesus, and the Holy Spirit in this struggle against the *isidliso.* But if the ZCC knew Madumo was consulting an *inyanga* and suspected that he was testing them, they would be angry. They don't like being tested, nor working with someone who is taking *muthi.* Yet they didn't sniff out the fact that he was already using *muthi* from Mr. Zondi. On the other hand, again, if Mr. Zondi knew that Madumo was busy with the Zionists, vomiting their FG coffee, he might not be pleased either. The whole treatment could be ruined.

"You know what amazed me yesterday?" Madumo said after pondering his dilemma. "Those two prophets, the second one and the third, came with the same story. It means they know something. It means there is *isidliso.*"

If the ZCC prophets were onto something with their diagnosis of *isidliso,* Madumo should go with them, to be sure, but he couldn't easily countenance that. He was deeply suspicious of the ZCC. He'd been born into the church. Both his parents were members. His brother remained an active member. But Madumo, like our interpreter Charles from the night before, was convinced there was evil within the church and saw his conflict with his brother as evidence of it.

Madumo was also convinced that the prescriptions handed out by ZCC prophets were sometimes false. In the early 1980s his parents had spent months traipsing around the mountains of Rustenberg seeking a place "where the waters meet" from which they could fetch water to bring to the church to be blessed in order to solve their problems. But they could never find such a place. "Do you know how hard it is to find the place where waters meet?" Madumo asked me when he told this tale. "And if you do find that place, it's too dangerous to take the water." For not only is there danger involved in getting to the center of a stream where waters meet, but such places are notorious as the resting places of the mystical snakes Mamlambo and Inkosi ya Manzi. These snakes possesses enormous powers and are widely reputed to carry people off to their dwelling places under the water. There they can be killed, or pass into another world. The most powerful healers claim to have spent years under the water with such snakes. Such snakes are not to be trifled with.

Indeed, in 1981, Madumo was himself nearly killed by a Mamlambo in Soweto, in the stream that passes through Protea before running towards Lenasia down between Chiawelo and the Avalon Cemetery. One afternoon before Christmas that year, at the behest of a prophet of the ZCC, Madumo's father sent his three sons to fetch water from this stream. Madumo was about thirteen years old, his brothers were a couple of years older and younger. They took a twenty-five-liter plastic drum and walked from Mapetla. It was about a forty-minute walk to the stream. Before they reached the water, however, the weather changed. A summer thunderstorm exploded on them. They were drenched.

"Now, in these rivers," Madumo explained when he told me this story many years later, "in fact in most rivers, there's a thing that witches do if they want to hit you with lightning. So there was a lot of lightning there. We didn't want to go on with that thunder. But my brother said, 'If we don't come at home with this water, we are going to be killed or at least lashed by our father.' So we decided to wait for the rain to stop. But it rained for maybe six or seven hours. Heavy rain. We waited in the scrap yard up there at the place of *maBosmen.* By sunset it was getting very dark. So we just took chances and went to the river. The river was flooding. We were frightened to shit, man. So, by luck, just by luck, there was a *Bosman* there who helped us and filled the scoop for us. That scoop was fucken heavy but we carried it home. When we got home my mother was outside in the street waiting. Waiting at the gate. And it was still raining. The water was up to our ankles in the street. We came to the house. When we arrived my mother said, 'Whoooooosh! You were nearly taken by that river.' She said she had become spiritually inclined after we left. She'd had a message from one of our ancestors telling her what was going on. And she had to pray to that ancestor to save us. She was told that the whole setup was done by our father and his family—the rain and all. Deliberately. Can you believe that? If that snake had been angry it was going to take all three of us. And that fucken psychopath, our father, he was waiting for that water. But our mother took that scoop and just destroyed it. Then my father just took his coat and left the house. She told us that our father was angry because, in the rural areas, if you want to be rich, one of your family members must die. You should kill one of your family. You see? So she told us he wanted to kill us, to make us into zombies and take us by *muthi* to his family's place in the rural areas where they would make us to plough fields." In the image of his torment, furrowed into his brow beneath his matted hair, I caught a glimpse of the courage this quest for healing must entail.

After our night of being propheted to the amen, Madumo suspended his distrust of the ZCC sufficiently to go ahead with the FG coffee treatment. He boiled the half-pound packet of coffee and chicory in a saucepan of water. When the brew was thick and black, he took it off the stove and allowed it to cool before drinking the whole half-gallon pot. He kept it down as long as possible before purging himself into the bucket. Then his battle with the *isidliso* began in earnest. He became weak, began hallucinating, felt he was going to die. . . .

15

DIAGNOSES, DOUBTS, AND DESPAIR

Shortly after Madumo began his battle with the *isidliso* I was called away from Soweto to make a trip to the Eastern Cape. While visiting the small university town of Grahamstown, I met the district surgeon, a doctor who, in addition to running the pediatric ward at the local hospital, held the job of performing autopsies in cases of unnatural death. I described to him Madumo's condition and the regimen of vomiting he'd been following to repel witchcraft. The surgeon's diagnosis was clear: The dark granular stuff resembling coffee grounds that my friend was vomiting up were blood clots. "He probably has bleeding ulcers brought on by the physical trauma of all that vomiting," he told me. The weakness and dizziness were probably the result of low blood pressure and impending kidney failure. And God alone knows what the pharmacological properties of the herbs might be. Unless my friend had been careful to drink plenty of water during the day, the surgeon told me, his constant vomiting over a long period of time would probably have caused him to become severely dehydrated, as well as damaging his esophagus, leading to low blood pressure and strain on the kidneys. Drinking half a gallon of extremely strong coffee under such circumstances could be enough to cause kidney failure.

I returned to Soweto dreading the thought of the state in which I would find Madumo. I was determined to take him to the hospital for proper medical treatment. The surgeon had suggested he would probably need to be rehydrated by intravenous drip. He'd also told me horror stories about the toxic substances administered by *inyangas* that he'd encountered in his autopsy work. I'd mentioned to the surgeon my alarm when I'd heard of Mr. Zondi rubbing mercury into Madumo's cuts, but he told me that would be the least of the problem. The real damage done by *inyangas,* the surgeon said, is caused by the constant emetics and enemas—especially enemas, as the colon is extremely efficient at absorbing toxins. Chemical poisoning by herbs administered by *inyangas* in the course of "curing" is common, he said. Of course, when the patient dies, witchcraft is blamed. For these healers are not simply administering some ancient wisdom of benign homeopathy but are constantly innovating in magical potions. He told me about encountering a case of chromium poisoning and discovering, after long inquiries, that an *inyanga* had been peeling chrome off a bumper bar and grinding it into dust—presumably to serve as an internal mirror, administered through enema, to reflect witchcraft. The surgeon told me he'd seen countless children die from being administered enemas by *inyangas* as cures for diarrhea. . . .

As I absorbed this information on the way back to Soweto, I worried that I'd been too simple-minded in endorsing Madumo's cure with Mr. Zondi; I'd been too ready to dismiss the physical procedures and substances administered as merely innocuous symbolic and ritual accoutrements of an essentially "psychological" cure. After all, I'd told myself, Madumo felt his curse to be real enough, and so long as he wasn't suffering any physical illness, it was clear that he stood no chance of getting his life back on track until he considered himself free of the curse. If these operations and emetics made him feel confident about that, they couldn't do any harm. . . .

Fortunately, Madumo is blessed with a strong constitution. When I found him in his room on my return he was looking fit and cheerful. The room was clean, his linen freshly laundered.

"What happened?" I asked. "Last time I saw you, you looked like death."

"False alarm," he said. He poured water from a red plastic jug to boil for tea.

"False alarm?" I asked, stunned by his transformation.

"False alarm."

"Did you talk to Zondi about it?"

"Yeah. There's nothing like that thing I was telling you about. No *isidliso.* He told me that thing was maybe brought on by nerves. Because when I'm at this church I get sort of spiritually inclined. Maybe I'm too much like my mother. Or then again, when I got back here that night, my room was smelling of *imphepho.* Maybe they were up to something in there next door."

Whatever it was, my friend had survived. I told him of the doctor's diagnosis and how worried I had been about him dying of dehydration and kidney failure. Madumo agreed that it sounded like a reasonable assessment: "That thing was probably just a natural sickness," he said. "You can never tell."

I suggested we go to visit Mr. Zondi. I wanted to get to the bottom of this *isidliso* business, and we had time to spare before the night vigil we were expected to attend at a neighbor's place in Lekoka Street.

Mr. Zondi greeted us from the window of his shack by the hostel as I edged the Dombolo over the gully outside. We were regular visitors to Mr. Zondi's place, and the other stall-holders and loiterers in the vicinity hardly paid us any notice as I parked the car close to the shack. Madumo was in a cheerful mood, bursting into the consulting room with warm lively greetings and cadging five rands from me in the process to buy a liter of Coke for our host. The windows were closed and the shack had the smell of old damp carpets. Mr. Zondi was passing time with his friend Mr. Masilo between clients. Madumo returned with the drink and organized a couple of glasses. He was keen to begin our discussion.

"So *Bab'u* Zondi," he said, addressing the older man formally in Zulu, "Adam wants to know more about this *isidliso* setup."

The healer nodded, without speaking. Madumo turned to me: "So, do you have a question?"

"Well," I replied, turning to Madumo, "what I want to know is did you have it, or were those ZCC guys just taking chances? And what exactly is this *isidliso* anyway? How does it work? "

Mr. Zondi replied, "Those people of the ZCC were wrong to tell you that story. They were just trying to fill their stomachs." The healer sat erect and still, his hands palm downwards on the table.

"Yeah," added Madumo, "they knew that we didn't come for a consultation, so they shouldn't just do that without knowing what our mission is in coming to the church."

"So you didn't have it?" I pressed.

"No," replied Madumo.

"Not at all?"

"No."

"So what was it that was nearly killing you then?"

Mr. Zondi intervened: "That thing was just a natural sick. A reaction to these herbs, because they are too much strong. There was no *isidliso*."

Madumo relaxed back into his seat.

"So, in general," I asked, "what is *isidliso* like? What's it all about?"

"It comes in many forms," said Mr. Zondi. "It can be in the form of a frog, or a crab. It depends how they mix the herbs and send them to you."

"So how do they do that?"

"Sometimes they can just pour that stuff and give it to you. Sometimes they send it through the night, then you can dream that you are drinking it in a cold drink, or liquor. Or it can appear in the dream in the form of meat."

"So, when this crab or frog gets inside you," I asked, "does it remain under the control of the person who sent it?"

"No," the healer replied, "once it is sent, it is under its own mission. But it depends on its mission, on the way it was formed. There are different categories. There's one sort of *isidliso* that's for causing misfortunes, general misfortunes, then there are others for killing. It depends on the herbs."

"But let's say I'm the witch," I pressed. "If I want to send you this *isidliso,* can I then use it to control everything you do?"

"No. No," the healer replied emphatically.

Madumo intervened: "So, the way Mr. Zondi says, it's automatical, this *isidliso.* It depends according to the mixtures used. Say they have put a mixture in your beer. Maybe they will start with the one to cause misfortune. Maybe it will cause you to lose your job. Or if you don't have a job, it will make it that no white man should look on you—favor you, like. So you won't ever get a job. Or maybe girls, it will make you unpopular with women. So it's automatical, it causes misfortunes wherever it goes. It just controls itself."

Mr. Zondi nodded in agreement, looking at Madumo with a paternal satisfaction.

"And there is no *isidliso* that is controlled by the witch like a remote control?"

Mr. Zondi shook his head. "It is controlled when it is started."

"But Madumo," I said, "you said last week that the *isidliso* was being controlled by that witch like with a remote control, that she was getting a 'printout' on your every movement and strengthening the *isidliso* when you began to fight it."

"Yeah. I was told like that," he replied, somewhat sheepishly. "That's what they told us at home."

"So what do you say, Mr. Zondi?"

Again, Mr. Zondi shook his head. "It's not like that," he said, leaning forward on his elbows. Then he explained, in deference to Madumo, that sometimes the herbs are different according to the various ethnic groups. As a Zulu, he is most familiar with the herbs of Natal. The *isidliso* there is not like a remote control. Other parts of the country, where people of different groups live, have different plants and animals, so the people have access to different herbs and are thus capable of creating different effects. Maybe it *is* possible for some witches to use *isidliso* as a form of remote control. He wouldn't rule out the possibility, but he'd never encountered it. The greatest problems for healers in a place like Soweto, he told us, are caused by witches mixing different herbs from different regions all over the country, because a healer cannot be expected to know all the different combinations and thus to know how to counteract them. The witch who moves from region to region gaining specialized herbs is the most powerful opponent. Soweto houses people—and, therefore, witches—from all over the subcontinent. The work of healing is hard here.

With the issue of *isidliso* settled, Madumo wanted to know more about the *tokoloshe*. The *tokoloshe* is deeply feared by its victims, but as well as being the instrument of witchcraft, the *tokoloshe* is also something of a prankster. And because it is best known for its enormous penis—which he carries slung over his shoulder—and voracious sexual appetite, it is also a figure of ribald humor. The *tokoloshe* in these parts mostly preys on women. Madumo said he wanted to get an idea of the "craftsmanship" of the *tokoloshe*. He wanted to know whether anything had changed in the way it was being made since the old days. For the *tokoloshe* is a pure fabrication by the agency of witchcraft, unlike other familiars such as the cat or the chicken (or the baboon, although such things are rare in Soweto), who have existences independent of the witches' craft.

Mr. Zondi was in an expansive mood. He gave us the whole recipe for making a *tokoloshe:* "First you have to get a black cat and kill it. From the cat you must remove its fat. The fat of a black cat. ["Or a black fat cat," Madumo chuckled when we repeated the recipe later to Mpho and Thabo over drinks in at Ncane's shebeen.] Thereafter, you go to the mountains. You must go to a peninsula, where the mountains go down into the sea—

like at the Cape Peninsula. On such a peninsula you will find certain shrubs. [He didn't tell us which shrubs, nor did we ask. Why would we want to know?] You take the herbs from those shrubs and mix them with the cat's fat. Thereafter, you must obtain the fat of an alligator, not the land alligator like they have in Botswana, but the alligator from the river. Or a crocodile. The one that stays in water. So, after mixing the cat's fat with the herbs from the mountain and the crocodile's fat, you must go to the place where two roads meet, a crossroads. There you must place your *muthi* in a container—maybe a bottle, or whatever—and you must bury that bottle in the crossroads. That bottle must remain in the intersection for a period of seven days. During that time, maybe a woman who is pregnant, or maybe a woman who is menstruating, will pass over the bottle. Then her shadow, her *isithunzi* [sometimes translated as "soul"] is going to pass into that bottle. From this, the *muthi* in the bottle is going to change into a monster."

"So what happens to the pregnant woman? What happens to her baby?" I asked.

"No," replied Mr. Zondi, "her child is born normally. But that thing in the bottle has the spirit of the child. On the one side there is a normal child, on the other, coming from the *muthi* in the bottle, is a monster." The two would normally never meet, and the mother would never know that she had helped spawn an abomination.

We didn't ask Mr. Zondi, "How come you know how to make a *tokoloshe* if you are not a witch?" And while it occurred to me that the healer might be making a joke at my expense, testing my credulity, it soon became apparent he was not. I dropped out of the conversation as Madumo engaged Mr. Zondi and his friend Masilo in an earnest discussion about the use of a certain kind of goat as a witch's familiar. My patience was wearing thin. After a while, I reminded Madumo that we had someplace to be and had to be moving. He rose, and we bade farewell to Mr. Zondi and his friend.

We arrived at the vigil shortly after eleven that night—Thabo, Mpho, Madumo and me—after priming ourselves, as is our custom, at Ncane's shebeen. In the front yard of the house, a few doors down the street from ours, a red-and-yellow striped tent had been erected. A single bulb hanging from the center of the empty tent illuminated the space with an eerie orange glow. Wisps of coal smoke cut through the air. We were here to remember Mogomotse. He'd died five years ago, when still just a small boy, and we'd all been fond of him. In the morning, shortly after dawn, we would join busloads of relatives, friends, and neighbors and troop down to the cemetery to unveil his tombstone. We greeted the women in the backyard, who were tending the three-legged iron pots of fragrant stew made from the meat of a pair of recently slaughtered sheep, and entered the house.

In the dining room, where the table had been removed and chairs placed against the walls, an old man was preaching from a battered Bible in the Sotho language. Beside him, a younger man waving a similar book was translating into Zulu, amplifying the old man's gestures and intonation as he went. The old man's eyes were closed and his grizzled, close-cropped head remained erect and still as his words streamed forth. The younger man's head—round, smooth and oily—was covered with beads of sweat from all his bobbing up and down. Together they labored over a vast opulent image of heaven that struck me as strangely squalid for a boy struck down so young. The child was killed five weeks before his sixth birthday. A sprinkling of neighbors and the girls I'd known as children in Mogomotse's day were huddled in blankets, waiting for the old fellow to finish before resuming their singing. At the end of the sermon, Mantja, a friend of the dead child's mother, began a hymn. We all joined in.

"Are you ready for this?" Mpho whispered as we took our seats after the song.

"I don't think so," I replied. "Hold them off for a while, would you?" Mpho nodded. I knew I would be called upon to speak. Everyone knew how fond I'd been of the boy. They would be expecting me to speak in his memory. I noticed Madumo was no longer with us. Since his mother's death he can't cope with funerals or the memory of grieving.

Someone said a prayer. Before she had finished, Thabo was on his feet. He cupped his hands in a gesture of piety, requesting a hearing. He spoke of Mogomotse. He told us the boy was surely in heaven and asked us to join him in prayer. I was grateful he'd resisted the temptation to mimic the theatrics of preachers as he's sometimes prone to do in these situations, especially after taking a few drinks. MaNdlovu, whom we know better in her guise as a drinker at Ncane's, began another hymn. We sang in Sotho about Jesus, the Lamb of God. Mpho stood to speak. He praised the memory of the dead child. He said he remembered how the little boy used to insist he was a Comrade, a fighter for the ANC. He spoke of what a man he would have made. He told us how he still misses Mogomotse when he sees the other children playing in Lekoka Street. "It seems unfair for such a boy to be taken from us so young," he concluded, "but who are we to question God's will?" Thereupon he launched into a spirited rendition of "Thula Sizwe," Mogomotse's favorite song, joined by the girls of Lekoka Street who remembered the little boy's singing in the days before they became women. The words of "Thula Sizwe" implore an oppressed nation not to weep over their dead, for they are gone to join Jesus. The chorus promises that freedom is coming.

The singing slowly ebbed into silence. I could feel everyone's eyes on me as I sank to the hard plastic chair and stared at my boots. I was in no mood for this. We had drunk nowhere near enough beer at Ncane's place in the Chiawelo flats. I remembered how this boy used to sing the songs of struggle. He couldn't have been more than three years old at the time I first met him, but he had the presence and the nerve to lead all the kids in the *toyi-toyi* and struggle songs until one of the older ones would lift him out of the way and take over in his place. They used to laugh at him for singing about *"Oli mathando"* instead of Oliver Tambo. Someone else began to preach.

I must have sat out a dozen prayers, hymns, and speeches

before I found myself on my feet requesting the right to be heard. A hissing chorus of "shhh!" circled the room, opening my way. I felt as if my racing pulse was beating a tatoo through the silence. "Wait!" commanded MaMama, a young neighbor, before disappearing to round up the others. The women from the kitchen and yard were crowding into the room. Mogomotse's grandmother took a seat directly opposite, studying me expectantly. The boy's mother stood amidst the throng from the kitchen. Mpho rose to translate.

"I remember when I first came here, to Lekoka Street," I said, "in 1990. . . ." I hadn't known my voice could be so feeble. "In those days, people weren't used to seeing a white man around the location—except for the police, of course. And whenever I walked the streets, the children would cry out *Lekgoa! Lekgoa!* It sounded like a warning, but I suppose they were just excited to see a white man, *lekgoa.* Then one morning, in 1991, I was walking past this house and a little boy came out and asked my name. "Adam," I said. "*Mr.* Adams," he insisted. After that, whenever I walked down Lekoka Street, that little boy would run to greet me. "Mr. Adams," he would shout. "Miiiiiister Adams!" He would take my hand and walk me to the shop. Though that boy was hardly any higher than my knee, with his hand in mine I felt safe. I didn't feel like a target. And whenever other children would see me and call *Lekgoa!* that little boy would correct them. "No! Not *lekgoa,*" he would say. "Mr. Adams." Before long all the children around here knew my name. And they made me their friend. Through the children of Lekoka Street, everyone else learnt who I was. Mr. Adams. And I was accepted, I think, for being the children's friend. Everyone made me feel that this was my home. For that, especially, I still thank Mogomotse. . . ."

I could say no more. Mogomotse's grandmother sprang to her feet and led the singing. Mpho left the room. When I had mimicked the boy saying Miiiiiister Adams, his voice had trembled and the translation had stopped. I sang along as best I could, but my mind had returned to that morning after Christmas Day five years earlier.

I had risen late, bleary eyed, from a hard night's festivity. On my way to the shop for milk, Ayanda came wheeling out to the middle of the street in her chair to greet me. "Mr. Adams, Mr. Adams," she gasped. "Mogomotse, he is dead."

"What?" I said, stooping to lean on the handles of her wheelchair.

"Mogomotse," she said. "He's dead. By an accident." Ayanda was nine years old; confined to a wheelchair three years earlier after being run down by a taxi. I looked down at her, still uncomprehending. She jerked her chin up at me and shrugged her shoulders. I caught a glimpse of something like terror in her eyes. She repeated herself in English. "Mogomotse. Dead." The boy had been run down by a drunken driver after a Christmas party.

The next day, MaMfete and I went to his grandmother's house to pay our respects. We entered without knocking, as is the custom. Inside, the newly extended house was still unfinished, the concrete floors were bare and there was no ceiling beneath the new tin roof. Everything seemed austere and exposed. No one was in sight. MaMfete began to sing an old Methodist hymn in an African cadence, firm and loud. She led me into the bedroom where her song was joined by a chorus of voices. The boy's mother lay exhausted on a mattress on the floor. Her mother sat beside her. I glanced towards them. They seemed oblivious to our presence. The room was crowded with neighbors and visitors, all women. The furniture had been removed. MaMfete seated herself on the floor while someone made space for me on one of the plastic chairs lining the walls. I sat there, stiff and stupid, fighting against tears, unable to utter a word. MaMfete began to pray. Her voice rose and fell in a gentle flow of consolation, punctuated at times by affirming amens. A solitary candle, burning in a jar on the floor, seemed to focus the stifling heat. Our shoulders were covered out of respect. I sat silent through the prayer; closed, screwed tight, bitter. MaMfete began to speak. She spoke of Mogomotse and of her sadness at his passing. "But if it is God's will," she said, "we must accept it." She introduced me to his family, gathered to share the grief. I knew only the grandmother. She described how I spent time with the children of Lekoka Street. She told them the child and I were the best of friends. The dead boy's mother roused herself to listen. MaMfete said I was teaching the children to read and write. She said that even when I couldn't speak their language, and they couldn't speak mine, we had found a way to communicate. She said that showed how God was great. She told them I had made a video of Mogomotse singing "Thula Sizwe." Hearing this, his mother broke down and wept. Huge inconsolable sobs. She cried alone. MaMfete talked on. I could no longer follow her words. In the battle against my own tears, my mind became enfolded in the rhythm of her voice as it steadily soothed the staccato gasps of a mother's grief. Another woman began to pray, then another, and another. Someone began to sing, and the whole assembly joined voices in a hymn. Their plaintive African harmonies, raising spirits above the pain, registered only a despairing threnody in my heart. I dared not unclamp my jaw to join them, for fear of the tears I knew I had no right to shed in the face of their God's will.

We buried Mogomotse a few days later.

16

BACK TO SQUARE ONE

Eventually, after weeks of vomiting, Madumo came to the end of the second phase of his treatment. The first phase had served to rid him of the evil despatched with the soil from the grave, the second phase was to protect him from further evil. On completion of the second phase, Mr. Zondi burnt his *imphepho* again and consulted the ancestors as to whether the treatment had been successful. It had been. Madumo was now set to complete the third phase, the discharge. For this, as well as rituals presided over by Mr. Zondi, the patient had to communicate with his own ancestors and re-establish good relations with departed kin. Principal amongst these ancestors, Mr. Zondi told Madumo, was his mother. The first anniversary of her death was approaching. On that anniversary, Madumo should make a feast and call his mother, tell her his problems, and bring her spirit to his home.

Were he still on good terms with his family, such a feast would have been a joyful matter. Indeed, as well as being a solemn commemoration of his deceased mother, it would have been an occasion for eating, drinking, and making merry with the neighbors, friends, and family who form the community within which the gifts of life are enjoyed. Unfortunately, Madumo was not on good terms with those people. In fact, his present unhappy condition, as Mr. Zondi had diagnosed, was directly caused by the action of his relatives. There was no one to whom he could turn who knew the names of his ancestors. And, because of witchcraft, friends were few and far between, too.

Madumo's problems in fulfilling the requirement of feeding his ancestors were compounded by the fact that he did not even have his own place. As a subtenant in an outside room, he was in no position to make a feast for his ancestors. He knew that if the people in the main house realized he was doing so, they would become extremely angry. A subtenant slaughtering in the yard risks awakening the landlord's ancestors and arousing their hunger. And if those ancestors are dissatisfied for any reason (which they probably are, for no doubt the landlord's family has been lax in their attention to ancestral needs), they can become angry and won't hesitate to make everyone aware of it. Thus the landlord's ancestors will vent their spleen on the landlord; the landlord will take it out on the tenant. As in life, so in death. Worse still, if the landlord finds you slaughtering in his yard without his permission, he can suspect you of practicing witchcraft. That suspicion can be deadly if the landlord decides to suffer not that witch to live.

"They'll say, 'He's witching us in our yard,'" Madumo said after we'd returned to his room following a visit to Mr. Zondi. On our way back from the healer's, we had stopped to buy some roast chicken, which we were now enjoying in Madumo's room.

"You'd better be careful," I said, tearing apart the greasy chicken and making a sandwich with a chunk of bread torn off the loaf.

"Hey," said Madumo, "this is really dangerous. But you heard him, I have to make this mini-feast for my mother."

Mr. Zondi had given Madumo precise instructions: Because of his circumstances, he should not make a full feast. No one inside the landlord's house should know what he is up to. He should buy two chickens—white chickens—one for himself, and one for Mr. Zondi. Mr. Zondi will take his chicken and slaughter it down by the Klipriver before dawn. Madumo should take his chicken into his room and keep it there overnight. He must cut its throat at dawn and let its blood seep into the soil of the yard without anybody noticing. Then the chicken should be cooked—without anyone knowing what it was in aid of. Madumo should eat only one piece and give the rest away. Mr. Zondi also instructed Madumo to buy some candles and two cartons of sorghum beer.

"Cartons?" I exclaimed, registering my contempt for the commercial variety of the indigenous brew after Madumo had itemized once again the *inyanga*'s shopping list.

"Well," Madumo replied, "it doesn't matter, so long as it is *mqomboti*."

"Can't you get someone to brew the real stuff for you?" I asked. To my taste, the commercial process for producing *mqomboti* transformed the gritty fragrant traditional brew into a sour sludge with the texture and odor of puréed vomit. The process was invented by local authorities in the 1930s, during the days of segregation when home brewing, along with bottled liquor, was prohibited. For Africans in urban areas, the city councils ran huge beerhalls to sell their own product, using the profits to build and administer segregated "Native Locations." In the early 1990s, these breweries were privatized and became for a while the largest black-owned industry in the country until corruption and incompetent management brought them to the brink of collapse.

Madumo thought that getting real *mqomboti* was a good idea. I suggested we go to my place in Mapetla Extension and ask the women there to brew him some. "MaMfete makes excellent *mqomboti*," I said. When we arrived at Lekoka Street, MaMfete was not at home, but we found Keitumetse inside busy with her studies. Since being forced by financial difficulties to discontinue her engineering studies and qualify as a teacher to support the family, Keitumetse has struggled to complete her technical degree part-time. Whenever she isn't cooking, cleaning, or earning a living, Keitumetse will be busy with her books. MaMfete was around the corner at the doctor's surgery, she told us. We said we wanted help in brewing sorghum beer and she gave us a list of ingredients to buy at the shop down the road: King Korn sorghum, maize, yeast. . . .

"So what are you two up to now?" she asked, her eyebrows raised. I explained that Madumo had to make a mini-feast for his mother, as it was one year on Friday since she passed away. "Oh, shame," she said and looked upon Madumo with kindness. "Mama will be home just now," she said.

When we returned from the shop with our packages, we found MaMfete at home in the red-and-white kitchen. She had been feeling unwell from an attack of high blood pressure but assured us she was better now. Dr. Mohasoane had given her something to bring it under control. Keitumetse had made her a sandwich and told her we needed help in the brewing of *mqomboti.*

"Madumo is having a problem, Mama," I said when we joined the two women at the table.

"I know," she said quietly. I was reluctant to raise the subject of brewing as she was in no condition to undertake extra work. Before I could say anything, however, she turned to Madumo and said quietly but firmly, "I can't help you with this thing. I can't mix that beer for you." I was taken aback. I know MaMfete as the most generous of souls. I was expecting that she would insist on brewing the beer while leaving me to complain that she was risking her health. She shook her head wearily and continued: "I can't do that. The reason is one: If I can be brewing that beer here at home and the ancestors of this house see that it is not for them, they will be disturbed. Perhaps they can even be getting angry. It's not right." Madumo was silently staring at the tablecloth. "You should be doing this at your home. Even *your* ancestors can become angry if they see me brewing this beer for you without their permission, behind their backs. And again, this thing of making a feast, it shouldn't be done without the seniors of your family being present. It is a wrong thing that you are doing. You must approach the elders of your family and do this in the proper way. Go and talk to your uncles. Surely they will help you. . . ." I tried to explain that he wasn't planning to make a feast here in Lekoka Street, just brew some beer. "It doesn't matter," she insisted. "It is not right." I didn't think it wise to mention that Madumo was planning to slaughter a chicken in his landlord's yard as MaMfete would surely have considered that outrageous. And I decided not to mentioned that he'd been instructed to make this feast by his *inyanga.*

Madumo returned to his room behind MaDudu's shebeen in Mapetla East depressed and dispirited. Of course it would be better for him if everything could be done according to protocol—"procedurally," he said—but such was not his situation. He had no choice but to follow Mr. Zondi's guidance. "I'm an orphan," he said. "An outcast. And I don't even know how to kill this fucken chicken in a right way. How can I call my ancestors without him helping me? Even if it's not procedural, I have to. MaMfete won't understand that. She won't. But I have to do this if everything is going to come clear."

So Madumo bought two candles and went to his mother's grave. After tidying the gravel on the mound, noting silently its gradual subsidence, he squatted on his haunches, lit a candle, and began to talk. He reminded his mother of his recent misfortunes and told her of his treatments with Mr. Zondi. He spoke highly of Mr. Zondi, crediting him with saving his life and setting him on a clear path. He asked her to look favorably upon his unorthodox procedures, informing her that in the morning he would slaughter a chicken for her and have a mini-feast in her honor. He explained that the paltry offering was "just for the meantime." When things came good, he promised, he would slaughter a cow and make amends with her and all of his ancestors in the proper way.

On his way home, he purchased a pair a chickens from the butcher near the hostel, delivered one to Mr. Zondi, and half smothered the other in a plastic bag so as to smuggle it into his room without anyone noticing. He stopped by the bottle store to buy two cartons of Joburg sorghum beer. Back in his room, he lit the other candle. The chicken, though tied at the ankles, scratched and squawked, and Madumo worried it was announcing to all the neighborhood that something was afoot. He had arranged with the woman in the house behind the neighbors to cook the bird, a woman who was not on good terms with his landlady and would not ask questions about the gift of a plump fowl.

In the morning, on a patch of unpaved ground behind the toilet, the chicken died, its throat cut. Madumo knocked on the door of the neighbor's shack and she accepted the bird without a word. A few hours later he dined on chicken and finished the beer. He was cheerful and tipsy and back to his old self when we met up later in the afternoon with Thabo and Mpho for our usual rounds of Soweto. It was just like the old days. . . .

On Monday morning he checked in with Mr. Zondi and the healer pronounced himself satisfied. "Everything should be starting to come good now," he insisted. Madumo was delighted. The curse was lifted. Of course, he might not succeed immediately. Obviously, without qualifications he would still be struggling to find work. But at least now he wouldn't have the additional burden of witchcraft dragging him down. He was back to square one.

Madumo may have been back to square one, but square one was a hardscrabble sort of place. His landlady had turned against him and his creditors were closing in. MaDudu had convinced herself that Madumo was up to no good with the white man who kept on visiting him in his room. The subtenant in the garage room next door had told her that the white guy was dealing drugs with Madumo as an accomplice. Shortly after the secret mini-feast she confronted Madumo. He angrily denied the story, spending the afternoon rounding up respectable citizens from around the location to testify that I was indeed a professor from New York and not a drug dealer. When the garage tenant arrived home in the evening Madumo confronted him and they nearly came to blows. The neighbor backed down, perhaps because Madumo suggested that if he were indeed a criminal, as the neighbor claimed, he must surely have access to guns and many accomplices who would not hesitate to shoot a rat like him.

MaDudu was in a bad humor. Though persuaded that Madumo and the white guy were not dealing drugs, she was not convinced that Madumo did not have plenty of money as a result of his friendship with the White. She arbitrarily raised his rent by fifty rands a month. On top of that, she started charging Madumo and her other tenants for the use of electricity, dividing the monthly bill equally between the house and the three outside rooms regardless of the fact that the house was four times the size of the rooms and full of refrigerators for her shebeen. Madumo was soon deeply in debt. He borrowed money to pay his rent, and then borrowed money to pay off his debt. Commercial money lenders in Soweto charge as much as fifty percent interest per month, sometimes more. Madumo was sinking fast. An old girlfriend came to his rescue with one month's rent. I helped out with another. His debts ranged from a few cents, for cigarettes, to a couple of hundred rands. He sometimes went for days without food. Still MaDudu did not relent. Eventually he had to move.

He took his bed and few belongings to an aunt's place for safekeeping and took himself to friends' houses to sleep on their floors. After some weeks of such living it began to become apparent that the change of fortune promised by Mr. Zondi in his treatment of the witchcraft was not eventuating. Madumo returned to his healer to find out what was wrong. Mr. Zondi gave him some more herbs to boil and vomit, but they didn't make much difference. Although he felt much more confident and in excellent health, Madumo was still suffering. He returned again to the healer. Mr. Zondi burnt his *imphepho* and consulted the ancestors. "The problem is," he announced, "the ancestors do not know where you are staying, so they cannot protect you properly. You must find your own place and settle down, or else return home." Until Madumo returned home and made a feast, Mr. Zondi told him, he could not be discharged from the healer's care.

Returning home was not an option. Madumo hadn't seen his brother or sister for months but he had no doubt that they were still as angry with him as ever. He could see no way of returning home. A few weeks later, after consulting the ancestors yet again, Mr. Zondi outlined the plan: he must return home and build himself a shack in the backyard. Madumo said he would think about it. Before long the idea had taken hold of him and it seemed like an obvious, indeed, inevitable solution to all his problems. By building such a shack he would solve his housing problem without having to find money for rent as well as being able to appease his ancestors and thus be discharged finally from his treatment with Mr. Zondi.

Madumo's ancestors, apparently, were uncomfortable about the fact that he was no longer living at home and was drifting about where they couldn't easily locate him. They were distressed, too, that he hadn't married and established a proper home for himself. Because of this he was unable to make an appropriate feast for the ancestors at a home where they could recognize him. They were thus unable to protect him fully. Mr. Zondi had also discovered that Madumo's deceased mother was pressing hard for reconciliation amongst her children. He conveyed to Madumo the ancestors' desire for him to return home and their suggestion that he should build a shack in the family's yard so as not to disturb the brother and sister living inside the house.

When Madumo recounted to me this plan, the idea of building a shack in the backyard of the Mapetla house struck me as sensible. Since being evicted from his room behind MaDudu's shebeen, Madumo had been sleeping on friends' floors and generally wearing out his welcome around the township. And as he was hardly in a position to pay the regular monthly rent required by landlords such as MaDudu, building a shack would at least afford him security from eviction if not a great deal of comfort. We talked at length about this project and I decided that if this all went well, I would help him build. We could buy scrap tin cheap and knock the thing together in a day or so. A couple of bags of cement would do for the floor. There was plenty of room in the backyard for a single room shack, and we would have but to run a line to the mains to get power. He would share the tap and toilet on the other side of the yard.

Before proceeding with the plan, Madumo decided that it would have to be cleared with the living elders of his family. He went to see his father's aunt in Orlando West, the oldest member of the family in Johannesburg. She endorsed the plan and agreed to accompany Madumo to discuss it with his brother and sister, the residents of the house. He'd not spoken to them since his last, thwarted attempt to return home. He was not certain of the reception he would find.

17

INTERVIEW WITH THE ANCESTORS

Having received the endorsement of his great aunt, the elder of the family in Soweto, Madumo wanted to clear the way one more time with the ancestors before approaching his brother and sister with the plan to build a shack. He conceived the idea that we should record on tape a consultation between the *inyanga* and the ancestors before proceeding with the plan. He was anxious to hear the ancestors' approval.

Mr. Zondi was happy to oblige. When we arrived at his place, Madumo asked if he would mind us recording a consultation. He smiled and agreed, instructing Madumo to bring him some *imphepho.* Madumo, who by this time was becoming such an acolyte that I occasionally wondered whether he might not do well to train as an *inyanga* himself, jumped from his seat and skipped into the anteroom lined with benches for patients and shelves for herbs. I set up the tape recorder. Madumo knew exactly what was needed, breaking off a handful of the dried leaves from a circular bale on the shelf near the door. Some weeks back Mr. Zondi had told us that his ancestors had instructed him not to use *imphepho* in his consultations anymore—except for Madumo. Perhaps that explained why there was still so much of the stuff on the shelf and why Madumo, casual and self-assured, returned to the room with a fistful of herbs to place in an old tobacco tin on Mr. Zondi's table. Mr. Zondi, after draping his red-and-black printed cloth over his shoulders, carefully set his horsehair whisk beside him on the table along with a silver police whistle attached to a wisp of an animal's tail, struck a match, and lit the herbs.

As the smoke of the *imphepho* plumed into the room, filling it with a sweet cloying incense, Mr. Zondi began calling the names of his ancestors. Before he could complete his invocation of the dead generations, however, the telephone rang. "Sorry," he said, answering the phone. He listened for a moment before opening the window to call a young man, his son, loitering with a group of friends nearby. We waited in silence, pretending not to listen, while the young man completed his call. Mr. Zondi began his invocation again:

"I am asking from you my ancestors the Ndabas," he said, his voice pitched slightly towards the incantatory but sounding positively conversational compared with the usual rantings of Christian preachers in these parts, "and the Zondis and you the Nhlabushenis and you the Luqas and you the Dedanis. I am praying to you, all you old and great ancestors. I pray for this young boy. You know him you beautiful ancestors. He's here amongst you. He wants to go home. As you have already told us, his mother is not happy that she's not seeing him at home." Suddenly he interrupted himself with sharp toot on the whistle. He paused for breath and continued: "We are asking you the old ancestors, we are hoping that, No! we *want* to see the light. We want to see that his coming back home meets with agreement, that there are no stumbling blocks that will stop him from going back home. And this man that's here amongst us, this young man that's coming from far places overseas, I'm happy that he's here and you, when you see him, welcome him with two hands. All the questions he asks, be free to answer him, you ancestors of old. So

I'm asking from you the old ancestors, speaking with you my old fathers, I who have paid *lobola,* I'm asking from you, you old ancestors the Ndondos"—another toot—"I'm asking that you give him light in his way."

His invocation complete, the *inyanga* fell silent. The ancestors now knew the agenda; they would reply in their own good time. A chorus of agitated voices spilled into the shack from the young men gambling with dice on the dusty ground near the hostel wall. A wisp of smoke curled upwards from the smoldering pile of *imphepho* on the table, licking the newly painted lemon yellow walls of the shack. Across the ceiling two lengths of red cord had been strung, knotted in the middle, to form a cross. The healer closed his eyes. His face relaxed into a mask, blank and monumental in the dim light. We waited. Suddenly Mr. Zondi turned to Madumo.

"This *mqomboti* you are talking about," he said, "you want to brew it at home?" No one had mentioned *mqomboti.*

"No," Madumo replied. "It's not to make a feast that I want to go home. I want to build a shack."

"It's a shack you want to build?" Mr. Zondi asked.

"Yes," said Madumo.

"But you haven't found the material for building a shack? You haven't found the iron yet?

"No, not yet. First we have to clear it with my family."

"Okay, so you're still thinking of doing it?"

"Yes."

Mr. Zondi closed his eyes again and we resumed our wait. His confusion about the shack puzzled me, for we had been talking about the project just a few minutes ago. Indeed, it had been his idea in the first place—at least, it was he who had conveyed what he said were the ancestors' wishes that Madumo should build a shack in the backyard of his family's home, where his brother and sister were still living. The feasting with *mqomboti* would come later.

"Ancestors, ancestors . . . ," Mr. Zondi began again, closing his eyes. He paused for a moment, deep in thought. "Yes, man," he said, returning his attention to Madumo, "let me just say that your mother . . . ," he paused to listen again: "as we talk the ancestors say she is sitting at the gate. She's sitting there waiting for you. Yes, she's waiting there hoping that you will come back home. And she's happy there now that she knows that you want to return home. Yes, she is very happy because you want to come back home. Yes, she's happy, she's happy. . . ." I glanced at Madumo; he looked rapt and radiant. "You are going to build that shack very easily, it's going to be very easy for you to build that shack."

Madumo settled back onto the old car seat that serves as Mr. Zondi's sofa. I glanced down at the tape recorder to check whether it was still recording. Mr. Zondi continued:

"But your brother," he said, relaying the words of the ancestors, "you must be careful of him. When you build that shack, watch out for them, your brother and sister; they'll have painful hearts. But after some time, when you are living there with them, they'll change. Then they'll laugh with you." Madumo, his attention fixed intently upon the *inyanga,* nodded in agreement. "You know what makes them to have bad hearts?" Mr. Zondi asked rhetorically, his eyes still closed. "They are saying that because you go with this man you think you are smarter than them. They say that you are saying they are 'nothing.'"

Although he didn't specifically mention *umlungu,* the white man, it was clear that Mr. Zondi was referring to me as the cause of Madumo's family discord. It's possible, I thought to myself. They could be resentful of me. Although I'd never witnessed Madumo inflating his self-importance on account of having a white friend, he wouldn't actually have to do so for others to believe that he was proud and hate him for it. As MaMfete says, when people see a white man, they see a money tree and want to shake it. If they see a black man standing next to the money tree, they resent him for the opportunity of shaking it first. In years past, my friends in Soweto occasionally had to weather political storms for associating with a white man. Now the resentment is purely financial and the danger greatly increased for all. In post-apartheid Soweto, a white person's black friends will be scrutinized intensely by their peers for signs of pride. Should they do anything, especially in the company of young men, that might give a legitimate pretext for anger—such as look at someone in the wrong way or speak with the wrong tone of voice—they can find themselves being set upon mercilessly and have few defenders. The fact that we had survived all these years together was proof to me, were I in doubt, that Madumo was not boastful about having a white friend. That, however, would have no necessary bearing upon his siblings' envy and resentment.

Mr. Zondi continued his intercession with the ancestors on Madumo's behalf: "You see, man," he said, opening his eyes and turning towards his client, "in your life there's nothing *really* bad that life gives you. You've woken up to that witchcraft. If you hadn't woken up, you wouldn't be here on Earth." He paused for a moment. "You know what, there *is* something you should look out for, in fact. It is being said by the ancestors now that there was a dream you were having—a long time ago. A dream that you were in the cemetery. What do you think made you have that dream of being in the cemetery?"

"That used to happen; that used to happen," Madumo said urgently.

"You nearly went mad. Crazy," said Mr. Zondi. "So you are very fortunate. Very much fortunate."

"There *was* such a dream, Adam," said Madumo, turning to me, his eyes ablaze. "It used to haunt me. I would dream that I was going to the graves, to the grave of my mother. So now what Mr. Zondi is saying is that because of that dream, if I had gone to her grave after dreaming that, I would have been made to go mad. Psychotic."

Mr. Zondi explained: "You know that all the time when you were thinking you just wanted to go to the graves, you were really being pulled by this thing. It wasn't just that you were going to the graves just because you were going. It was this thing that was pulling you. That's how they wanted to get you. They wanted to make you crazy."

I was puzzled again. Clearly the "thing" of which Mr. Zondi spoke was some class of witchcraft, but I couldn't understand how the dream and the grave were connected nor who was behind the evil plot.

Sensing my incomprehension, Madumo, who had clearly been over this ground before with his healer, explained: "So what is happening, Adam," he said, "is that these people were putting more *muthi* on the grave."

"Who were?" I interrupted.

"Relatives," he said. "They could see that I am going there to clean the grave, so their plan was to hit me in that way. I would have come into contact with that *muthi* when I went to visit the grave. So if I'd gone there to the grave when I had that dream, it would have made me to go mad."

"Right now they are saying . . . ," said Mr. Zondi, returning his attention to the ancestors.

"That it will go away?" interrupted Madumo.

"No. It's gone already," Mr. Zondi said. "It's just that the hatred that they now have is because you are under this man. That's what they hate you for." Again he used the honorific *indoda,* man, as he nodded in my direction rather than the more usual, but less respectful, *umlungu*—white man. He added that because I had helped Madumo finance his cure and protection from subsequent witchcraft, thereby thwarting their evil plans, the brother and sister were doubly angry.

"So when I go there with my granny from Killarney and Adam," asked Madumo, returning to the shack-building project, "will there be a problem? Will we be fighting each other?"

"No! No, no, no, no. . . ." Mr. Zondi's ancestors, reporting the opinion of Madumo's, seemed clear on the point. "There's nothing like that. And don't mind what they do, your brother and sister, for their hearts are still paining them."

"Because I'm still alive?"

"Yes."

"Because being under this man is what is making me continue to live?"

Mr. Zondi nodded but said no more. The ancestors had spoken; the interview was over. Mr. Zondi removed his shawl and began repacking his equipment. I packed up the tape recorder. Three middle-aged Zulu women entered the waiting room and greeted Mr. Zondi through the open door.

After Mr. Zondi had dismissed the interlopers, Madumo leant forward and earnestly addressed his healer: "This means they are going to *inyangas,* my brother and sister? There are people taking them to *inyangas* to work on me?"

"That is right."

We bade Mr. Zondi farewell.

18

THE HOMECOMING

Madumo knew, without his healer having to tell him, that his siblings' search for witchcraft *muthi* would be futile. He was not perturbed. He was protected. Mr. Zondi's words relaying the ancestors' confidence in the shack-building project gave him renewed courage. He was elated and eager to proceed with negotiations. We were both encouraged by the interview with the ancestors.

"He seems to have helped you a lot," I said as we drove away from the hostel. "Mr. Zondi."

"He has," replied Madumo. "The only thing is, he can't fully discharge me until I've made a feast for the ancestors. And I can't do that until I am at home."

"Ancestors or not," I said, "he seems like a solid sort of man."

"Yeah," affirmed Madumo, "and did you hear what he said about my mother waiting for me at the gate? That means everything is given the green light. It's full speed ahead."

"What about that stuff about your brother and sister trying to bewitch you?"

"No, that's nothing. Even if they try, they won't make it. I'm too much strong now."

"So tonight's the night?" I asked.

"Tonight's the night," he said. "Tonight's the night." We resolved to fetch his great aunt from her house after dinner and take her to Madumo's family home in Mapetla to discuss the plan for building the shack. Normally such negotiations would take place on a Sunday, but the old lady is a staunch churchgoer and couldn't possibly miss a Sunday's observance. Madumo's strategy was to arrive at his house in the evening after eight, at which time his brother and sister would surely be home and not yet asleep.

Madumo may have been too strong for the evil forces attacking him, but whatever it was that was after our Dombolo was on the winning team. The Zionists' holy water treatment was wearing off and the Mazda was ailing. Every day something else was going wrong, from the cylinder head to the door handles, despite the loving care lavished upon the old car by Thabo. My abiding fear was that the car would die while I was alone somewhere in Soweto in the dark. Fortunately Thabo had joined a *stokvel,* or savings club, devoted to the preservation of these old cars. Through the Dombolo Stokvel we managed to obtain parts and the services of a dedicated self-trained mechanic named Jimmy, whose friends described him as the "scientist of Dombolos." For Jimmy, the preservation of Dombolos was an ethical calling of the highest order. He was training to become an ambulance driver, but he swore to his friends and customers that he would continue as a mechanic on the side. Whenever he felt we were neglecting the proper maintenance of the Dombolo, he would subject us to withering abuse. In the past two weeks the steering had failed, the clutch had dissolved, the brakes had disintegrated, and the accelerator had developed a tendency to jam at full throttle at the most disconcerting moments. We were calling upon Jimmy daily. As I drove down the track away from the hostel a strange clanging noise began under the hood, and I realized that another visit to Jimmy was imperative.

Jimmy operates his workshop on the newly paved driveway

that is the unused back entrance to the Pimville Civic Center. The ground is caked hard with dried oil and the area is littered with discarded engine parts, oil drums, spare part packaging, and broken bottles. Four cars, in various stages of disrepair, awaited his attention. Music blared from the radio in Jimmy's blue Dombolo. That car is a work of pure love. Jimmy was on his back underneath a yellow Dombolo. He slid out quickly when we greeted him and said, "Look at that!" pointing in horror to some mechanical abuse whose enormity I failed to comprehend, though I nodded in agreement nonetheless. I described our problem and he settled down with his spanners. "I'm going to shoot Thabo if he doesn't replace that timing chain," he said. I clucked in feigned disapproval, too. And so we passed another afternoon loitering in the sun while Jimmy poked around under the hood of the Dombolo in between fielding questions from a constant stream of customers seeking his aid.

With the car returned to health, we drove to Thabo's house, where I drank a warming measure of brandy. Madumo stuck to tea, conscious of the impropriety of breathing liquor on his father's aunt—the "granny" who was going to preside over the negotiations for his shack. We watched television and shared Thabo's dinner. At eight we drove to the aunt's house in Killarney, the section of Orlando West not far from Winnie Mandela's house that is nicknamed after a white suburb where similar hills and rocks are found. We found the old lady already in bed. While I settled onto a plump apricot sofa and chatted with Madumo's cousin's husband, Madumo went into the bedroom to talk with the old lady. Her daughter didn't want her to go out so late, relenting only on the condition that her nine-year-old granddaughter accompany us.

As we drove towards Mapetla it seemed to me that we were finally about to see a turn for the better in Madumo's fortunes. I was sure that if he could only get himself settled in a place to call his own he could think about his future and dispel his obsessions with witches. And while I was not particularly inspired by Mr. Zondi's reporting of the ancestors' intentions, the fact that we now had the old lady with us, the family elder, gave me confidence that we had every reason to hope for success. My previous experience of these sorts of negotiations was that after the hosts had served tea or cold drinks, the family elder would present her case. The children would listen respectfully, perhaps interjecting a few reservations and minor objections before acceding to her wishes and restoring peace. I have seen MaMfete wield the formidable authority of the African grandmother to resolve such crises many times in the past.

"How are you feeling?" I asked Madumo. "Are you nervous?" I wasn't.

"Actually," he replied, "I'm quite paranoid."

When we arrived at Madumo's house we found the heavy steel gate closed and locked. The air hung heavy with the smell of a burnt-out grass fire from the railway reserve. I can't say that I detected the presence of Madumo's mother waiting nearby, as Mr. Zondi had forecast, but I'm not an expert in these things. The old lady got out of the car. "Ouma!" she called, her voice small and feeble. "Ouma!" Two young men walking down the street passed close by the car and Madumo greeted them, inviting himself to share their cigarette in the process. Ouma appeared at the side of the house. Peering into the darkness she recognized the old lady at her gate and greeted her with joy. Returning with the key to the heavy brass padlock securing the gate, she opened the gate hugged her granny. My greeting was returned coolly. Her brother was ignored completely. I parked the car in the front yard while Madumo relocked the gate. We followed his sister into the house and seated ourselves in the sitting room. The sound of a football match, highlights of an earlier game, spilled out of a television in the front bedroom.

Ouma disappeared into the bedroom. A short while later she returned, perching herself on the edge of a sofa. "Prince," she called, summoning her brother.

Prince did not answer. Ouma called again. He replied that he was coming but took time to appear. He came to the sitting room when his sister called a third time and sat himself on the plastic-covered couch, remote control in hand, without greeting anyone. The couch gave off a crackling static sound as it settled under his bulk. His eyes remained fixed on the television in the next room, never glancing towards the corner where he knew his brother must be sitting. Like most Soweto sitting rooms, this one was crowded with big furniture: two sofas against the walls, an overstuffed matching armchair in the middle of the room, a coffee table, and room divider. Madumo sat at the furthest extreme of the room from his brother, beside the young girl who sat beside the old lady. I was on the armchair. Behind me, in the windows, were the photographs of the ZCC bishops. Ouma fetched a pillow from her bedroom and sat on the floor at the end of the couch, beside Prince. I was beginning to feel uneasy about our mission.

The old lady began to speak. Her voice was quiet but firm as she carefully outlined the reasons for our visit. She said that she knew how difficult things had been since their mother's death but that it was her wish, and she was sure it would be their mother's wish, too, for them all to be reconciled. She spoke of Madumo's hardships and his desire to build himself a shack in the yard. She gave the plan her blessing. She asked her children to extend the hand of friendship to their brother.

She took her time. Prince's attention remained glued to the football match on the television while she spoke. Every so often he would aim the remote control into the bedroom to raise the volume on the set so as not to miss an important point of commentary. Madumo remained quiet, staring straight ahead and away from his brother.

Although the old lady spoke deep Sotho, I quickly grasped the essence of her message and as her words droned on, circling around and around her central plea for reconciliation, I relaxed from the effort of translation and sank back into the armchair. The plastic cover emitted a soft slow sigh as the air escaped behind me. I studied the room. I noticed that Prince had gained weight since last I saw him, which must have been four or five years ago. He was no longer the slim youth I recalled, but a solid, somewhat bulky man in his late twenties with a smooth face and close-cropped scalp—much more substantial than Madumo. He had always struck me as shy when I came to this house in the old days, when their mother was alive. Usually I would find Prince at home with a message that I would find Madumo somewhere out in the neighborhood. He had always been friendly, but we never really talked. Prince never seemed to leave the house, and I never met him on the streets or in the shebeens of the neighborhood. On the wall behind the sofa where Prince sat, a big ersatz wagon wheel served as a casing for a small clock. The room was cluttered with ornaments, knick-knacks, and bric-a-brac. The cabinet was stocked with cheap liquor—part of the family's way, Madumo had told me when I was puzzled by the display after my last visit, of paying homage to the ancestors. The doilies were gone.

While Prince stared at the television, Ouma gazed up at her granny from her pillow on the floor. I thought I could see the beginnings of tears forming in her big brown eyes as the old lady spoke. Perhaps she is feeling some sympathy for Madumo's plight, I thought. Or perhaps she is sad about being squeezed between two implacable brothers.

The old lady's speech ended. Prince replied:

"No!" he said, his voice firm, abrupt, directed towards the television in the other room. "There will be no shacks built in this yard. And that one has no right to come here with you, Grandmother." He nodded sidelong towards the place where his brother was sitting without averting his eyes from the television. "If he really wants to solve these problems in our family, let him come with Peter and Kabelo." He paused. The room was silent save for the soccer commentary and the roar of the televised crowd. By referring to their father, Peter, by his English name, Prince was underlining his contempt for the whole family. Kabelo is the eldest brother. Prince continued, turning to his great aunt, his face remaining strangely blank and passive despite the intensity of his words: "We are not working here at home. We have no jobs. How can we support him? Who is going to pay the electricity? No, if he is having money to build a shack, let him go and fetch our father, then they can call our brother. Then let them sort out the problems here. Because they are part of this thing, too." Nobody spoke or interrupted him, so he continued, rounding upon the old lady: "If you are so concerned about this one, why don't you let him build a shack in *your* yard? Huh? Why not? No! *You* must look after him. Or this white man can. Not us. During all the years when our mother was alive and we were suffering here, we never saw anyone from your family. No one ever came to give assistance. So no one can come here now and tell us what to do."

The old lady sat still, her shoulders wrapped in her blanket, staring at her hands. As Prince's anger grew and his harsh words rained upon her like blows, she turned her face from him and seemed to shrink into her bent arthritic bones. She clasped her hands tightly on her lap.

Madumo said nothing. I said nothing. I hadn't expected to participate in the discussions and I hadn't prepared any remarks to offer the gathering. As soon as Prince began his speech I could see that our mission was futile. There was no point in trying to argue with him. He would never be persuaded that accommodating Madumo in the backyard of this family house was the right thing to do. The old lady didn't try either. After her speech aroused such an angry disrespectful response, she spoke no more. As Prince's speech to the old lady began winding down I began searching about in my mind for some way of changing the topic, some way of deflecting the brother's resentment at our intrusion, something to say that would allow us to extricate ourselves from this situation without more grief. It occurred to me that I should take a bold initiative and ask Madumo's brother and sister straight out why they hated their brother. As a brother of seven siblings, my experience of family quarrels in the past had led me to believe that siblings are often more than willing to berate one another, accuse each other of perfidious wrongdoing, denounce one another for every kind of failing . . . but when pushed to admit the inadmissible, will deny hatred. "I don't hate *him,*" they will say, "I just hate what he has *done*. . . ." Perhaps it's a peculiarly Christian form of hypocrisy, but a useful device nonetheless for opening an avenue of reconciliation when all else seems hopeless. So I waited for Prince to finish, then took my chance.

"I don't think this is going to work," I said, sitting forward upon the plastic-sheathed armchair. Prince returned his attention to the soccer highlights and the Play of the Week. I turned towards Ouma: "It's obvious this idea of the shack is not going to work, at least not now, so I think we should just forget it. Madumo will just have to find other accommodation." Nobody spoke; nobody moved. To kill the silence, I continued. "But there's a question I want to ask you: Why do you hate your brother so?"

"We don't hate him . . . ," began Ouma. Before she could finish her sentence Prince put out a hand to silence her. He turned to me and spoke, addressing me in clear, fluent English.

"I'll tell you why I hate him," he said, spitting his words like hard bitter seeds into the room. "One, he has never worked. Why doesn't he look after himself? Me, I don't have any education, but I'm a *man*. I can look after myself. I'm not working, but still I can look after myself. I've fixed up this house, bought the room divider, the TV . . . everything. I have no education but I'm proud of what I am. I can look after myself. Not like him. He's nothing. And I can beat him in every department. I can beat him. . . ."

Prince paused for a breath and Ouma intervened: "Look at him, he's nearly forty and he's still schooling. When is he going to finish? Why can't he get a job and look after himself? Where is all the education getting him?" Years ago she had begun studying herself but was forced to withdraw when their father disappeared and stopped paying her fees.

Prince joined her and together they recited a litany of their brother's inadequacies, linking him in the process to a cabal including Kabelo and their father. He embarked upon a long account of how their father left them in the early nineties and never supported them when their mother was ill. He told me how their older brother left home in the eighties to work for the Broadcasting Corporation, never returning until he was retrenched. Then, when he received his retrenchment package, he used the money to "buy a wife" rather than help his family. After marrying, Kabelo was required to move out of the house. Their mother insisted. So he took a room with his wife and never returned. The point of the story, I inferred, was that once you leave this place you do not return. But his arguments, and Ouma's, were strangely inconsistent. On the one hand they were berating their brother for his inability to look after himself as they were, on the other they were denouncing him for refusing to find work and look after them.

"And this one, your friend," said Prince with another contemptuous flick of his head towards his brother, "he's just a socialite. When we were suffering here at home, when our mother was alive, he was just roaming around, the man-about-town, going to our relatives and telling them funny things, having girlfriends, drinking, going around with a white man . . . being a playboy." This image of Madumo as a playboy would have made me laugh were it not for the bitterness with which it was expressed. Prince's face, which had been strangely impassive at first, was now flushed with anger. He seemed to be saying that his brother's social prowess, a moral failing in comparison to Prince's own righteous isolation, was something valuable gained at his expense. My friendship with Madumo grew into a central theme: "He thinks he's better than us because he's at school and going around with a white man, that a white man is financing his education. But he's not, he's nothing. He can't even look after himself. That's why he wants to come back here. But he won't make it. He won't. If he comes to stay in this yard, either he will have to kill me, or I will kill him. And I've got guns. *Plenty* of guns . . . Plenty!" His final words were spat forth with undiluted venom: "He will kill me or I will kill him."

While Prince was speaking, Ouma was clamoring to intervene. She would raise her hand like an eager schoolgirl awaiting her teacher's nod, but whenever she began Prince would silence her with an imperious wave, saying, "No, that's irrelevant." Finally she got her chance:

"No," she snarled, her face twisting into an ugly sneer, "I do hate him. I hate him. I *hate* him." She paused for a moment, her acid words raising a toxic cloud in the room. "You know, Adam, when our mother was dying, he couldn't even lift her up. She was lying on that bed in there, and I had to go to school. He would just sit in here with his friends—Mpho and the others—and not even lift her out of the bed. . . ." She embarked upon a long, bitter, and convoluted story about the last days of her mother's life, how Madumo had not cared, how he'd gone to the Indian doctor at the shops near Merafe Station and told him stories about their mother being a "basket case for twenty years—a couch potato."

"So you're sure you are not just trying to take over the house and exclude the others?" I asked, addressing Prince. Their self-righteousness was beginning to annoy me. I knew how sorely grieved Madumo had been during his mother's illness, which had, indeed, lasted years. He'd felt bitterly restricted, as an African son, precluded from the intimacy necessary for nursing a mother. I suspected, too, that he'd been frustrated by her insistence upon spiritual malaise and her reluctance to seek medical care.

Prince looked taken aback. "No," he said. "This is a family house. It belongs to the family. We are not going to stay here." I'd clearly struck a nerve. He sat forward on the couch and addressed me intently: "As soon as I get money I'm going to buy a stand and build a shack. Because this place is not safe for us. In fact, it's dangerous. Very dangerous. Because this one is busy going around telling stories about us. We can't stay here. And when we leave here I am taking nothing. Even though I've paid for everything, I'm taking nothing. Not this room divider, not the television. Nothing. Maybe I will take my ID book. That's all. Just take my ID book, and I'll just go. And did he tell you who paid for these improvements? Huh? Did he say? Of course not. He wouldn't. Because *I* did. I spent a lot of money building that wall out there. Putting in these windows and everything. But when I leave, I'll just leave. He can have this house then. But not before."

I nodded as if in sympathy as Prince spoke, but I must have been looking skeptical nonetheless for he insisted on explaining more:

"This thing is not about the house," he said. "You wouldn't understand. This problem goes back a long way in our family. Because our father and mother were having many problems, and this thing stems from many years ago. From back in the seventies. You see after '76, this one and our older brother, they were taken to the rural areas. To our father's place in fact, where his mother stays. And that old lady taught them things there that are not in our culture this side." He paused for a moment as if wondering whether to continue. "You are a white man," he said quietly. "These are things of we Africans. So you won't understand. But that is when this thing started." He paused again, staring at me with a look of challenge and scorn.

I may be a white man, but I've been around Soweto long enough to know what Prince was speaking of: witchcraft. There was no need to say the word, no need to elaborate. He was implying that their father's mother was a witch and that she had instilled witchcraft in her two older grandsons in order to attack her daughter-in-law along with the younger siblings who had remained at her side. Presumably this was the reason for the discord within the parent's marriage and for the mother's untimely death.

"So why does that make you hate your brother?" I asked, "since he's not to blame."

Prince glared at me for a moment as if resisting the urge to answer before replying: "I was having problems, too. In the eighties I had to go to Moria for three years because of him. I couldn't finish my schooling because of those things. Then last year I was arrested. Where was he? What was he doing then? These are things of we blacks. You won't understand, but *he* knows what I mean." He still couldn't bring himself to mention his brother's name nor look in his direction while recounting the misfortunes caused by Madumo's witchcraft. He must have been seriously afflicted as a youth if he'd had to spend years undergoing treatment at Moria, the headquarters of the ZCC. Madumo's crimes, it seemed, were grievous. As he spoke, I could see the tendons on his neck stretching tight and his face seemed to swell with rage, but his voice stayed weirdly, preternaturally calm.

By now my naive hope of eliciting a denial of hatred in order to open a possibility of future reconciliation had been thoroughly demolished. I found myself face-to-face with unapologetic hatred and had no notion as to how to proceed. The old lady seemed to have retreated into her blanket in horror at the young man's onslaught. Madumo was keeping quiet, mercifully. A word from him would set off an explosion. Somehow I had to find a way to close the interview. I had never before witnessed pure hatred in the flesh. Anger, rage, violence have been common in my experience of life. Love, too. But hatred of the sort I was witnessing here, a hatred born of intimacy and nurtured over long years of contact, was completely new to me. And at this my heart also trembled. I'd seen it in the movies, of course, read of it in books, so I was able to recognize its face before me in Prince. But I had no idea what to do or say. Eventually Madumo's brother ceased his denunciation. He stared at me steadily, confident I could say nothing to rebut his case; Ouma, too. I had to say something. I wanted to look behind me to Madumo, to connect with him against this onslaught, but I didn't dare turn. I couldn't take my eyes from Prince. I found myself trying to imagine what my mother in Australia or MaMfete would say in such a situation. They would probably appeal somehow to the Christian gospel of love, the basis upon which they live their lives and recommend others to live theirs too. Perhaps it was just a rhetorical ploy on my part to calm a difficult situation since I knew that Prince was a staunch member of the Zion Christian Church, or perhaps Prince had shaken me into a recognition of some sort of core values in myself. I cannot say. Whatever the reason, I found myself appealing to the message of the Gospels:

"How can you carry such bitterness in your hearts?" I asked, flailing about in my mind for the courage to make these platitudes seem sincere. "You are Christians. Both of you. Think of the message of Jesus, the message of love. Forget about Madumo for a moment. Just look at what this bitterness is doing to you. It's a poison. A poison in your hearts. Okay, I can see now that this whole thing was a bad idea. We'll leave you now. But please, think about yourselves, look out for yourselves. If you don't overcome this hatred, this bitterness, it can kill you. . . ." I was not allowed to finish and I doubt I could have found more such words. They seemed to me like so many mouthfuls of foolishness.

"I *am* bitter," said Prince, scorning my feeble homily. "I'm bitter, but I'm happy. *Happy!* I am happy. I haven't spoken to that one for two years, and if I don't speak to him again for two hundred years, I will still be happy. And I have no guilt. I am not the guilty one. I was at Moria when they told me my mother had died. I came back to bury her. I did what I had to do and I didn't shed a tear. Not one tear. But I didn't kill her. Believe me, I have been through hell. Hell! But I am strong. I'm not afraid of him." His grievous words settled over the room, spreading a dreadful silence in their wake. I prayed Madumo wouldn't respond.

"Well think of your mother then," I said, grasping for one last chance of appeal. "When she was alive she loved Madumo. He is her son, your brother. Surely she doesn't want this bitterness in her family now that she has passed away?"

"No!" spat Ouma, half rising from her pillow and staring directly at Madumo. "Our mother *is* happy. She hates him too."

"You know," added Prince, a malicious smile spreading across his face, "our mother once said to him—back in 1982—she said, 'One day I am going to die, and you are going to suffer.' So now she is dead. And look at him!" In his glee at trumping my argument, Prince was again too proud to spell out the accusation. His implication, however, was obvious. Their mother was seeking vengeance for her wrongful death, a death caused by witchcraft. "When he dies, he will have to have his people to bury him. When I die, others will bury me."

I couldn't help feeling that their mother, perhaps inadvertently, must have abetted this ill feeling while she lived. She was surely the source of the fear of their grandmother's witchcraft.

"Let's go," whispered Madumo to me, quietly rising from the couch.

"You see!" snarled Ouma, as Madumo settled back onto the couch when I failed to follow his lead. "Look at him! Sitting there with his cap on inside the house. He's just plain rude. You have taken off your cap, but not him. He's too arrogant. And in those days when you used to come and fetch him here to go out with you, he would just go out even if he hadn't washed, in dirty football shorts, or whatever. How could he go out like that? He doesn't have respect. He's just rubbish."

"Let's go," said Madumo firmly, rising again.

I rose from my seat, too, fearful that Madumo would say something and provoke his sister further. I beckoned for him to move ahead of me and he left the room without a word. I followed him out, bidding farewell as best I could.

"It's bad," said Madumo when we were safely in the car. I nodded. "It's bad, but it used to be worse. When I was still staying there? Oh boy! You should have seen them then." I had nothing to say.

The old lady, assisted by the little girl, hauled her painful bones into the car, and we drove back to her home in Orlando West through the deserted streets of Soweto. Nobody spoke. Madumo helped her into the house. "She was crying," he told me when he returned. "It's witchcraft," she'd said to him. "This really is witchcraft."

19

A FEAST FOR THE ANCESTORS?

After that dreadful night Madumo slumped into a despondent lethargy. Although he bravely insisted that his siblings could never undermine him, now that he was protected from witchcraft, he couldn't mask his disappointment. His faith in his healer had been shaken. He was still homeless, sleeping now on his friend Meshack's kitchen floor and surviving on handouts from wherever he could find them. All the plans we had been discussing about ways of securing his future collapsed. He seemed once more to be losing interest in life itself.

Madumo and I drifted apart for a time. We became irritated with each other and kept to ourselves. I can't say exactly why. It was as if we would have had to face some unpleasant reckoning were we to spend too much time together, would have enunciated things better left in silence. After that night I felt that my own sense of how the world works was pathetically inadequate. My first glimpse of the power of hatred had shaken me more than I care to admit. There had been something poisonous in the air at Madumo's place that night, something obscene, grotesque, and I can't say it would be absurd to talk of it possessing an agency of its own. That something forced me to admit that my long-cherished understandings of what people are made of, presumptions about how and why they act and notions of what they are really capable of doing, were plainly naive. It was as if I'd discovered the true superficiality of sophisticated notions about power, which I'd long presumed needed no reference to anything resembling this thing they call here Witchcraft nor invocation of an animated entity called Evil in order to make sense. Whatever it was that I had witnessed, I realized I had no name for it. And I had no wish to name it, almost feared to. To call it "Hatred" would have been easy enough. But that was like trying to encompass something unfathomable within a familiar term, reducing it thereby to an elementary factor in the reckoning of motives—the commonplace opposite of Love. But this was more than just the motives of particular squabbling individuals. To name it "Evil" would be to endow it with the familiar form of well-known enemies conjured up in stories by those who claim to know the "Good." Neither was satisfactory. By trying to imagine how I might feel were one of my brothers to kill our mother, I could begin to perceive the outlines of something perhaps analogous to Madumo's brother's rage. But no sooner had I glimpsed this image of anger than I recognized it as a paltry counterfeit of the familial resentments that Prince had laid bare on that night. His was a compendium of injury spanning generations of the living and dead, enmeshed in traces of invisible powers of harm. Madumo had a name for it sure enough: Witchcraft. But that was opening a path upon which I hesitated to tread.

A couple of days after the meeting with his brother and sister, Madumo went to visit his healer for advice. He walked in the early afternoon to the hostel but discovered the shack locked and Mr. Zondi nowhere to be found. A woman selling vegetables in a nearby lean-to told him the healer had left town for some few weeks. Madumo knew Zondi's business was growing around the country—he had been spending much of his time lately attending to clients in far-off places—but he was frustrated, nonetheless. A few weeks later Mr. Zondi returned. Madumo waited in line at his shack, listening to the mumbled miseries of supplicants in need. After nearly three hours of waiting in the herb-filled anteroom, his turn arrived. Mr. Zondi greeted him warmly, heard him tell his story, then told him that the ancestors had in fact planned all this pain in advance. He said they wanted Madumo to see just how angry and dangerous his siblings really were. He said their jealousy was too strong and he must be vigilant against their evil. He dispensed some more herbs for Madumo to vomit and moved on to the next patient. Madumo was not completely convinced.

I was even less impressed. He told me the healer's story later that afternoon. "That's bullshit," I said sharply. We were sitting in the Dombolo in Lekoka Street outside my place. I sat forward, trying to pull the broken driver's seat up behind me to ease the strain on my back. The pain in my neck was making me even more irritable than usual. Madumo was smoking, so I opened the window. A cold draught blew into the car. "That's just plain bullshit, Madumo," I repeated, winding up the window again. "I've got it all on tape, every word those ancestors said—*supposedly* said—and there's nothing like that there. Zondi said your mother was at the gate waiting for you to come home. Clear and simple. I'll play it back for you if you want. You even asked him straight out if there'd be any problems with them at home about building a shack and he said no. Now he's just making up excuses."

"Yeah," said Madumo sadly, "maybe." His voice trailed off. I could see that he didn't want to give up on Mr. Zondi, that he hadn't completely lost faith in the enterprise of divination. After all that vomiting, all the money we'd spent, I couldn't really blame him. Yet something about the failure of our plan troubled me deeply. I had been so confident that his brother and sister wouldn't object to Madumo building a shack in the yard of the family home; hopeful, too, that my friend's trials were coming to an end and that I could be released from my duties towards him without feeling I'd let him down.

"So what does he say you should do now?" I asked.

Madumo stared straight ahead to where the children were playing soccer in the street, boys versus girls. "He says I must still make that feast for my ancestors," he said quietly. "He says they're still waiting."

"Fuck this shit, man," I snapped. "A feast for the ancestors? What've the ancestors ever done for you?" I was almost shouting. "What have they ever done that you should waste your money feeding them? Nothing. And they never will. Do something for yourself for a change. You could pay six months rent with the money it will take to make that feast. Even start a business. Get off your arse and solve your own problems instead of blaming witches for everything that goes wrong and waiting for your ancestors to rescue you. Dead people can't help you get a life." Two of the youngest children in the street were clamoring for attention at the door. Surprised by my own vehemence and needing air, I jerked open the door, causing the children to fall back in surprise.

"No," replied Madumo calmly, "I have to finish this thing. I've started it, and I've pushed it through this far. Now I must finish. Okay, maybe Mr. Zondi was mistaken about that thing of the shack. Maybe that was a mistake, yes. But he *has* helped me. Truly, he's helped me. I know it. He's helped me in many ways. You know it yourself. And you've helped me too, Adam. You should have seen them at home before. I mean, that time was bad, but before, it used to be worse. Worse. It could have been a serious homicide. I'm lucky to be alive. In a true sense, I *am* lucky. Because those people can do anything. Anything. So now I must go through to the end. I must. After that, I'm on my own. Until then, I must follow what he says."

I had nothing to say. He was right. And he didn't need to add that if he was indeed going to finish this treatment, I would have to pay. I was beginning to feel as if I'd suffered him to impose on me too long. But he knew me too well to ask for more. I didn't offer. Perhaps he realized that if he broached the subject he would open himself to another tirade. Madumo's financial dependence had begun to grate on me in recent weeks, all the more so since I couldn't see any end to it in sight. It galled me that in all the years I'd known him, indeed in all his thirty-three years, he'd only ever worked for a total of three months and showed no inclination now to find a way of making a living. It's quite an achievement, in a way. But I wasn't in the mood to revel in Madumo's quixotic ways by funding his life as a layabout while he pursued his quest for higher knowledge.

I was beginning to better appreciate his brother's resentment. Just last week, when we began discussing his future in the light of the shack-building debacle, he'd asked me if I could advance him money to re-enroll at UNISA. It was then I discovered that the money I'd sent him last year for his school fees, which he'd assured me long ago was safely set aside in a fixed-term deposit account at the bank for the day when he would resume his studies, had been used as capital to underwrite his ill-starred drug and counterfeit trading.

"I thought you said you had that money in a fixed deposit," I said. Madumo studied the back of a hand and said nothing. He rearranged the sheaf of UNISA enrollment forms he'd brought to demonstrate his intentions and their cost. "So what are you telling me? That you've spent it? That you lied?"

Madumo paused for a moment. We were sitting in my room in Lekoka Street. MaMfete was busy in the yard outside. I had guessed from the moment he arrived that something was up because he'd made a point of making a date to come and see me. Usually, because I had the car, I would call on him.

"I lied," he said quietly. "I did spend that money. I don't have it anymore."

"So what did you spend it on?" I asked. It had been a substantial sum, enough for his year's college fees. "What did you do with it?"

—

"Don't tell me," I said. "That was the money you were using for the fakes." This is what Mpho had told me on the first day I arrived.

"Yeah."

"So why didn't you tell me before?"

"I couldn't. I was too ashamed."

"So what happened?"

"We lost it when they arrested Lucky."

"You lost it?"

"Yeah."

"Lost?"

"Yeah. That was what we used to buy the fakes that were confiscated by the police. When they took the fakes, that was the end of the real money."

"So what was your sister talking about when I went to your place that time looking for you, when she said you'd borrowed six thousand from a relative?"

"We lost that, too."

"Lost it?"

"Yeah. It was your money, plus that six thousand from my relative that we used to buy those fakes. It was like a syndicate; that cousin in Diepkloof was our partner. She was putting up some of the money, I put in some, and Lucky, too—we had shares, like. Then Lucky was arrested. And we needed money for the lawyer. So it's gone. Finished."

"Finished?" The word came out like a sneer. We were back where we'd started months ago. I was angry; Madumo was a mess.

"So if I can only be going back to school, like," he said, "I know things will come right. And then there's my cousin in Mafikeng. That one I told you about who is having the job with the police that side. When I went there last year he was promising to get me a job with the police. So maybe if I can enroll for even one course, at least . . ."

"Yeah, Madumo," I said, cutting him off. "I know."

"Serious," he said. "I just need one course, then I can get the student card."

"You call that serious, do you? Serious? You haven't got a

clue what serious means. For a start, how can that cousin in Mafikeng get you a job? Huh?"

"I don't know. He says if I come that side he can organize me a job in the police."

"He's talking shit. He's your cousin and he's older, so he feels he has to promise you something. So he makes promises and then he can say he's looking after you because he's making promises, even though he knows you're not going to go and live out there so he'll never have to deliver. Everyone's full of empty promises here, from the president down. But that cousin can't get you a job with the police, not in Mafikeng, not anywhere. Police are recruited by a central office. Remember? Last year they advertised nationally and were swamped with applications. At least a hundred for every position. Now they're not even recruiting anymore. Besides, you need a matriculation certificate *and* a driver's licence to get a job with the police. And you don't have either. And even if you did your cousin couldn't get you that job. Forget about it. In fact, you want to be serious? Let's talk about serious. If you're serious, tell me this: Who is *ever* going to give you a job? Huh? Who?" Madumo didn't answer. He leant forward as if hanging on my every word. I was surprised to see that he didn't seem angry or resentful. My tone softened: "Face the facts, Madumo. You're not going to get a job. You're a Soweto guy. Who's going to hire you? Employers don't like Soweto guys. You know that. And you have no qualifications. No experience. Any job you go for there's going to be twenty *kwerekwere* willing to do it for half the pay you'd need, a quarter—even less. Even if you did have qualifications, you're thirty-three years old and you look like a thug. Even if you finish that degree, you'll be forty years old and still no experience. Do you think someone's going to hire you then? Look around you. How many graduates are there now who can't find jobs? And what's it going to be like in ten years' time? And meanwhile, while you're studying for your degree, how are you going to pay rent? Am I supposed to sponsor you? I can't. And people aren't going to let you sleep on their floors forever. Meshack's wife is going to keep feeding you when your own family won't?"

While I spoke Madumo shuffled his papers back into a neat pile and folded them into their tattered brown official envelopes. Earning a degree might be a pipedream, but having a valid student card had real benefits on the streets of Soweto. A card-carrying student, even one advancing in years like Madumo, was at least not a hobo. It might not get him a degree or a job, but if only he had such a thing, he might at least persuade a woman that there was some point to being his girlfriend. That was a dream worth having.

"Madumo," I continued, "what are you going to do with your life? Let's say we make this feast for your ancestors. So then the witchcraft is off, you're cured, the ancestors are fed . . . then what? How will you survive? Because let me tell you something I've noticed about this place lately: life is getting tougher for guys in your position. People don't want to share anymore. In the old days, they would never have chased you out of that house. They could fight you to hell, but they wouldn't let you starve. And life wasn't so expensive then—no rent, no electricity . . . so there was more in the pot. Everyone had some useless old uncle or a brother in the Struggle . . . someone who needed a hand. So they shared. Either everyone was hungry or no one was hungry. But now it's every man for himself. Now you're on your own. Even if your mother hadn't passed away you'd be in trouble now. Am I wrong?" I was exaggerating, but not much. Every family I knew seemed to be torn apart in recent years by conflicts over money and responsibility. For all the talk of *Ubuntu,* or "African humanism," by the new African elite, on the streets of Soweto the practice of everyday life was tending ever more towards the dog-eat-dog.

"Am I wrong?" I insisted.

Madumo pondered his answer for a minute and then said, "What can I do?" That expression in this place usually accompanies a throwing up of hands in despair, but Madumo sounded sincere. "You're right," he added. "This thing of getting a job with the police is nonsense. But what can I do?"

"I don't know," I replied. "I really don't. But we've got to think of something. I'm telling you, forget about getting a job. You have to find some other way to make money, some kind of business. And forget about crime. You're hopeless at crime."

He laughed. "I know. You need that appetite for blood to do crime these days."

"Think about it," I said. "Think about something you can do as a serious project."

"Well," said Madumo quietly, "I'm having this idea of selling clothes." I looked up. "You know, Meshack has this friend who is having a connection for secondhand clothes. I'm thinking that maybe I can get some secondhand clothes and do business." He began to form a plan and it seemed to make sense. Clothes are his great passion. If he could find a way to supply himself with decent stock, he could surely sell at a profit to people in the neighborhood, like teachers and criminals, who had a little money but not enough to buy new clothes at the stores in town. Across South Africa, as across the rest of the continent, indeed the rest of the world, an enormous trade in recycled clothes from the wealthy countries is carried on by people like Madumo, who resell clothes bought from bulk importers. It would take little capital to start. He said he knew of a Polish man in town who was such an importer. He would start inquiring right away. . . . Talking his way through this plan Madumo seemed reinvigorated, as if he had suddenly acquired a sense of a future. When it came time for us to part, he turned abruptly to me and took my hand.

"Thank you," he said. "Thank you. You know, Adam, we Africans we usually won't talk to someone straight like that. Maybe we'll come from this side, then that. Or if someone tells you straight that this and this and this . . . then you'll think he's undermining you. And then you'll want to argue, to fight. But you Westerns? Oh boy! Straight, straight, straight. No nonsense. So I want to thank you, sir. You have told me something true. Like a brother. I won't forget it."

A month or so later I suddenly experienced a piece of extraordinary and unanticipated good fortune. I was offered, without having applied, a marvelous job. Madumo was delighted: "This is the work of the ancestors, my man," he said. "No doubt about it. No doubt at all. They are thanking you for all the help you've given me." MaMfete, too, was overjoyed and saw in this turn of my fortunes the hand of her God, motivated, so she said, by gratitude on her behalf. I was not so churlish as to ask why I was the one being so blessed when their needs remained infinitely greater than mine. It seemed to me that I was the one who should be grateful to them, for it was the world they had opened to me that had made my good fortune possible. In an excess of celebratory cheer I agreed with Madumo that we should make an ancestral feast. "For you and me both," he said, "you and me both."

I can't say that I immediately regretted my offer, but I did procrastinate. Weeks passed. The date of my departure for New York drew nearer. Every time we talked about the feast I discovered new reasons to delay. Money was only part of the problem. Because Madumo had been banished from his family's home around the corner in Mapetla, the only option he had for making a satisfactory feast was to return to the place of his father's family in the rural areas, a day's journey to the west via Mafikeng to Ga-Kunuana, near the border of Botswana. I had other things to do.

Then the Dombolo died. I was driving in the suburbs far from Soweto where the streets are all named after dead Afrikaner presidents when it stopped. In a sign of how the style of township life was inexorably spreading to the suburbs, I only took five minutes to find a backyard mechanic's workshop run by a Polish immigrant called Mike and a Zimbabwean called Agrippa. Agrippa got the car running sufficiently to return to Soweto, where Thabo's crew would be able to refit it with parts of dubious provenance, but he warned against driving it to Mafikeng. Mafikeng was only half-way to Madumo's ancestors and the road to the village near the border was unsealed. We would have to take the bus, but I had left it too late. Madumo had to go on his own.

Climbing off the bus in downtown Mafikeng just as dusk was settling and the Saturday bustle of the taxi-rank was beginning to clear, Madumo asked the young woman he'd met on board to direct him to the nearest police station, where he thought he might be able to contact his cousin Papi—the one who'd promised him the job as a policeman. At the police station he discovered that his cousin was sick at home in his village some twenty miles away, so he decided to press on with his journey to Ga-Kunuana, the place of his ancestors. He returned to the taxi-rank, found a van heading in that direction, and waited while it filled with passengers for the dusty bumpy six-hour trip through the villages to the south. Fortunately for Madumo, the drivers on these routes through the countryside know the villages well, so if you tell the driver the surname of the family you are visiting, he will drop you at their gate.

Madumo arrived at his uncle's home shortly after midnight. The four-room house, constructed of homemade bricks and tin, along with two rondavels across a dusty yard and a cattle kraal ringed with thornbush were situated on the outskirts of a settlement consisting of about fifty such homesteads. The family greeted him warmly and were not at all surprised to hear he'd come to make a feast. Nobody makes the trip from Johannesburg just to be sociable. And despite the problems that propel such visits, the arrival of guests from the city is always welcome. For not only does it break the monotony of rural life, it signals an opportunity for the whole village to eat and drink at someone else's expense. So Madumo's uncle listened to his story and, despite the lateness of the hour, immediately set out to walk to the next village to fetch the family matriarch—Madumo's father's aunt, the last surviving daughter of the man after whom Madumo was named.

The "granny" arrived before dawn and Madumo, who had

fallen asleep, was roused to tell her his story. In the flickering light of candles he told her of his troubles and of how he'd consulted an *inyanga* who had instructed him to make a feast for his ancestors. He wanted to give thanks for their protection and to open the way for their aid. The old lady listened to his story. When she spoke at last, she was reluctant. She told him he should have come with his father—who was living in a village about a day's journey away. She told him he should go there first and fetch his father. Madumo was insistent. In the most polite and respectful way, he told the old lady and his uncles the whole story of the conflict with his father. He stressed that his father would almost certainly refuse to assist him. Moreover, his father would most likely not have any money. He would probably demand that the money Madumo had raised for the ancestors be given to him first. He would cause the plan for the feast to fail. Loath to miss the opportunity for a feast, Madumo's uncles endorsed his every argument. Eventually the old lady relented and gave her blessing for the feast.

In the morning preparations began. The women went off to neighbors to organize the heavy black iron three-legged pots. Young girls began grinding sorghum for the beer. Madumo had to go to the next village to buy candles and paraffin and sundry other supplies at the store. Someone went to buy vegetables. Being the middle of the month, money was scarce and supplies were low. Madumo paid for everything. On Monday, Madumo and his uncles boarded a donkey cart for the ten-mile trip to the auction yards to buy a beast to slaughter. The cheapest one they could find was a ram—the biggest ram Madumo had ever seen—but it was expensive nonetheless, costing three hundred and fifty rands, half Madumo's budget for the feast. When they returned with the ram, they housed him in the family's kraal and proceeded to the cemetery with snuff and a candle to meet with those whom Madumo was here to appease. Crouching beside the grave of his great-grandfather, his namesake, he told his ancestor all his problems, reciting a litany of trouble and misfortune going back to the days of his youth.

When they returned to the house, the newly brewed beer was beginning to bubble. They gave him a stick and told him to stir the big drums of beer and talk to his ancestors. For two days, whenever the spirit moved him, he stirred and talked and talked and stirred and the dead to whom he talked came to seem as if they were with him. Then on Wednesday, early in the morning, they roused him to come outside to the kraal. There the men slaughtered the ram and spattered Madumo with blood. Then they took the gall and some undigested grass and washed him with it before returning to the graves for a final consultation. Meanwhile the ram was hacked into pieces and set to boil in the iron pots. Throughout the preceding days, word had passed around the village that a feast was on, and by the time the food was ready more than a hundred and fifty hungry people were waiting to eat. Following the food, pots of sorghum beer were passed around to groups of men. Everyone ate and drank till all was finished. Everyone except Madumo. He was not allowed to touch the meat or the beer. The ancestors were adjudged to be satisfied.

"I mean, it's a jackpot for these people," said Madumo when giving me his account of the feast. "You know, when you're from Joburg people just can't understand that you don't have money. They thought that I'm working and I was there to give them money and what what. So my cousins there, they were wanting everything. Money for cigarettes, beers. I had to leave those shoes, the white ones. The other pair of jeans. My red jersey. They all wanted something out of me, those cousins, and we wear the same size. Hey, the others were giving me their sizes so that next time I should bring them clothes. That seven hundred you gave me? Gone. Psssshoo!"—he whisked his hand across his whistling lips—"gone. I didn't even have money for the taxi from Mafikeng to Joburg, so I had to borrow from my cousin there."

"So what did you tell them when you first arrived in the middle of the night?" I asked.

"No, those people are used to people coming from Joburg. But you have to be procedural. They're like the ZCC; the elders have to give their permission. You can't just communicate with the ancestors. And nobody will take a decision without consulting an elder. So I had to tell everything, how this and this and this happened. And they always want to know more. So I had to tell them how it's hard for me to survive. How I don't have a wife, or even a place to live. I told them about Mr. Zondi and how he'd been helping me. In fact, they could hardly recognize me since I was there last time. They said that last time I was looking horrible, like a hobo."

"Did you tell them about the witchcraft?"

He paused for a moment. "Well, not really. I told them that I've been having troubles. But these people are used to these stories. That side there's a hell of a lot of witchcraft. A hell of a lot of witchcraft. In a high volume. And these people specialize in *isidliso.* Everyone that side is having *isidliso,* having to have it taken out. So they know about witchcraft. They'll have it taken out, then again they will get *isidliso.* Time and again."

"And Mr. Zondi, what did they say about him?"

"Well, they are used to *inyangas* that side. Generally, they live with *inyangas.* Whenever there's a problem, there should be an *inyanga.* In fact, my family is having its own special *inyanga.* So they also said I should come back and do some sort of ritual and be introduced to this family *inyanga.*"

"Another feast? Damn! These people are hungry."

Madumo smiled. "No, not a feast. A small ritual, like, just so that *inyanga* should be knowing me. But I should tell my *inyanga* here about that one, so there mustn't be any misunderstanding. They shouldn't have jealousy, or their *muthis* will clash. And they were wanting to see you that side, too. Because I was telling them about you. I told them my story, that I was helped by you. And they wanted to say something to the graves and acknowledge you and give you some power through mixing my surname with your surname, praising the names. Like, maybe saying, 'This is our son with the son of Ashforth.' Something of that sort that will give you the light." I looked at him quizzically. "They weren't going to give you *muthi* or cut you with a razor or anything. Just something to light your way, to make you powerful to your seniors at work. Something like that. So they've done that, introduced you to the ancestors. Well, you Westerns, you don't believe these things, but I'm telling you, you'll notice a change in your life. Things will be just smooth. Looking back, one day, you're going to wonder how did you reach the stage that you did, and then you'll know it's because of ancestors."

"Well," I replied, grateful again to be spared a cutting with a razor, "thanks anyway. So you didn't mention anything about the witchcraft?"

"No," he replied. "It's not necessary."

"So what else did they tell you to do?"

"Smoking and drinking, that was one thing," he replied. I laughed. "I mean, they told me that I must *stop* smoking and drinking. That is the point they stressed. Because in my family, we don't smoke and we don't drink."

"Really?" I said, looking dubious.

"Well, that one, my great-grandfather, the one that I'm named after, he was a priest. Anglican. So they said that if I want things to come good from his side, if I want to succeed in life through the ancestors being with me, then I mustn't be smoking or drinking."

"So you're going to do that?"

"I am," he said. "Well, smoking is difficult. I just had one. But liquor is finished."

"I'm glad to hear it." My own love of drinking has been sorely taxed by witnessing the toll it has taken on my Sowetan friends, male friends more particularly, over the years. I doubted Madumo could survive without the conviviality offered by smoking and drinking, but was glad to hear him acknowledge it as a goal.

"And another thing," he said. "My granny that side told me that I should be really careful with my relatives this side, in Meadowlands. In fact, anyone linking with my blood grandmother, my father's mother. Pshew! She's the biggest witch. Everyone's accusing her of witchcraft. And that aunt in Meadowlands, she's a collaborator."

"Your father's mother is still alive?

"Yes, she is. And she's strong that one. She's 'round about eighty-two years old, but she's still running around. Very strong. She can do anything. And she's well known as a witch. So I must be careful on that score."

"What about the one we went to your brother and sister with, is she a witch too?"

"No, that one's okay. Because she's not related by blood, she's my grandfather's wife's sister. So she's clear." I was relieved to hear it. "So now I'm ready to start with this business of selling. And they told me that side that I should come with clothes and household things, because there's not too many people selling that side, not like here in Joburg. And they told me that I must build a house that side in the place where my great-grandfather used to have his house. Nowadays there's just rings there on the ground. . . ."

I looked at my friend spinning out his new plans and dreams and couldn't help feeling a touch of sadness. The following day I would be leaving Soweto to return to work in New York.

20

DEPARTURES AND BEGINNINGS

"So, my man," said Madumo as we made our way down the crowded airport concourse to Departures, "you're going to write that book. I know it. And it's going to be a hell of a book. I'm telling you. Everything is going to get the green light. Mr. Zondi told me. He's sure of it!"

I quashed a malicious urge to remind him how wrong his Mr. Zondi had been in predicting our reception when we returned to Madumo's family home and diverted myself by pretending to attend to traveler's matters in my bags. A young Indian boy steering the mountain of his family's baggage on a trolley crashed into my ankle. I cursed harshly. Madumo laughed and scooped up my bag. He had come to my place in Mapetla Extension that afternoon for the usual farewell drinks, bringing with him his notebooks and journals. He had even brought his homemade poster of *My Daily Prayer,* which satirizes the pious kitsch found on Sowetan walls and begins, "Anybody who troubles me will be killed without warning. . . ." This he used to hang on his wall to suggest to passing creditors, of whom there were many, that he was a dangerous psychopath who shouldn't be pressed too hard for repayment of his debts. As he handed me the collection, he told me to use them in my book. I packed the documents into my bag along with the box of audio tapes recording our many hours of conversation about his struggle against witchcraft. In the same bag I carried the jar of "white" Vaseline and the heavy green briquet of Sunlight soap blessed by the Zionists for my good fortune. I had no idea what to do with it all.

We pushed our way through the crush of the concourse. Madumo was elated. I was depressed. He'd been to see Mr. Zondi the day before and had been told by the *inyanga* that his treatment had been successful. The herbs had worked; the ram had not died in vain. The ancestors were pleased, although they would always require appeasement in the future when things improved further—as things surely would, despite that minor setback over the plan to build a shack. The ancestors were united behind Madumo. The witches were defeated; their evil spells turned back upon themselves. Madumo was protected against further onslaught, ready to start life anew. He seemed healthy, confident, and refreshed.

I was sad to be leaving Soweto again, leaving South Africa. I always get depressed at departures. I can't remember how many times I've made this trip to the airport from Soweto with my friends. Sometimes I leave not knowing if I'll return. Other times the leave has been taken with the return date already set. In the early days of my life in Soweto, great fanfare marked the moment of my departure. In 1991 they held a farewell party that entertained the whole neighborhood, with performances by the Mapetla Drum Majorettes; the Sandinista Choir from the ANC Youth League in Phiri; Noise Khanyile's traditional Zulu band, AmaGugu aKwaZulu; a brass band; a choir of church ladies; . . . and feasting for everyone. These days I mostly prefer to slink off to the airport quietly. Usually I try to drink as much as possible and see if I can maintain a stoic disposition at least until the plane takes off and the lights dim. No matter how I do it, it's always too much like heartbreak, and this time was proving no exception.

The formalities of departure passed in a blur and I found myself alone in a crowded plane awaiting takeoff for New York, wondering what it was that I had been doing these past months. As usual, I was departing with more questions than answers. More than ever before, those questions were about witchcraft. For months it seemed that talk of witches and witchcraft had been the major part of life. I had been swept up in Madumo's struggle against the curse of witchcraft, sometimes against my better judgement.

A nice, middle-aged, English-speaking, white South African lady sat down beside me and began struggling with her seatbelt. I made the mistake of making eye contact as I assisted with her buckle.

"Are you going home?" she asked.

"Sort of," I replied.

"How did you enjoy your visit?"

"Fine," I said and hurriedly reached for my headphones, inserting one of the Madumo tapes into the recorder. Madumo's voice droned along with the steady hum of the engines and I closed my eyes. I have spent so much of my life in this place that I am leaving, I thought to myself. Yet even when I leave, my life and thoughts remain anchored there, or perhaps I should say they swirl around and endlessly return to the problem of how to understand life, my life, in Soweto. Yet still, I find myself incapable of resolving the basic question: What am I to make of it? Over this past decade, the last of the twentieth century, I've been made to feel at home in Soweto. Yet still I feel the need to write of my life there, as if it were something out of the ordinary. Am I any different, I wondered, from the legions of "whites from overseas" throughout these long centuries who have come to these parts and left with the makings of books?

As I settled into that jet-propelled dreamworld of waking sleep that is international travel, a world fueled by a narcosis that seems borne in miasmas seeping from the carpets and galleys of these craft as they leap time zones and hemispheres, none of the dispositions of professionals writing about Africa seemed to make much sense. And yet I know I am heir to all of them, just as Madumo is living in a world made by the ceaseless passage of people like me into Africa. Although Soweto has come over the years to be a home to me in ways that are certainly not trivial, and people there are like family, I cannot pretend to be a Sowetan. Proclaiming a desire to tell an insider's story about that place to outsiders would be unbearably pretentious. Nor can I pretend to the usual justification of people like me poking about in places they don't belong, the professional disposition of seeking to improve or assist people—neither the bankers, the missionaries, nor the revolutionaries would recognize me as one of their kind. I have tried to be kind to people who have been kind to me. More than that, I cannot say.

Madumo is part of the same world that I am, a world that is simultaneously everywhere and nowhere. Were he sitting next to me on this flight to New York he could disembark at Kennedy Airport like the millions before him and make a life for himself in New York City without skipping a beat. And when he missed home, he could get on the phone like the rest of us. Most of what I know about his life, and he knows of mine, is easily understandable in the same ordinary terms we can find and use anywhere on the planet today. And even when Madumo and I discuss those aspects of life in which we seem to differ the most, such as this whole witchcraft business, the terms we use are already translated from one language and culture to another and back again, over and over through generations. There is no pristine vocabulary of difference available to Madumo to describe his experiences with witchcraft that I could translate and then present to the world in terms familiar to the West; no language to make the words seem unique, or the effort of translation worthwhile. The words, like the worlds, are already pre-translated. And yet, there remains something radically and irreducibly different in his experience of these matters from mine, a difference which is not just our peculiar preferences and dispositions as two particular individuals, nor is it systematizable into some uniform scheme of difference between, say, Africa and the West.

I wondered what the woman next to me would make of the fact that I had spent my vacation at home in Soweto working with a friend who'd been bewitched. Would it just confirm a suspicion, commonplace in the folk wisdom of Western modernity, that Africans are backward and ignorant? What if I insisted that my friend actually had been bewitched? Would she reply that there are no such things as witches, so while my friend may have *believed* himself to have been bewitched, this belief was in fact mistaken and if I insist on accepting his belief at face value, I am a fool? Would she regale me with stories of her own about superstitious Africans?

Perhaps my neighbor would not be so ready to jump to conclusions about the evident stupidity of talk about witchcraft as I imagined. Perhaps she would adopt the position, commonplace now in anthropological studies, that talk of witchcraft is not an index of primitive ignorance and superstition but an idiom through which other realities are expressed, realities such as social stress and strain, unemployment, capitalist globalization, the collective fantasizing of popular culture, and so on. Perhaps she would insist that when Madumo talks on and on about witchcraft, he is not really talking about witches but is simply finding an idiom for expressing the meaning of his misfortune as an unemployed black man missing the gravy train in the new South Africa. It suddenly occurred to me that perhaps I should ask. . . .

I glanced across at my neighbor and found her studying the advertisements for duty-free goods in the back of the in-flight magazine, perfumes and cigarettes arrayed in a parody of Indiana Jones searching for exotic loot in the African savannah. The fine tracery of lines in the sun-dried skin around her eyes reminded me of the faces I had lived with in my youth in Australia. I felt a sudden warmth towards my fellow traveler, another white person left out too long in the sun. I was on the verge of asking her about witches and their craft when I found myself checked.

What's the point? I asked myself. Why would I want to risk exposing myself and my friend to ridicule by attempting to tell his story?

I realized I had no idea how to tell Madumo's story anyway; decided there was no point in talking about witchcraft with my neighbor. Perhaps these things can't be spoken of with strangers. I closed my eyes and returned my attention to his words on the tape. I found a strange comfort in the sound of his voice patiently explaining to me the manifold dimensions of his complicated predicament. . . . *The problem is with this ancestorship, Adam, when I, or we Africans, are in trouble we normally think of these people, but when life picks up, when something just comes up and life becomes normal, we normally forget about ancestors and say, because of this Western culture and trying to follow Western culture, and say, no, if I didn't go out and find a job and talk to Whites, or bosses, and say here is my experience, they wouldn't give me a job, so there was no ancestors whilst I was negotiating for the job, but when the job is finished I'll go back and say, Oh my ancestors, my ancestors. . . .*

Madumo is not a stupid man. Although he is not as well educated as he might have been had he the sorts of opportunities that have been afforded me, he is by no means illiterate or incapable of analyzing and questioning the nature of his worldly experience. Indeed, he is one of those people, rare in my experience, who are blessed with the capacity for philosophical reflection—or, perhaps more accurately, cursed with a readiness to doubt. He does not speak of witchcraft because he is imprisoned in some closed system of thought or because he lacks the ability to comprehend alternative explanations for his experience. He speaks of witchcraft because he is worried about the work of witches.

During our discussions, Madumo once told me, "Most of the time I try to Westernize my mind and not think about witchcraft." He was explaining why it is necessary to be discreet when you suspect yourself to be bewitched so as not to create an atmosphere of gossip and fear around you. At first I was rather taken aback by this approach to the idea of belief. As a simple sort of Westerner, I had assumed that believing or not believing was an either/or proposition: either you believe in witches, as Madumo does (in which case, you take precautions), or you don't believe, as I don't (in which case there is nothing to be done). But for Madumo, "belief" is not simply the passive acceptance or rejection of a cognitive "idea" but a form of action in itself.

The reason he tried to think like a Westerner, he told me, was because fearing witchcraft didn't just make him feel paranoid, and thus miserable, it also strengthened the actual power of the witch. The witch's power works on and through that fear. This understanding of power involves ontological presuppositions regarding the natures of thought, mind, and action radically different from those commonplace in the West, at least insofar as these presuppositions surface in the "official" discourses of modern life. I can see no arguments sufficient to persuade someone that the form of action Madumo speaks of as "belief" is not valid and efficacious in relation to witches. (Nor can I see a way of confirming for a believer that prayer is not a form of real interaction with the divine.)

For Madumo, "Westernizing the mind" is not a way of denying the reality of witchcraft but a mode of combating the real powers of witches. Perhaps for someone who's mind is sufficiently "Westernized," someone like MaMfete, say, who succeeds in maintaining a degree of unbelief in the face of a generalized fear of witchcraft, the "cultural" rituals, prohibitions, and procedures that for Madumo are a life-and-death struggle against the powers of evil become healthy affirmations of an African identity in a world dominated by Whites. When educated Africans talk about these matters to outsiders they typically render the indigenous categories in the language of modern Europe. *Inyangas,* for example, are transformed into "traditional doctors" and their herbs are accounted for as a pharmacopeia into which scientists would be well advised to inquire in pursuit of new drugs. But this seems to me to involve a serious misrepresentation of the politics involved in the business of healing, the power struggle waged by the healer and his ancestors, using herbs as weapons, against the evil forces deployed by the witch. These power struggles engaging living humans and spiritual entities can have disastrous results, as when the witch is killed. They can also leave someone like Madumo in a long, expensive, and wearing campaign against an incurable misfortune. It's no small task to transform a matter of security, physical security from the assault of malicious supernatural powers such as confronted Madumo, into a matter of identity.

I cannot begin to count the number of times I have been asked the question, "Do *you* believe in witches?" I don't believe in witches, and, mostly, I say so. But I don't believe that whatever it is my friends worry about when they worry about witchcraft can be dismissed by asserting that witches cannot exist. Madumo and Mr. Zondi, when they worked against the evil forces derailing my friend's life, were not simply confused about the way the world works. They were not merely pursuing mistaken ideas of causation and irrational suggestions about human powers in defiance of proper rational scientific explanation. I have no doubt that if Madumo had spent a few more years in a science classroom, with a decent teacher, some of the stories he has heard about the powers of herbs and other substances might seem less plausible. But even a master baker can believe in the transubstantiation of the host. The qualities and capacities of substances as mobilized by witches and healers are not reducible to properties measured in a chemist's laboratory. Nor can their effects be discounted as "psychological" by assimilating them into that catch-all of confoundment in contemporary Western medicine: the placebo effect. Yet neither can they be reduced to some sort of symbol system in which the qualities and powers of substances can be accounted for by a single authoritative cosmology with fixed doctrines and dogmas like the theology that accounts for transubstantiation. When Madumo's ancestors got their feast at last, I doubt if they were merely eating air and promises.

From my discussions with Madumo and Mr. Zondi, along with many others, it seems clear that even if there were once authoritative traditions (and I'm not convinced that there were) specifying the precise nature of the powers involved in witchcraft and the capacities and methods of witches, most people today are less than perfectly aware of them. The social and cultural dislocations of urbanization over the past century or so in this region, along with the impositions of apartheid and the turmoil of political struggle, have meant that if there ever were ancient authorities and old traditions in these matters, they have not been handed down intact. The intermingling in cities of people from different civilizations, religions, and cultures has also produced a ferment of spiritual life. Innovation and imagination are the key ingredients today in the struggle against the ailments wrought of malice and spoken of as witchcraft, just as they are in the struggle for salvation.

As I pondered Madumo's predicament it became clear that the question "Do you believe in witches?" when asked in Soweto is not at all simple. It's not just a question about how events are caused but is also at root a question about meaning, about the meaning of life. At the end of the day, Madumo and I differ fundamentally over the degree of meaningfulness there is to be found in the world. Beyond explicitly directed human action, I am not predisposed to find meaning or purpose, neither higher nor hidden, in the workings of the world. Divine Providence and witchcraft are, to me, equally abstract and empty hypotheses. Though I doubt that it all boils down to physics, I feel no impulsion to make sense of the world, the cosmos, by reference to any sort of sentient Supreme Being, nor to find evidence of the supernatural powers of jealous neighbors in the ebb and flow of my worldly fortunes. I do not talk to dead relatives and I do not fear the secret malice of the living. I have no fear of the envious inflicting wounds to the soul, nor salve for the scrapes I might find there. As far as I am concerned, there are no invisible forces or beings that shape the lives and destinies of the living, although I sometimes feel a sort of envy, a feeling of tone deafness, when witnessing others communicate with beings beyond my ken. I am free, too, of the fear that the invisible realms of which we humans are a part might not be an ethical order in which truth and justice prevail. And I've no need to wonder why God tolerates Evil in the world. I am thus spared the problem of identifying whether the invisible forces that are busily shaping our destinies are agents of Good or forces of Evil, and I never have to wrestle with the problem of interacting with such beings and entities in meaningful ways so as to bend their actions towards the best. I have no Sabbath to keep, and when I look to the heavens, I see only the sky. But I know no one in Soweto who dwells in such emptiness.

I opened one of Madumo's notebooks and began to read the tale of his tribulations. A piece of paper, tightly folded, fell from the book and disappeared into the detritus at my feet. I retrieved and unfolded it to find a carefully stenciled outline of his foot. He'd made the image while we were drinking this afternoon so that next time I come I could bring him a pair of All Star sneakers. For years he'd been nagging me for All Stars. I usually excused my negligence in meeting his request by claiming I didn't know his size. (When I learnt it was 9½, I had to say the sizes are different in the U.S.) I smiled as I folded the paper back into the notebook. Maybe he'll be lucky next time.

Usually when I reach this point in the flight home I find myself overwhelmed by the knowledge that someone I love will probably die before I return to Soweto. In the years I've been engaged with Soweto I have buried more friends there than I have lost in the many more years I have lived in England, Australia, and America. I have buried victims of political violence and witchcraft, road accidents, murder, and disease. Once or twice I've even attended the funeral of someone who had died of "old age"—that is, over sixty. And I hate funerals. I find no solace in the conviction that the deceased are beginning a new kind of life. Sometimes, when I contemplate the amount of tragedy that has marked my friends' lives in Soweto and which I, by accident of birth, have avoided—except through my connection with Soweto—I think that to reject, or deny, as I do the proposition that the world as we live it is part of a larger purpose is an egregious affront to those who have suffered, and are suffering still, with the hope, the faith, that it all has a point. But that is how it is.

For Madumo, like everyone else I know in Soweto, the world *is* full of meaning, of signs of the presence and purposes of invisible powers. To empty it of meaning would be as absurd as to empty it of air. The problem is, rather, how to interpret the signs which loom large every day. And the work of developing a plausible reading of the signs, as I witnessed in our months working with Mr. Zondi, is rarely easy. Nor is it easy, once you have found someone you trust to tell you what is what, to retain the faith in one reading against another. There are radically different interpretive schemes available in contemporary Soweto, embodied in the persons of the *inyanga,* the prophet, the minister, and the doctor—in all their bewildering varieties. Holding fast to the readings of any one of these figures is never easy. In perilous cases it is irresponsible not to consider all the options, and people typically do, for failure to read the signs correctly can result in death. While I cannot share my friend's sense of the urgency of this work, the imperative of deciphering signs of invisible power, I can, I think, see in vague outline some of the contours of the problem.

Invisible powers only make their presence felt through visible or tangible signs. These signs, of which the world and all it contains are made, are inherently ambiguous. The gnawing pain in the stomach might be *isidliso* sent by a witch, it might be a reminder from a neglected ancestor, or a punishment for sins. . . . Then again, it might just be a simple ulcer with no greater significance at all—a "natural sick" as people here call it. Yet even if it seems like an ulcer to the surgeon, it might still be a sign of the invisible agency of *isidliso,* which the surgeon is unqualified to detect. Such signs are always open to a variety of interpretations. Interpretations derive their validity from distinct forms of authority. Ministers and doctors, grounding their practices in the massive institutional solidity of Western religion and science, have their own structures of authority specifying truths and rights, and their own institutions of education and accreditation.

Mr. Zondi, like all such healers, draws his authority from communication with his ancestors, the ZCC prophets from their spirits. I can see no grounds for suggesting that these latter two are not real relationships just because I have no access to them and cannot imagine what they might consist of. But just as the signs are ambiguous, so are the powers behind them uncertain. Invisible entities originate the signs for their own purposes, but their powers, by definition, extend far beyond the limits suggested by any apparent manifestation. So in interpreting a particular given sign one can only guess at the nature and motive of the originating power—unless direct communication by speech is proffered. But even then the utterances of spirits or ancestors are subject to interpretation, whether they are fed or not. This uncertainty can become a source of considerable anxiety when someone is faced, like Madumo was, with the imperative of interpreting the meaning of signs presaging imminent death.

The cabin lights were out; the meal had long since been cleared away. Calling for another bottle of wine seemed like a bad idea. Madumo's words were still droning on in my headphones. I was into the third tape and he was explaining to me again the powers of ancestors. Most of the time when we were having these conversations, I would listen patiently. Every so often I would chip in with a skeptical question or comment. For many years I have read extensively in the literature of African ethnography. I've studied southern African cosmology from books written by Christian missionaries bent on understanding the people they were seeking to convert. Much of what Madumo says can be found in such books, although much of Madumo's lore would be unrecognizable to the ancestors of whom he speaks. The ancestors themselves, since the political kingdoms to which they belonged while living were broken up and transformed under white rule, have changed their roles in society. In Soweto today it is rare to find someone outside of the ZCC or the other larger independent churches who pays homage to an ancestor outside of the immediate family. And yet the ancestors remain vital members of the living community, having lost none of their salience in everyday life. Madumo might have been practicing half-baked rituals when he surreptitiously slaughtered that half-smothered chicken in the yard, but he did so in relation to beings who present themselves to him as real and immediate, pressing for attention. Similarly for the witch, who presents himself or herself today in radically different guises, though with undiminished intensity. The traditions of dead generations may weigh like a nightmare on the brains of the living, as Karl Marx wrote, but they do so because we are still living the nightmare.

And witchcraft *is* a nightmare. I have no doubt that my life is the better for not having to worry about witches, and certainly for not having to worry about being accused of witchcraft. But I can't explain adequately why I fear them not, for I cannot fully subscribe to the folk wisdom of Western modernity that exults in the triumph of enlightenment over superstition. Occasionally I have found myself trying to describe to people outside Africa the implications of living in a paradigm of witchcraft, in a world where a meaning for misfortune is sought in the actions of ill-disposed people nearby. It is almost impossible to convey an adequate sense of how life is mostly lived on the same sorts of terms as anywhere, until suddenly the perils spoken of as witchcraft become terrifyingly present. Sometimes friends outside of Africa see the supposition that misfortune is socially motivated, the idea that *someone* has caused me to suffer and that malice must be counteracted, to be comforting. In some ways it is. When Madumo began his quest for cure with Mr. Zondi, I persuaded myself that the enterprise was equivalent in some general sort of way to a course of treatment with a psychotherapist, a slow sort of realignment between the jumbled contents of a mind and the possibilities of meaningful existence offered by the actually existing realities of the given social world. Perhaps that is a useful analogy, but it's a poor sort of description of the battles those two waged together against the invisible evil forces of the witches.

After all these hours of talking about witchcraft, I cannot truthfully say I really understand it. I can describe what people say easily enough and trace the implications of their actions. But the core of the matter eludes me still, though I suspect it involves ways of working in the fertile fields of hatred and fear. Perhaps I should follow the strategy of the serious ethnographer and apprentice myself to a healer to learn fully the nature of the work. But I would feel ridiculous doing such a thing. Besides, the work of the witch is cloaked in utter secrecy. No matter how much you know about witchcraft, you can only know *what* is possible (and I know enough now to know that anything is possible); you can never know *how* it is done. Only the witch can know that, and the witch doesn't talk to anyone who is not a witch too. Despite the enormous enterprise of divination involving hundreds of thousands of *inyangas* and prophets, the secrecy of witchcraft can never be penetrated. Ultimately, it seems to me, the question of witchcraft involves something akin to a religious mystery, a matter for contemplation and spiritual action but which defeats all efforts to comprehend in clear and distinct ideas. Madumo and I can talk endlessly about witchcraft and understand each other perfectly. Where we part company, however, is when he marches into the realms of the ineffable. As I listen to his voice on our tapes I am reminded of a comment by Saint Augustine to the effect that the ways in which a soul clings to a body are entirely wonderful and cannot be understood by man. Whatever else he is doing as he vomits Mr. Zondi's herbs, my friend is working with something meaningful in relation to this connection between what a Westerner would call body and soul. He is also wracked by fear that others, who hate him, might be able to interfere with the proper relation between his bodily presence and that unknowable, unrepresentable something that is "out there" in the heavens and the cosmos while being also "in here" in the heart, the soul, or the spirit . . . in life itself. That I cannot follow him into this domain results, I have no doubt, from a lack of imagination rather than from superior intelligence or enlightenment.

Madumo's voice on the tape is receding into the distance as I resolve that once I am settled back in America, I will transcribe these tapes and study the journals of my friend's struggle against the curse of witchcraft and see what they add up to. Perhaps I *will* write that book Madumo was so enthusiastic about. I could never write a case study in the classic sense. But I know I won't be able to work my way through the labyrinth of questions these past months have raised without writing something. I cannot separate thinking from writing. My life in Soweto has forced me to question assumptions I'd never even realized I took for granted. So for years I have been writing about little other than Soweto. Perhaps someone might be interested in reading of Madumo's plight. For Soweto, while in many ways a world unto itself, remains yet a part of the same world we all inhabit at the close of the twentieth century. And Madumo's story, while unique in its particulars, is not unheard of elsewhere. Of course, if I were to think about publishing this stuff I would have to change all the names and places so that any resemblance to actual persons is purely accidental. Perhaps I could take advantage of the late-twentieth-century blurring of literary boundaries between fiction and nonfiction by making it all seem made-up while insisting that the story is true—or by making it all seem true while suggesting it has been made up. That's the way it is in a world full of witches, anyway: you never know what is really real or true. Whatever happens, I must remember to smear a bit of the ZCC's magic Vaseline on the manuscript before I send it off. As the tape machine clicks itself into silence at the end of the cassette, I fall asleep content, still wondering whether such a story could ever be properly told but grateful for having lived it.